PRAISE FOR
PROJECT-BASED LEARNING ACROSS THE DISCIPLINES

"The lessons and PowerPoint presentations in this book clearly describe what students have to do and give them different ways of learning the subject. Students can be more expressive in how they present their assignments. It may look like a lot of work, but it is the right amount for the student to fully understand the subject. The project-based learning techniques demonstrate active learning rather than passive learning. Active learning challenges students and is a simple yet effective method of teaching."

—*Ian Brewer, Tenth-Grade Student*
Sacred Heart Cathedral Preparatory
San Francisco, CA

"We are at a pivotal time in the history of education, where questions about inequity, accessibility, and bridging the achievement gap undergird the conversations of the political pundits. The dire pronouncements focus on the extent to which current educational practices are not preparing our students to be analytical and critical thinkers. To this end, *Project-Based Learning Across the Disciplines: Plan, Manage, and Assess Through +1 Pedagogy* has made a tangible contribution to the field of project-based learning.

"Dr. Warren has an acute understanding of what it takes to guide our students into becoming autonomous learners with the skill set to work collaboratively in a team setting, skills that are integral in a global economy. For the educator, the lessons, activities and resources remove the guesswork and allow for creativity and individualization. This book is filled with a plethora of topic ideas and transcends mere interdisciplinary conversations while also providing a road map for students to become difference makers. It takes a critical look at what positive contributions students can make, not only to their immediate neighborhoods, but also to their society and country."

—*Ruth Brown, Educator, English Language Arts/*
English Language Development
Harry Bridges Span School, LAUSD
Wilmington, CA

"THIS is what I've been waitng for. With +1 Pedagogy, Dr. Warren lays out so clearly a framework for teaching in the 21st century classroom. It is an elevated level of teaching and learning to which I aspire as a teacher, and it is exactly how I want my own children to learn."

—*Adreanna Clark, Elementary School Teacher*
Kekaha Elementary School
Kekaha, HI

"As the principal of a middle school, I found that +1 Pedagogy helped build the capacity of my teachers by providing solid instructional tools for students to engage in PBL. Dr. Warren's book is a step-by-step process for building classroom environments that are rich in learning and guided by PBL. This book is a must for all instructional leaders on a school campus.

"As we expand STEAM/STEM programs on our campus, we are doing so with hard work, dedication, and Dr. Warren's guidance on PBL. Her book enables us to use frameworks and models that support our teachers and learners in all classes, from physical education to language arts, with projects that are models of effective instruction across the content areas. This book is helping bring all departments together by providing interdisciplinary frameworks and rubrics that teachers can use.

"The most valuable sections are the sample frameworks provided because they contain important standards for student mastery that beautifully transition into student inquiry, activities, presentation, assessments, and reflection. Simply stated, +1 Pedagogy allows teachers to let their students create, discuss, design, and show mastery of the content being taught by creating a project that prepares students to be college and career ready. Powerful!

"+1 Pedagogy is helping to provide the foundational part of a learning environment that assists students in meeting the demands of the 21st century. Thank you, Acacia Warren, for providing a wealth of tools that are valuable and applicable to teachers and students who engage in PBL."

—*David Herrera, Principal*
Enterprise Middle School
Compton, CA

"An effective mathematics program requires students to collaboratively engage in making sense and reasoning about meaningful mathematics through real-world contexts. Although the enormous challenge of connecting mathematics to authentic 21st century experiences can become a reality through project-based learning, many math teachers have yet to embrace this approach because it can be difficult to implement. Dr. Warren's book on +1 Pedagogy provides an invaluable framework and practical resources that address PBL management and organization, technology implementation, and the mathematical practices through incorporating high cognitively demanding tasks. Mathematics teachers and leaders looking to achieve effective and relevant math instruction should make +1 Pedagogy a key part of their daily planning."

—Travis L. Holden, Secondary Mathematics Coordinator
Local District Central Los Angeles Unified School District
Los Angeles, CA

"The theories and methodologies in relation to pedagogy are vast, but +1 Pedagogy synthesizes these methods and fosters a healthy disposition towards learning. Dr. Acacia M. Warren is an educator who has sacrificed her time and energy to reform curriculum and academics for teachers and students. This book is designed to provide students with the same level of educational opportunities, despite socioeconomic status. Students are more inclined to learn because they are engaged in topics that interest them.

"Great educators are lifetime learners and *Project-Based Learning Across the Disciplines: Plan, Manage, and Assess Through +1 Pedagogy* offers a series of steps in the direction of solving one of the most important issues facing our modern society—how to help teachers and students become successful in the classrooms of the future."

—*John W. Horton, III, English Teacher*
Rikkyo (St. Paul's) Junior & Senior High School at Ikebukero
Tokyo, Japan

"Educators nationwide believe in the general purpose of project-based learning. +1 Pedagogy puts these beliefs into action. This is a transformative framework that is imperative for 21st century teachers and learners."

—*Nicole Jacobson, EdD, Assistant Principal*
Westminster School District
Garden Grove, CA

"Acacia Warren has written an exceptional piece that will improve teaching and the lives of all students. She has been a thoughtful practitioner throughout her career and her research ensures more rigorous classrooms for the future. Using research, best practice, and a theoretical framework around learning theory, she has provided the pathway for teachers so that they can create not only powerful learning experiences for them but guarantee that they are prepared for the 21st century. Dr. Warren's clear guidelines to create a new pedagogy will inform the field for years to come."

—*Antonia Issa Lahera, EdD, Program Coordinator School Leadership Programs*
and Director CASLA and ISLI Grants
California State University, Dominguez Hills
Dominguez Hills, CA

"This book serves as an innovative, interdisciplinary teaching and learning guide. Schools and districts will rethink project-based learning by learning how to seamlessly weave essential 21st century inquiry, application, collaboration, and research skills into their curriculum design and prepare students to meet the rigors of a globally competitive society!"

—*Donna Stewart Lewis, EdD, JD, Founder and CEO*
ETHOS Academies
Woodland Hills, CA

"This is a well-researched and thoroughly written guide for implementing +1 Pedagogy. Dr. Warren includes step-by-step guidelines, templates, guiding questions, and other resources that provide teachers with the necessary tools to carry out the +1 Pedagogy with success. Additionally, her clearly written text and examples make this book a valuable resource. With the guidance of this book, I can see myself bringing +1 Pedagogy to my classroom."

—*Tara Winberry Litt, Fifth-Grade Teacher*
Beverly Hills Unified School District
Beverly Hills, CA

"In her discourse on project-based learning, Dr. Warren accomplishes a work vital to education in the 21st century and beyond. Her concept of +1 Pedagogy is thoughtful and masterful and provides an invaluable resource for educators. As a post-secondary music educator and online instructor, I applaud her demonstrated passion for bridging the gap across the disciplines at every level, skillfully addressing technology and the arts. Dr. Warren generously provides a universal framework ready for immediate application and—beyond that—motivates and inspires us to greatness. Bravo!"

—*David Shawn Valcárcel, MM, Music Educator,*
Author of History of Rock Course Resource Pack
San Bernardino Valley College
San Bernardino, CA

"As a student I always ask the question, Why? Why is this assignment important, how will it benefit me, and how do I successfully complete it? The guided presentation and templates demonstrated in the book help me to understand the purpose of a project and eliminate confusion. I know exactly what to research and how to complete the study. If more teachers used this method, it would help students achieve a good grade more efficiently. I need to be challenged and prepared for college-level work, and this method will help me reach that goal."

—*Akemi Williams, Ninth-Grade Student*
Dublin High School
Dublin, CA

PROJECT-BASED LEARNING ACROSS THE DISCIPLINES

PLAN, MANAGE, AND ASSESS THROUGH +1 PEDAGOGY

Acacia M. Warren

Foreword by Maria G. Ott

CORWIN
A SAGE Publishing Company

FOR INFORMATION:

Corwin

A SAGE Company

2455 Teller Road

Thousand Oaks, California 91320

(800) 233-9936

www.corwin.com

SAGE Publications Ltd.

1 Oliver's Yard

55 City Road

London EC1Y 1SP

United Kingdom

SAGE Publications India Pvt. Ltd.

B 1/I 1 Mohan Cooperative Industrial Area

Mathura Road, New Delhi 110 044

India

SAGE Publications Asia-Pacific Pte. Ltd.

3 Church Street

#10-04 Samsung Hub

Singapore 049483

Senior Acquisitions Editor: Jessica Allan

Senior Associate Editor: Kimberly Greenberg

Editorial Assistant: Katie Crilley

Production Editor: Amy Schroller

Copy Editor: Jocelyn Rau

Typesetter: C&M Digitals (P) Ltd.

Proofreader: Sally Jaskold

Indexer: Judy Hunt

Cover Designer: Scott Van Atta

Marketing Manager: Jill S. Margulies

Printed in the United States of America

Library of Congress Cataloging-in-Publication Data

Names: Warren, Acacia, author.

Title: Project-based learning across the disciplines : plan, manage, and assess through +1 pedagogy / Acacia Warren.

Description: Thousand Oaks, California : Corwin, a SAGE Company, 2016. | Includes bibliographical references and index.

Identifiers: LCCN 2015042330 | ISBN 978-1-5063-3379-3 (pbk. : alk. paper)

Subjects: LCSH: Project method in teaching. | Interdisciplinary approach in education.

Classification: LCC LB1027.43 .W37 2016 | DDC 371.3/6—dc23 LC record available at http://lccn.loc.gov/2015042330

This book is printed on acid-free paper.

16 17 18 19 20 10 9 8 7 6 5 4 3 2 1

CONTENTS

Foreword   xi

    Dr. Maria G. Ott

Acknowledgments   xiii

About the Author   xvii

Introduction   1

    The Purpose of This Book   2
    To Plan Is to Lead   4
    How to Use This Book   4

INTERSECTION 1   PLANNING   7

Chapter 1: Road Map to Success   9

    +1 Pedagogy™   12
    Project Learning   13
    Transformation of PBL   14
    Projects   16
    Contextualizing the Learning Experience   17
    Frequently Asked Questions   19
    A Plan of Action   21
    Planning With the End in Mind   22
    Philosophical and Psychological Rationale   24
    Fidelity to +1P   24
    Professional Development   27
    Summary and Most Important Concepts   30

Chapter 2: Navigating the Road   33

    Checkpoint 1: +1P Planning Rubric and Standards   35
      Standards   35
      Common Core State Standards   38

Next Generation Science Standards	44
History/Social Studies Standards	47
Physical Education Standards	51
Visual and Performing Arts Standards	52
Your Turn to Practice	54
Checkpoint 2: Topic Selection and Big Ideas	55
Topic Selection	56
Your Turn to Practice	58
Motivation	59
Big Ideas	60
Your Turn to Practice	61
Checkpoint 3: Universal Concepts and Essential Questions	62
Universal Concepts	62
Your Turn to Practice	65
Essential Questions	66
Your Turn to Practice	70
Summary and Most Important Concepts	71
INTERSECTION 2 MANAGING	**73**
Chapter 3: Route to Project Management	**75**
Checkpoint 4: Project Objective	76
Your Turn to Practice	78
Checkpoint 5: Focused Inquiry, Learning Activities, and Investigation (Research)	79
Focused Inquiry	80
Your Turn to Practice	83
Learning Activities	85
Your Turn to Practice	88
Project Management	90
Investigation (Research)	94
Your Turn to Practice	102
Summary and Most Important Concepts	105
Chapter 4: Crossroads of Technology and +1 Pedagogy	**107**
SAMR Model	108
Digital Pedagogy	110
+1 Pedagogy and Digital Pedagogy	111
Cloud Management Systems	112
Learning Management Systems	123
Social Media	125
Apps	130

+1 Pedagogy Without Technology   130
Summary and Most Important Concepts   132

INTERSECTION 3   ASSESSING   **133**

Chapter 5: Exit at Assessment   **135**

Accountability   136
Formative and Summative Assessments   140
Common Core Assessments   142
Checkpoint 6: Recommendations and Presentation   144
    Recommendations   144
    Your Turn to Practice   145
    Presentation   148
    Your Turn to Practice   154
Checkpoint 7: Writing Assessment,
    Reflection, and Commitment   156
    Writing Assessment   157
    Your Turn to Practice   162
    Rubrics and Grading   163
    Reflection and Commitment   171
    Your Turn to Practice   177
21st Century Skills   185
Differentiation   186
Summary and Most Important Concepts   188

Chapter 6: Final Destination   **191**

Self-Assessment   192
    21st Century Skills Checklist
      for Teachers and Administrators   192
    Mindset   196
    Final Thoughts   197
Most Important Concepts   198

Appendix A   **199**

Appendix B   **203**

References   **235**

Index   **241**

FOREWORD

The twenty-first century learner enters the traditional brick and mortar classroom with unique skills, interests, and learning needs. In her book, Dr. Acacia Warren provides educators with the tools needed to bridge learning for the student raised with technology. Technology takes the student beyond classroom walls, and the tools and instructional approaches she describes transform traditional facilities constrained by physical space. Her insightful book is practical and addresses the challenges of new curriculum, including the Common Core, to support teachers in mastering the steps that lead to great teaching and that promote rigorous learning.

Dr. Warren describes her learning model as a bridge to twenty-first century skills. Her approach is user friendly and provides historical context for understanding the importance of project-based learning in the current educational environment. The learner is the center of the planning process, achieving learning outcomes by doing and experiencing. Dr. Warren utilizes technology tools to tap into the communication and problem solving inherent in self-directed learning.

Dr. Warren designed +1 Pedagogy (+1P) as an interdisciplinary framework to support educators in implementing project-based learning across the curriculum, integrating the tools of the twenty-first century to transform the educator as facilitator and designer and to ignite the potential of the learner through self-direction, problem solving, and by connecting knowledge through integrated learning experiences.

Project-based learning is not new to education; however, teachers have been challenged in finding ways to sustain curriculum integration during an era of standards and assessment. Dr. Warren's +1P approach provides an invaluable solution and shifts the focus from knowledge as rote learning to knowledge as creation of solutions and new information.

In her book, Dr. Acacia Warren demonstrates how to design and implement twenty-first century experiences that promote authentic learning, guided by expert teachers committed to the learners of this century. Teachers guide students through complex problem-solving tasks such as researching, collaborating, presenting, and reflecting. Students learn to research and utilize technology as a tool to accelerate acquisition of knowledge.

Dr. Warren challenges educators to abandon artificial constraints that limit student potential to rote learning. She envisions students as independent learners guided by skilled teachers who promote connections across the curriculum. Her book describes the steps that lead to proficiency in project-based learning approaches. Teachers regularly engage in reflection about the purpose and outcomes of lessons and students learn to make recommendations related to their projects and to adjust their work based on evidence from their research and observations.

The +1P classroom is a dynamic place that transcends the constraints of brick-and-mortar walls. It is a place that lives within the context of the twenty-first century and maximizes the potential of learners born into endless possibilities that invite them to create, invent, explore, and problem solve the complex challenges of an increasingly connected world. Dr. Warren envisions engaged learners who cross the *Bridge to 21st Century Skills, Technology, and Achievement.*

During a study trip to Beijing, China, in 2013, Acacia Warren stood on the steps of the Great Wall and wondered if astronauts could view this man-made object as they orbited the Earth in the Space Station. She reflected on the challenges of preparing youth to create twenty-first century world wonders in an age of technology, inspiration, and invention. She envisioned educational accomplishments, accelerated by new ways of teaching that would spark learning breakthroughs for all students. Her vision for +1P took root on the Great Wall. Her book builds the bridge needed to accomplish the vision.

Maria G. Ott, PhD
Professor of Clinical Education
USC Rossier School of Education
Co-author of *A Culturally Proficient
Society Begins in School: Leadership for Equity*

ACKNOWLEDGMENTS

This book has two honorary co-authors—my husband and best friend, Delvin Warren, and my twin sister and best friend, Fawn Hutton. They are both equally cherished and appreciated for believing in my talents and expertise, for offering honesty and constructive criticism, for edifying and encouraging me throughout this process, for listening and cultivating my ideas, and for sincerely reading every page of my numerous drafts. I thank Delvin for his entrepreneurial spirit, ambition, artistic talent, and optimism. I thank Fawn (and her husband David) for coaching me, persevering with me, and ensuring that I stayed the course. I thank my parents, Dr. Elliott C. Osborne and Sonia M. Osborne, for their invaluable expertise in teaching and learning and for staying up late nights to offer feedback. I thank my other parents, Charles and Ernestine Warren, for their patience, support, and positive reinforcement. My brother, Meshach Osborne (secondary PE teacher and coach), and his wife, Brenda Flores Osborne, have also been instrumental during the construction of this book. I thank them for their willingness to assist in any way possible, even if it was taking me out on their boat to give me a break from writing. I thank my other two sisters, Keziah Davis and Berniece Osborne, for understanding my passion for education and for sharing resources and/or advice when needed.

I am especially grateful to Dr. Maria G. Ott for guiding me in the direction of publishing. Her responses to my e-mails at all hours of the day (and night) were and still are impeccable. I thank her for adding clarity and calmness to my publishing journey. Dr. Ott's intelligence, kindness, and leadership are truly inspiring. On a more personal note, climbing the Great Wall of China together was an indelible experience that I will cherish forever (smile for the memories!).

Every now and then, a special colleague brings new life, energy, and support to one's aspirations. That special colleague is none other than

Dr. Nicole Jacobson. I thank her for reading every page of my first draft and offering actionable feedback. Dr. Jacobson's skills and expertise in mathematics influenced every sample unit in this book, from vessel operations to roller coasters to famous painters. I also thank her husband, Mike, and two kids, Jack and Rachel, for allowing me to "borrow" her time for advice and writing sessions. Nicole's friendship is worth more than words can express and I am proud to have worked by her side.

I would be remiss not to appreciate my Los Angeles Unified School District (LAUSD) family. Their devotion, resilience, flexibility, and craftsmanship speak volumes, despite what the media depicts. May this book represent what's good about LAUSD and inspire others to publish. When you belong to the second-largest district in the United States, you come across incredible talent, precious diversity, and countless educators. Some LAUSD colleagues who have been particularly influential during the creation of this book, are as follows: Travis Holden, Wen-Wen Cheng, David Gonzalez, Youssef Elias, James Centeno, Bernice Caan, Leigh Ann Orr, Sonia Vargas, Dr. Denise Pereyra, and Ruth Brown. Regarding my educational journey, I am profoundly grateful to those who have served as personal mentors: Julie Love, Susan A. Van Buren, Jennifer Scargall, Mylene Keipp, Dr. David Baca, Angela Tenette, Dr. Jared DuPree, Dr. Linda Lee, and Isabel Nino. My former Secondary ELA Coordinator team is just as vital to my professional growth: Dharma Hernandez, Jaimi Krielaart, Eric Grow, Toya Tate-Rose, Jina Virtue, Michael Swanston, Dr. Nicolas Mize, and Laura Cavalli. I also pay tribute to my Local District Superintendent, Roberto A. Martinez, an exemplary and charismatic leader who puts students first. I am also grateful to the district administrators and principals who granted me the opportunity to work with them: Natividad Rozsa, Dr. Darnise Williams, Dr. Frances Gipson, Davie Devereaux, Lou Mardesich, Kendra Wallace, Dr. James Downing, III, and Linda McClellan.

My sincere gratitude goes to those who have enlightened and motivated me to push the boundaries of what is possible. I begin with Stacey Knox. His counsel and expertise is without a doubt the *best* in Los Angeles. I thank him for introducing me to "new words" and for extolling the teaching profession to the highest degree. Next, I extend my heartfelt appreciation to Dr. Tim Esposito and his office staff. I thank him for keeping me "aligned" after typing for hours and hours and hours. I want to recognize David Herrera, a mentor whose leadership, passion, and resourcefulness are admirable. Special thanks to the talented website designers and graphic artists for their contribution to the website that supports implementation of this book: Alan Armijo, Debra Bradfield, Montae Scott, and Drew Lewis. I am also indebted to the following friends and acquaintances for their "extra boost" of encouragement: Tunde George-Tay, Michael Chankay, Molly Scargall, Dr. George L. Blankinship, III, MD and Asha Kamali May, Alan Clark and Adreanna Clark, Uzoma Okoro and Dr. Melanie Okoro, Noor Mitchell and Phyllis Mitchell, Janessa Barnave, Ralph Knowles, George Brewer and Seretha Brewer, Rodney Pamphile and Dawn Arceneaux Pamphile, Lowell Henry, and my favorite magician—John George. I thank the following professors for shaping my practice as an educator: Dr. Paul Green, Dr. Della Peretti, Dr. Paul Ammon, Dr. Antonia Issa Lahera, Dr. Rudy Crew, Dr. Kenneth Yates, Dr. Julie Marsh, Dr. R.J. Pat Gallagher, Dr. Guilbert Hentschke, and Dr. Sandra Kaplan. Their expertise and leadership in the field of education is highly commendable, and their words of wisdom fortified my desire to teach, lead, and write a book that starts a conversation about best practices for teaching and learning.

Finally, I thank Jessica Allan for trusting in a new author with innovative ideas. I am grateful to the Corwin editing team for their tireless dedication and high-quality work. Completing this project would not have been possible without them. They supported my journey to publication with sincerity and efficiency.

PUBLISHER'S ACKNOWLEDGMENTS

Corwin gratefully acknowledges the contributions of the following reviewers:

Marcia Carlson
Sixth-Grade Teacher
Crestview School of Inquiry
Clive, IA

Susan Leeds
Gifted Specialist
Winter Park High School
Winter Park, FL

Frank Chiki
Principal
Zuni Elementary School
Albuquerque, NM

Susan E. Schipper
Primary Grade Teacher
Charles Street School
Palmyra, NJ

Mari Gates
K–5 Instructional Coach
Henry B. Burkland
    Elementary School
Middleboro, MA

Thomas Shiland
Science Teacher
Saratoga Springs City Schools
Saratoga Springs, NY

ABOUT THE AUTHOR

 **Acacia M. Warren**, EdD, is currently an assistant principal in the Los Angeles Unified School District (LAUSD), where she has served as a teacher, coach, Gifted and Talented Education (GATE) Coordinator, Response to Intervention (RtI) Expert, Common Core Facilitator, and District Coordinator. She has extensive expertise in facilitating professional development for hundreds of schools, promoting literacy across the disciplines, Common Core planning and curriculum design, and integrating technology with instructional practices. Dr. Warren's passion is providing teachers/educators with strategies and tools that accelerate achievement in the classroom and equipping administrators with strategies for leading these efforts. Prior to Dr. Warren's professional experiences in LAUSD, she served as a teacher for the Oakland Unified School District. Dr. Warren is also the president of Acacia Tree Learning Services, an educational consulting business that thrives on project-based learning, technology-integrated instruction, professional development, and global competence.

Dr. Warren credits her educational career and academic successes to her alma maters—University of California, Riverside (BA); University of California, Berkeley (MA and Teaching Credential); California State University, Dominguez Hills (MA); and the University of Southern California (EdD). She is grateful for the knowledge, research, and networking opportunities that each institution has provided. Dr. Warren can be reached through her educational website, **www.acaciatreelearning.com**, a digital resource that supports implementation of the contents presented in this book.

Dedicated to my parents, Dr. Elliott C. Osborne and Sonia M. Osborne.

*Thank you for being the first to model great teaching in
your own classrooms, for supporting me in attaining four college
degrees, and for always encouraging me to aim high.*

*This book is also dedicated to every teacher on this planet.
Your passion, innovation, and dedication inspire me every day.
The following poem was written in honor of you.*

I Am a Teacher

I am a teacher
A believer
A thinker
A philosopher

I am a teacher
A creator
A designer
A constructor

I am a teacher
A coordinator
A manager
A collaborator

I am a teacher
A calculator
A problem-solver
A common denominator

I am a teacher
A social worker
A caretaker
A counselor

I am a teacher
A police officer
A firefighter
A doctor

I am a teacher
A lawyer
A debater
A negotiator

I am a teacher
A successor
A conqueror
A survivor

I am a teacher

—by Acacia M. Warren, 2014

INTRODUCTION

An investment in education is an investment in our future. A good return on this investment requires thoughtful attention to curriculum and instruction, professional development, and leadership. The significance of this book stems from over a decade of experience perfecting these principles. My teaching career began in the Oakland Unified School District, where I took an early interest in strategic planning and curriculum design. My lesson plans were carefully constructed and I spent hours designing my own templates/worksheets. I took advantage of professional development opportunities by attending conferences inside and outside of the district. Even as a novice, I recognized the need to enhance my practice through professional development. I was especially intrigued by professional development that related concepts and ideas directly to the classroom. This type of relevance and application is a key ingredient for immediate transfer.

After two years in Oakland, I accepted a teaching position in the Los Angeles Unified School District (LAUSD). I credit LAUSD for propelling my career in teaching and leadership, namely as a GATE and Data Coordinator, Response to Instruction and Intervention (RtI^2) Expert, Common Core Facilitator, and administrator. My career experiences have resulted in facilitating professional development for hundreds of teachers and schools. It was not long before I became acutely aware of the need for interdisciplinary models that accelerate achievement through 21st Century Skills. These truths, along with my passion for project-based learning, were instrumental in the development of this book. I felt compelled to utilize my knowledge and expertise in curriculum planning, professional development, and leadership by creating +1 Pedagogy™. The timeliness of this book meets the demands of a Common Core–aligned curriculum and sets the bar for exemplary practices in education.

The standard competencies within the Common Core necessitate new norms for teaching and learning. Students are challenged with going deeper for conceptual knowledge, employing critical thinking skills, and using computer-mediated technology, while teachers are tasked with facilitating this process. Today's workforce reflects these same skill requirements. Many jobs require a college degree, certifications, and/or technological skills. For this reason, schools across the United States and around the world are adapting instruction to mirror college and career readiness. A college education is advantageous and can increase career opportunities. To prepare students for meeting these expectations, an interdisciplinary approach to learning that elevates consciousness, accelerates achievement through 21st Century Skills, and builds the capacity of our nation's youth to compete in a global economy is essential. This approach is defined as +1 Pedagogy™ (+1P), a framework that pushes the boundaries of what is possible in the classroom by bridging technology and innovation in education. This framework amplifies student potential and transforms instruction to better meet the academic and social needs of students.

+1P is an instructional model that leverages achievement through project-based learning (PBL). Despite the popularity of PBL, I know firsthand that it is not as prevalent in schools as one may think. While educators may utilize certain aspects of PBL, such as inquiry and investigation, more comprehensive models are needed. The +1P framework is interdisciplinary, integrates technology, and spans all grade levels, making it applicable to students of all ages and interests. Students can study a broad range of topics across any discipline. Critical components include authentic tasks, inquiry, research, 21st Century Skills, technology, problem solving, collaborating, writing, presenting, and reflecting—necessary skills for college and career readiness. This style of content delivery and academic rigor prepares students to apply concepts beyond the classroom, thus contributing to their development as action researchers and global competitors.

THE PURPOSE OF THIS BOOK

The purpose of this book is to provide educators with an invaluable resource for planning, managing, and assessing +1P. To accomplish this goal, a practical guide is needed to streamline implementation. This book serves as a road map for guiding educators through the process. You will find that this framework is feasible on *all* levels, regardless of budget, minimal or advanced technology, and grade level. One highlight of +1P is the cost-effectiveness of implementation. Educators are encouraged to use the resources already within their possession, along with the resources provided in this book. For your convenience, concrete strategies and techniques for engaging in a cycle of inquiry and investigation are included. By the end of this book, readers will be fully equipped to implement the framework. Figure A includes a diagram of the +1P framework. The remaining chapters explain this diagram in further detail.

Far too often, educators are introduced to new curricula, pedagogical practices, and strategies without a comprehensive guide for implementation. This book is intentionally designed as a turnkey model for facilitating and implementing +1P. To build your capacity, the "I do, you do" approach is utilized. As I unpack an example unit of study, you will simultaneously create your own unit of

Figure A   +1P Diagram

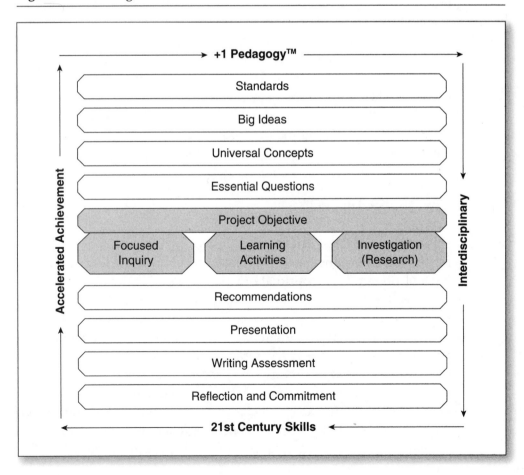

study. You will also process your learning through a strategy called "Think-Question-Transfer." This user-friendly strategy is the impetus for application and transfer to the classroom. After reading this book, you will be prepared to start your own +1P journey. You will understand the process from beginning to end. Written primarily for K–12 educators, the strategies and ideas in this book are equally applicable to college professors and parents.

TO PLAN IS TO LEAD

I firmly believe that the quality of your planning is a reflection of your performance and leadership. A plan of action is necessary for achieving goals and sustaining outcomes. Without a coherent plan of action, pursuit of goals/objectives/outcomes may be disjointed and misguided. Educators also need to be supported in their planning. They need time to plan (compensation for planning is not a bad idea either) and a repertoire of tools/instructional methods/strategies that foster planning. The first section of this book provides an entry point for +1P planning but does not stop there. Once a plan is in place, instruction must be delivered and managed accordingly. The second section of this book provides an entry point for +1P implementation and management but does not stop there. The final section of this book addresses +1P accountability, assessment, and reflection. All three sections of this book—planning, managing, and assessing—are vitally important for successful implementation of the +1P framework.

HOW TO USE THIS BOOK

Optimal practice makes perfect—this phrase is packed with implications for teaching, learning, and applying knowledge. Teaching and learning are enhanced with optimal practice, and performance is enhanced when you apply *what* you practice. This book is designed to guide your repeated practice of applying the +1P framework to your classroom. Rarely are new initiatives implemented with perfection the first time around. Even as a veteran teacher, you will need to practice to become better at facilitating the process. The key to +1P is getting started and persevering through the process. This book includes a myriad of strategies to bolster your success with implementation. Each section of this book—planning, managing, and assessing— emphasizes practical techniques to streamline implementation. The concepts presented in each chapter build on one another. For this reason, the chapters are best read in chronological order. There is a compelling logic to the layout of this book. The first chapter sets the foundation and is grounded in theory and research. Chapters 2 and 3 define the +1P framework and start to blend theory with practice. The fourth chapter integrates +1P with computer-mediated technology. Chapter 5 elaborates on +1P assessments and the use of rubrics for mastery. The final chapter ties everything together and starts a conversation about implementing the +1P framework into classrooms.

Most importantly, you will have multiple opportunities to process and practice as you read. It is recommended that you highlight salient points in the chapters, write copious notes in the margins, and complete the practice tasks. Your experience with this book is meant to be interactive, engaging, and applicable to your students. Take full advantage of planning a completed unit of study and building your capacity to implement +1P. Whether you are a teacher, instructional coach, coordinator, administrator, or parent, use this book to generate conversations about rigor and instructional strategies that prepare our students for college and career readiness. The +1P framework is designed to yield the best results for teaching and learning in a highly competitive world. Together, we can accelerate achievement as we invest in the future of our students.

INTERSECTION 1

PLANNING

*"Planning is bringing the future into the present
so that you can do something about it now."*

—Alan Lakein

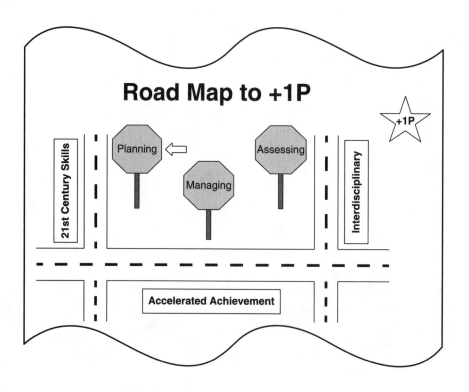

1

ROAD MAP TO SUCCESS

Initiatives such as Common Core and computer adaptive tests for K–12 mark the dawn of a new era in education. Schools are progressively shifting their assessment practices from those that measure students' short-term recall of information to higher-level thinking. To compete locally and globally, students need skills that support an information-driven and technologically powered society. The 21st Century Skills movement is transforming teaching and learning practices in today's classrooms. In an effort to challenge educators to redefine what is meant by a rigorous curriculum and schooling experience, Wagner (2010) outlines seven survival skills needed for learning, literacy, and life.

1. **Critical Thinking and Problem Solving**—Students think critically when they engage in real-world problems, question ideas or issues within their environment, and refine their understanding after new learning. To develop problem-solving skills, students must grapple with academic challenges and real-world problems.

2. **Collaboration Across Networks and Leading by Influence**—Social interaction and networking, whether digitally or face-to-face, develop a student's capacity to collaborate and lead by influence. This process of networking enables students to learn from each other and build confidence as they acquire their own voice.

3. **Agility and Adaptability**—Students who are agile, flexible, and adaptable are more adept at handling change. These students learn to apply different strategies and techniques to diverse learning situations. Because change is inevitable, it is better for students to master these skills *before* they go to college, enter the workforce, or go into business for themselves.

4. **Initiative and Entrepreneurialism**—An entrepreneurial mind-set involves taking initiative to make things happen instead of waiting on others to make things happen. Students with this mind-set are self-directed learners, proactive, innovative, and not afraid to take responsible risks. In addition to preparing students to compete locally and globally, these skills increase a student's chances of being successful and reaching his or her full potential.

5. **Effective Oral and Written Communication**—College and career readiness, along with global competitiveness, demands that students master skills in communication. Effective communication is predicated on verbal, written, technological, and presentation skills. Students must develop efficacy in articulating their thoughts, intentions, and rationale for any given situation.

6. **Accessing and Analyzing Information**—Information is power when it is accessed *and* processed. While there are multiple ways to access information through printed text and digital media, students need additional skills in how to analyze and interpret the information. Once students have accessed information, they must know what it says, what it means, and why it matters.

7. **Curiosity and Imagination**—It is imperative to honor the inquisitive nature of students. Educators can use awe and wonderment to foster inquiry and active engagement in the classroom. Students are more inclined to use their imagination when they are given opportunities to explore and be creative, which may also increase student motivation.

Figure 1.1 includes a representative symbol and questions for each skill, making it easier for students to recall and apply the skills throughout their learning.

The symbols in Figure 1.1 are visual reminders that students can easily draw, replicate, or refer to as they engage in the +1 Pedagogy™ (+1P) process. The questions in the checklist are designed to foster

Figure 1.1   21st Century Skills Checklist for Students

Critical Thinking and Problem Solving	1. How am I thinking outside the box? 2. How do I consider multiple perspectives? 3. Do my questions generate more questions? 4. How do I find answers to my questions? 5. Can I go about solving this in a different way? 6. What more can I say, find, or do? 7. What methods am I using to problem solve?
Collaboration Across Networks and Leading by Influence	1. How am I collaborating across networks? 2. How does teamwork help me collaborate? 3. How do I use technology to interact with my peers? 4. In what ways am I showing leadership? 5. How do I lead by influence?
Agility and Adaptability	1. How do I show that I am alert and ready? 2. Am I being responsive and is it quick enough? 3. How do I show that I am flexible? 4. What does being adaptable mean to me? 5. Why should my team and I be adaptable?
Initiative and Entrepreneurialism	1. How do I show that I am self-directed? 2. How do I show that I am taking initiative? 3. How do I achieve success? 4. How do I show that I am learning from others? 5. In what ways am I being proactive and innovative?
Effective Oral and Written Communication Power of Words	1. How often do I engage in dialogue? 2. Are my conversations intellectually stimulating? 3. How do I present information effectively? 4. In what ways do I express my thoughts in writing? 5. What does it mean to communicate effectively? 6. How do I use technology to communicate?

(Continued)

Figure 1.1 (Continued)

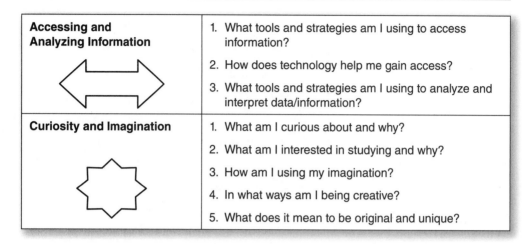

Accessing and Analyzing Information	1. What tools and strategies am I using to access information?
	2. How does technology help me gain access?
	3. What tools and strategies am I using to analyze and interpret data/information?
Curiosity and Imagination	1. What am I curious about and why?
	2. What am I interested in studying and why?
	3. How am I using my imagination?
	4. In what ways am I being creative?
	5. What does it mean to be original and unique?

metacognition and adherence to the skills. By answering the questions, students are better able to process and transfer the 21st Century Skills to their projects. Wagner's (2010) model, also referred to as 21st Century Skills, captures the essence of teaching and learning for this generation of students. Educators can leverage learning by integrating these essential skills into their instructional practices. The ubiquitous nature of these skills makes them applicable to any school, curriculum, and discipline. 21st Century Skills translate across disciplines and can help students achieve success in life and in the workplace. There are numerous variations of 21st Century Skills, but for the purposes of +1P, Wagner's model will be emphasized.

Think about an educational or life experience related to one or more of the seven survival skills. How did this experience shape who you are today? How might you utilize the 21st Century Skills Checklist in your district, school, or classroom?

+1 PEDAGOGY

The paradigm shift toward 21st Century Skills has become an international phenomenon. But how do we prepare students to consistently *apply* these skills inside and outside the classroom? The answer is +1 Pedagogy. +1P is an interdisciplinary framework for elevating consciousness, accelerating achievement through 21st Century Skills, and building the capacity of our nation's youth to compete in a global economy. The framework includes a cycle of inquiry and investigation where students manage their own acquisition of learning through projects that incorporate rigor, technology, and real-world application.

Grounded in research, +1P is a turnkey model that blends theory and practice for a comprehensive project-based learning experience that is cost-effective. Schools worldwide can use +1P to transform teaching and learning in the classroom. The +1P framework supports *learning* (critical thinking, collaborating, and communicating), *literacy* (reading, writing, speaking and listening, and digital), and *life* (goal setting, problem solving, and self-directedness). The structure and design of +1P prepares students for college, career, and life. If we (educators) are serious about maximizing student potential and capacity, we must focus on instructional practices that meet these outcomes. +1P is one avenue for accomplishing these goals. The remainder of the chapter explores the historical context, purpose, and rationale for +1 Pedagogy.

PROJECT LEARNING

William Heard Kilpatrick, an esteemed professor at Columbia Teachers College, invented the concept of project learning in the early 20th century. Kilpatrick (1918) advocated the use of projects that engender purposeful activity and student interest. He believed in learning environments that cultivate meaning-making and student engagement. The latter is indicative of a constructivist approach to learning, where learners engage in authentic tasks and create meaning through active learning (Jimenez-Eliaeson, 2010). Bonwell and Eison (1991) popularized project learning in the early '90s and coined a new term— project-based learning (PBL). PBL is an instructional model that focuses the responsibility of learning on the learner. PBL has since become an innovative approach to fostering student-directed inquiry of topics or problems in a real-world setting (Barak & Dori, 2005). PBL supplements the regular course of instruction with projects that promote inquiry, collaboration, critical thinking, and problem-solving skills. Overall, PBL is designed to enhance existing instruction by providing more flexibility, responsibility, and accountability to students as they engage in research and inquiry (Wolk, 1994).

The "learning by doing" approach to learning is understood as a reform effort that challenges traditional components of instruction—namely, confinement to a single classroom, limited face-to-face interactions, textbook dependency, and teacher-initiated tasks—all of which may inhibit creativity and access to enhanced communication with the outside world (Wolk, 1994). Due to its interactive communicative function, PBL presents more opportunities to transform the way students communicate and problem solve. PBL also involves a public audience that goes beyond the teacher and the classroom, most of which is orchestrated on the Internet. The Internet allows students to simultaneously interact with their peers through blogs, e-mails, chats, and/or video conferencing while completing their project (ChanLin, 2008). Because PBL creates independent thinkers and learners, the outcome is greater conceptual understanding of a topic by self-directed learners.

TRANSFORMATION OF PBL

Over the years, research on PBL has expanded from a specific kind of problem-based learning in schools to a wider variety of practices, subjects, and grade levels (Walker & Leary, 2009). Taken as a whole, PBL has proven to be effective because it adds a dimension of learning that influences *what* students learn and *how* they learn it. Statistically, the number of schools receiving PBL training and materials has more than tripled since 2001 (Ravitz & Blazevski, 2010). Evidence of heightened interest is provided by the growth of websites that highlight PBL as a sound pedagogical practice and the inclusion of PBL in policy documents from the National Middle School Association (Yetkiner, Anderoglu, & Capraro, 2008) and the National High School Center (Harris, Cohen, & Flaherty, 2008).

To a large extent, PBL has been embraced as a reform model that is a central component of instruction (Pearlman, 2002; Newell, 2003). In a sense, PBL demands that we rethink power relations between students and teachers. By design, PBL is more collaborative and less hierarchical (Stommel, 2013). Teachers are encouraged to facilitate learning, while students are encouraged to take more ownership of their learning. Instead of teachers dispensing all the knowledge, students play an active role in studying, researching, and presenting content.

PBL organizes learning around projects. These projects include tasks primarily based on inquiry, investigation, and problem solving.

Inquiries for PBL projects can originate from societal problems, economic/political/social/media concerns, or curiosity about a topic of interest. PBL projects generally culminate in realistic products or presentations. Through these presentations, students utilize communication skills, collaborative skills, and creativity skills. Ultimately, students gain a deeper understanding of the concepts and standards at the heart of the project, build vital workplace skills, and adopt lifelong habits of learning (Boaler, 1997).

According to Thomas (2000), five criteria are necessary for determining the authenticity of projects:

1. **Centrality**—Projects are central, not peripheral to the curriculum.

2. **Essential Question**—Projects are focused on essential questions that prompt students to go deeper with the concepts and principles of a discipline.

3. **Constructive Investigation**—Projects involve students in aggressive research.

4. **Autonomy**—Projects are student driven to a significant degree.

5. **Realism**—Projects address real-world problems and concerns in society.

Exemplary projects are predicated on these five criteria. PBL projects are also the "main course" in learning (Larmer & Mergendoller, 2010). They serve as vehicles to encourage student motivation and to provide a means for demonstrating and explaining what students have learned (Ravitz & Blazevski, 2010). The rigor and depth of a PBL project goes beyond simply applying what students have learned from traditional instruction. PBL projects relate to students' lives and are connected to inquiry that is organized around a phenomenon. Students discover ideas and relationships that enhance understanding and critical thinking. They learn to relate activities to everyday experiences and dispel previous misconceptions about their topic of study. Most importantly, when students are asked to explain the results of their study outside of school, they can easily recall and retain information about their topic of study. This style of constructivist learning, where students make meaning through projects that stimulate conceptual understanding, is relative to +1 Pedagogy. Grounded in research, +1P equips teachers with tools for *how* to plan, manage, and assess learning that blends theory, practice, standards, technology, and 21st Century Skills. This comprehensive framework heightens teaching and accelerates achievement through constructivist learning. More about +1P is explained in the next section.

Think about a topic that you would like students to explore. How would project-based learning deepen student understanding of that topic? How might you transfer knowledge about the five criteria for determining authenticity of a project back to your district, school, or classroom?

PROJECTS

The term "project" has become the standard activity in many instructional units. The question is, "Are students constructing knowledge as they construct projects?" There is more to developing a meaningful project than simply choosing a topic and writing a paper or completing an activity for that topic (Lamb, Johnson, & Smith, 1997). Students need to engage in tasks that require them to think deeply about important concepts, as opposed to only carrying out procedures. There is a long-standing tradition in schools for doing projects, incorporating hands-on activities, developing interdisciplinary themes, conducting field trips, and implementing laboratory investigations (Thomas, 2000). However, Tobin, Tippins, and Gallard (1994) assert that activities characterized as "hands-on" may not necessarily be "minds-on." In other words, achievement gained from a hands-on activity does not guarantee the use of critical thinking and problem-solving skills. +1P projects are "minds-on" because they are inquiry based, research based, technology based, and literacy based, and they incorporate 21st Century Skills. The relevant learning experiences gained from +1P encourage the transfer of knowledge to real-world situations while preparing students for college and a career.

+1P projects require a level of cognitive demand that goes beyond "hands-on." At minimum, students practice verbal, written, and digital communication; engage in inquiry; conduct research; present their recommendations and findings; and reflect on the process.

definition of +1P work

Figure 1.2   Characteristics of General Projects and +1P Projects

General Projects	+1P Projects
• Standards based	• Standards based *and* interdisciplinary
• Task driven	• Goal driven
• Hands-on and Minds-on	• Hands-on and Minds-on
• Does not require in-depth inquiry and investigation/research	• Requires an in-depth cycle of inquiry and investigation/research
• Students acquire factual and procedural knowledge of the topic	• Students acquire factual, procedural, *and* conceptual knowledge of the topic
• Does not require Internet/technology	• Internet/technology is required
• Collaboration is not required	• Collaboration is required
• Does not require a presentation	• Presentation is required
• Does not require reflection and commitment	• Reflection and a commitment are required
• Does not require a writing assessment	• Writing assessment is required
• Does not require use of 21st Century Skills	• Use of 21st Century Skills is required
• Learning is specific to the project	• Learning is applicable and transferrable to other situations

These skills and competencies not only prepare students to compete locally and globally, but they are prerequisites for success. For clarity, it is necessary to highlight the difference between projects in general and +1P projects. Figure 1.2 indicates characteristics of both. It is important to note that there is a place for both types of projects in schools. General projects are completed in a shorter amount of time, while +1P projects may take longer because students are intentionally going deeper for conceptual knowledge.

CONTEXTUALIZING THE LEARNING EXPERIENCE

Context matters. According to Teemant, Smith, Pinnegar, and Egan (2005), responding to the needs of students who are diverse in culture, language, and/or learning is paramount if schools are to equitably serve all students. High-quality instruction that responds to the needs of students considers the context of its recipients (learners). Without a context of the learner, enhancing student success may be misguided and disjointed. Bottom line—*know* your students so you can *know* how to teach them. Students bring funds of knowledge and cultural capital that are essential to the learning process.

As schools experience unparalleled cultural, linguistic, and ethnic diversity, teachers are tasked with contextualizing learning for students of diverse backgrounds. +1 Pedagogy is one model for contextualizing learning through authentic experiences. Students are given opportunities to "travel" through time with research and the Internet, allowing them to "travel" beyond the walls of their classroom and learn about diverse perspectives. Throughout the process, students are making meaning, relating their own experiences, deepening understanding, and learning new information. This type of exposure helps level the playing field in education, especially for those students who encounter more limitations to their schooling experiences. By limitations, I mean less access to resources, digital devices, field trips, programs that require additional funding, and parent involvement. Despite these limitations, cognitively, students are capable of achieving and making progress. Limited exposure and access to resources does not constitute or justify limited instruction. Because teachers control the discourse in their classrooms, it is incumbent upon them (and the school) to provide learning opportunities that accelerate achievement, integrate 21st Century Skills, and prepare students to compete in a global economy. These opportunities and skills require an interdisciplinary approach to teaching and learning. Students can learn whatever is taught, but it is hard to learn what is not taught. This does not mean that students must receive all knowledge from their teacher or school, but few experts achieve their status without some form of education and schooling experience. Through interdisciplinary projects, students are taught to make connections across content, explore multiple resources, and apply learning in diverse situations. Because +1P is predicated on interdisciplinary projects, learning is purposeful, meaningful, and applicable.

At its root, the purpose of learning deals with the central question of what is worth knowing, experiencing, doing, and being (Schubert, 2010). In other words, learning should be strategically situated to engage students in authentic experiences. McTighe, Seif, and Wiggins (2010) attribute positive changes in behavior/student perceptions to authentic learning experiences that enhance student engagement and understanding of important facts. The question remains, "How do educators stimulate the highest level of achievement in students?" We can start by promoting instructional models that embed inquiry, research, critical thinking, going deeper for conceptual knowledge, and 21st Century Skills. +1P ensures that these skills and practices are executed in the classroom. In summary, the stated research is necessary and appropriate for contextualizing the +1P framework and learning in general.

Think about the quote, "Contextualize if you want me to internalize." Why does context matter? How might contextualized learning benefit our students? How might you transfer knowledge about contextualized learning back to your district, school, or classroom?

FREQUENTLY ASKED QUESTIONS

Now that you have some background knowledge about the +1P framework, you may still have questions about implementation. This next section addresses six common questions/concerns that may surface in regards to +1P implementation.

1. **Does my school need a budget to implement +1P?**

    No. +1P is specifically designed to enhance teaching and learning, with or without additional funding. A hallmark of the framework is its cost-effectiveness. With this book and the resources at your disposal, you can fully implement +1P and transform instructional practices.

2. **Can my students still engage in +1P if our school does not have a computer lab and/or digital devices for every student?**

    Yes. Although it is ideal, students do not need their own digital device to engage in the process. If there are fewer than two or three computers/laptops/digital devices in the classroom, students can take turns or the teacher can set up a rotation chart for different days. Teachers may also consider assigning one digital device per group of students or encourage students to conduct research outside of school. The school library is another place where students can access the Internet. Pending approval by the teacher or school, smart phones can also be used to conduct research. Lastly, teachers can use their school-issued computer/LCD/laptop/digital device to assist students in their research. While the teacher uses his or her digital device to help one group, other groups can work on a different task related to their project.

3. **Does +1P require that I collaborate with other teachers, or can I just plan and implement the framework by myself?**

    Collaboration with colleagues is highly encouraged and always best, but some teachers may not have that luxury. In that case, pace yourself. Implementation is positively intense and can be challenging to organize alone. Do not overwhelm yourself to the point of frustration and giving up. Use the templates, strategies, and techniques offered in this book to mitigate anxiety and boost enthusiasm around planning, managing, and assessing +1P.

4. **Since research is an essential part of the +1P process, what do I do about students who struggle with reading or cannot read altogether?**

    All students deserve a high-quality education and exposure to rigorous instructional methods, regardless of a disability or gaps in their reading development. Students who struggle with reading can be grouped with stronger readers. Teachers can also use scaffolds, visual media, technology, and other supports to enhance reading comprehension. If you teach primary grades, especially kindergarten and first grade, consider using videos, pictures, and technology to supplement reading a lot of text.

5. **How do I ensure mastery of the material and concepts that students are studying?**

    Student mastery cannot be measured in one snapshot. For that reason, +1P includes a diverse range of learning activities and student outcomes. Teachers would determine mastery through the use of rubrics, observations, student journals, and learning activities. The culminating tasks (presentation, writing assessment, and reflection) will assess student mastery as well.

6. **How do I find time to implement +1P, especially if my schedule is already impacted?**

    +1P is designed to supplement the curriculum already in place. Teachers can explore ways to connect concepts and themes currently being taught in the classroom. There is flexibility regarding how and when you choose to implement the framework. For instance, you could introduce +1P at the beginning of the year, towards the middle or end of a semester, or during the last few weeks of the school year. Elementary teachers could also dedicate the last hour of the day for +1P. Secondary teachers could implement +1P during an extended advisory/homeroom period, seventh period (if applicable), elective period, or any other period. The most time-consuming elements, such as learning activities, research, and preparation for the presentation, can be extended through homework. More importantly, teachers of any discipline need to ask, "If I do not teach +1P, what other framework(s) do I use to engage students in a cycle of inquiry and investigation, practical use of 21st Century Skills, writing assessment, presentation, reflection, and commitment around a topic of study?"

A PLAN OF ACTION

Highly effective teachers are strategic about their planning. Without a plan of action, desired goals are less attainable. This applies to +1P as well. There are numerous considerations and strategies to guide planning. Tyler (1949), an originating author of the basic principles of curriculum and instruction, presents three absolutes for student learning:

1. Students acquire an understanding of the subject at hand.

2. Students can apply what they have learned to new situations.

3. Students have a desire to continue learning.

Students benefit when they are engaged in sophisticated learning opportunities that are rooted in conceptual knowledge, application, and a compelling desire for more. Tyler's (1949) recommendations for student learning capture the essence of education and the mission of +1P.

Tyler (1949) also recommends four objectives when planning a comprehensive unit. Following is a discussion about each objective.

1. **Forgetting vs. Retaining**
    According to Tyler (1949), acquisition of knowledge is increased with real-world application. Students are less likely to forget subject matter that pertains to their daily lives. Consequently, students experience an increase in their retention of knowledge. +1P is similar in that students deeply engage

with subject matter through authentic learning experiences, making it easier to retain what is studied.

2. **Time**

   Tyler (1949) contends that it takes time to bring about certain changes in young people. As a result, we need to honor the time it takes for students to grasp critical concepts and content knowledge. It is better to spend quality time going deeper for conceptual knowledge through an extended unit than a cursory review of knowledge and facts in one or two lessons. +1P is intentionally designed to support a cycle of inquiry and investigation around a specific topic. At minimum, a completed cycle should take four to six weeks.

3. **Multiple Outcomes**

   Tyler (1949) asserts that enhanced learning experiences include multiple outcomes. Students need multiple opportunities to demonstrate mastery, because learning is multifaceted and dynamic. +1P is a multifaceted instructional model that includes conducting research, responding to inquiry, interpreting data, drawing conclusions, presenting, and most importantly, a change in behavior resulting from a deeper understanding about the topic of study.

4. **Consistency**

   Tyler (1949) indicates that learning requires consistency and reinforcement. Learning activities that share these characteristics result in sustainable outcomes. The +1P cycle follows a consistent pattern that enables students to retain core concepts, make meaning about them, and apply what they know in new situations. Learning is also reinforced through repeated checks for understanding and real-world application.

PLANNING WITH THE END IN MIND

Steven R. Covey, author of *The 7 Habits of Highly Effective People* (1989), presents a framework for personal efficacy through seven habits. The following habits contribute to one's success:

1. Be proactive

2. Begin with the end in mind

3. Put first things first

4. Think win-win

5. Seek first to understand, then to be understood

6. Synergize

7. Sharpen the saw

While all seven habits are valuable, the first two habits are directly applicable to +1 Pedagogy. First and foremost, implementation requires educators to be proactive. These educators are driven by an innate passion to do what is best for students and to use their resourcefulness to maximize learning. Proactive educators do not make excuses; instead, they find solutions and develop a plan of action. The second highly effective habit relates to planning—*Begin with the end in mind*. Planning necessitates knowledge of where we are going before we start our journey. Just as we would never plan a trip without knowing our final destination, the same applies to teaching. Educational planning requires knowledge of long-term goals to reach intended outcomes. When teachers plan backward from the desired outcomes within a lesson or unit, clarity is established and everyone benefits. Planning ahead allows teachers and students to anticipate challenges because they are cognizant of where they are going. The key is purposefully planning for desired results. In terms of +1P, it is highly recommended to plan around project outcomes *before* starting a project. Implementation is less challenging when a clear vision of desired outcomes is expressed and understood by teachers and students.

Think   Question   Transfer

Think about a successful experience that was directly related to your thoughtful planning. How might the outcomes be different if you had not planned accordingly? Why does planning "with the end in mind" matter? How might you transfer knowledge about this type of planning back to your district, school, or classroom?

PHILOSOPHICAL AND PSYCHOLOGICAL RATIONALE

Our job as educators is to carefully foster environments that stimulate growth in students as they construct meaning for themselves. First, we must substantiate our curriculum and instruction with a philosophical and psychological rationale. This requires intentional planning around values and human development. A philosophical rationale speaks to basic values aimed at enhancing the educational program of a school, while a psychological rationale enables educators to distinguish a change in human behavior as a result of the learning process (Tyler, 1949). Philosophically, students are encouraged to value what they learn. Psychologically, students experience a change in perception toward a topic of study because they are interested, engaged in authentic tasks, and involved in the learning process. Through +1P, learning is rooted in a philosophical and psychological rationale, where students experience a better understanding about the world around them.

Spector (2008) is another researcher who presented the psychology of learning as a critical foundation area. He argues that behavior and development of knowledge and skills are the "bedrock" on which education rests. Educators can use this knowledge to facilitate the learning process and accelerate achievement. +1P provides opportunities for students to engage socially and cognitively. Students prepare for global competence by finding creative ways to study a phenomenon. Teachers and students can then use these learning experiences to achieve anticipated outcomes of learning.

FIDELITY TO +1P

Teaching and learning should be grounded in frameworks that are applicable and transferable. Students need to apply what they know and learn in a variety of contexts. It is imperative for students to understand the purpose of learning, along with the application of concepts. +1 Pedagogy provides a practical framework for contextualizing learning and enhancing overall teaching practices. Frameworks that contextualize learning must also be applied with consistency and fidelity. Given that +1P is interdisciplinary, comprehensible, global, coherent, concise, and relative, fidelity to the framework is warranted. It pays to invest in a framework that prepares students for college, career, and life.

As educators, we take more ownership of enduring frameworks that increase application and transfer, which is enhanced with practical tools for support. Figure 1.3 is one of many tools that support +1P implementation. The border of the diagram features outcomes and expectations of +1P, while the inside of the diagram includes twelve essential components. These essential components are needed to complete a full cycle of +1P for any discipline or topic. Successful implementation is dependent on utilization of all components and fidelity.

The twelve essential components of +1P are highlighted and defined below:

1. **Standards:** Projects are grounded in standards that clarify what students should know and be able to do. Standards provide a common language and compass for student understanding.

2. **Big Ideas:** Large in scope, big ideas are interdisciplinary concepts related to the +1P project. Students can use big ideas as focal points for their investigative study.

Figure 1.3   +1P Diagram

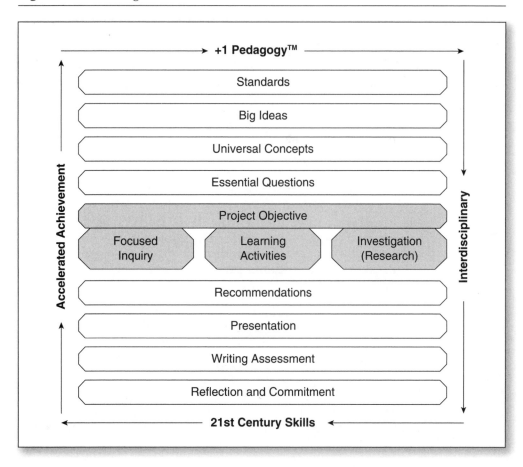

3. **Universal Concepts:** Projects include broad statements that are thematic in nature and designed to deepen conceptual understanding of a topic. Universal concepts are applicable within and across disciplines, include big ideas, and are purposefully intended to stimulate and stretch student thinking.

4. **Essential Questions:** Projects are framed by overarching questions that are transferable, debatable, and generate more inquiry. Essential questions include big ideas and can be discipline specific or interdisciplinary.

5. **Project Objective:** The project is a call to action related to the topic of study and defined by an objective that encompasses *think, know, source,* and *do.*

6. **Focused Inquiry:** Students engage in a cycle of inquiry related to big ideas. Focused inquiry includes *general, specific, elaborate,* and *sourcing* questions.

7. **Learning Activities:** Students experience multifaceted tasks that are designed to contextualize learning for students. Learning activities range in complexity and rigor.

8. **Investigation (Research):** Projects include a cycle of investigation/research. Students analyze primary and secondary sources of information as they conduct their research, while attending to Look Fours (*trends over time, multiple perspectives, technological advances,* and *forecasting*), Credibility 4, and questions from the focused inquiry component.

9. **Recommendations:** Students make recommendations for improving and/or changing a situation related to their project, based on evidence from their research. Students also explain the benefits of their recommendations.

10. **Presentation:** Students present their project to their peers or an audience beyond their classroom. Presentation options include *oral, kinesthetic, visual,* and/or *written* products. When students present, they will use techniques for persuasion (ethos, pathos, logos—EPL) and presentation (projection, eye contact, attire, confidence, engagement, and succinctness—PEACES).

11. **Writing Assessment:** As a culminating task, each student writes a short essay that addresses the following: importance

of topic of study, major findings from the research, and significance of each finding supported by evidence from the research.

12. **Reflection and Commitment:** Students reflect on how the project experience deepened their knowledge, and they consider what could be done differently the next time. Students also commit to extending and sharing the project with others.

Teachers do not have to follow the exact order stated above when planning for +1P implementation. For example, teachers may choose to brainstorm big ideas and universal concepts related to the topic of study before choosing standards. What matters most is that teachers plan for and execute all twelve components with fidelity.

Think about the instructional implications of +1 Pedagogy (+1P). What purpose does fidelity serve in implementing frameworks? How might you transfer knowledge about the +1P framework and diagram back to your district, school, or classroom?

PROFESSIONAL DEVELOPMENT

Professional development can assist educators with understanding the true purpose and rationale for +1P and fostering implementation. Once teachers are equipped with tools for planning, they are ready to implement the framework. Guskey (2000) defines professional development as those processes and activities designed to enhance the professional knowledge, skills, and attitudes of educators so that they, in return, improve student learning. In other words, professional development facilitates learning in a way that enhances instructional practice, professional growth, and student achievement. Professional development also serves the purpose of building a collaborative school culture. Oftentimes, teachers are confined to their classroom throughout the school day. Professional development (via staff meetings, grade level meetings, department meetings, Personal Learning Community [PLC] meetings, etc.) allows educators to collaborate and plan around a common purpose or goal. This book is strategically designed as a professional development resource for +1P implementation. Educators are encouraged to collaborate with each other as they engage in the +1P process.

According to Guskey (2000), there are three defining characteristics of professional development—*intentional, ongoing,* and *systematic.* Figure 1.4 illustrates these defining characteristics.

In addition to the three characteristics of professional development, Guskey (2000) lists seven major types of professional development.

Figure 1.4   Characteristics of Professional Development

Three Characteristics of Professional Development

An *Intentional* Process

- Should be purposeful and intentional
- Consciously designed to bring about change and improvement
- NOT a random or haphazard process
- Professional development is a deliberate process, guided by a clear vision
- Includes planned goals
- Recommended steps:

  1. Begin with a clear statement of purposes and goals

  2. Ensure that the goals are worthwhile

  3. Relate professional development purposes and goals to the mission of the school

  4. Determine how the goals can be assessed

  5. Evidence needed to determine if the goals are attained; multiple indicators may be necessary

An *Ongoing* Process

- Education is a field with a continually expanding knowledge base.
- To keep abreast of the expanding knowledge base, educators must be continuous learners throughout the span of their professional career.

A *Systematic* Process

- Without a systematic approach to professional development, organizational variables can hinder or prevent the success of improvement efforts, even when the individual aspects of professional development are executed appropriately.
- When viewed systematically, professional development is seen not in terms of individual improvement but also in terms of improving the capacity of the organization to solve problems and renew itself.

1. Training

2. Observation/Assessment

3. Involvement in a Development/Improvement Process

4. Study Groups

5. Inquiry/Action Research

6. Individually Guided Activities

7. Mentoring

The specified professional development types present a wide variety of options and opportunities to enhance professional knowledge. Schools/teachers can choose a professional development type from the above list (or use all seven!) to guide +1P implementation. Once a structure for professional development has been chosen, it is imperative to evaluate its effectiveness. A precise process of evaluation is needed after professional development to highlight what is effective and what needs improvement. Guskey (2000) outlines five critical levels of professional development evaluation.

1. Participants' reactions

2. Participants' learning

3. Organization support and change

4. Participants' use of new knowledge and skills

5. Student learning outcomes

Schools need to establish professional development environments that foster this kind of trust and constructive feedback. If teachers are not provided with constructive outlets to plan, revise, and reflect, successful implementation of any framework can be diverted. The more prepared educators are at delivering, revising, and reflecting about the +1P process, the better they will become at reaching intended outcomes, which are acceleration of student achievement, application of 21st Century Skills, and global competence. Overall, the discourse on professional development exists to promote professional growth that is meaningful, purposeful, and applicable. Professional development is paramount to transferring best practices into the classroom and building capacity and efficacy around teaching and learning. The remaining chapters focus on building teacher capacity to implement +1P.

Think about a professional development session (inside or outside of school) that benefited your instructional practice. What about the professional development was applicable and transferable? How might you transfer Guskey's (2000) model of professional development back to your district, school, or classroom?

SUMMARY

+1 Pedagogy stimulates learning through 21st Century Skills and creates multiple pathways to inquiry and research, making it a powerful instructional model for teaching and learning. Even as global competiveness and college and career readiness is fostered in schools across the nation, schools still need a framework that brings these ideals to fruition. This chapter extends conversations about theory and practice and their application to teaching and learning. As educators, we regularly encounter shifting paradigms. For this reason, we need frameworks and books grounded in the latest theories and practices. Chapter 1 uses research to contextualize and rationalize +1P implementation, thus maximizing the transfer of +1P to the classroom. +1P blends past and current research with Common Core State Standards and 21st Century Skills that accelerate achievement for students. The next chapter explores these concepts in further detail and examines four of the twelve essential components of +1P.

═══════════════════════ MICs ═══════════════════════

MOST IMPORTANT CONCEPTS

- 21st Century Skills
  - Checklist for Students
- +1 Pedagogy (+1P)

- Transformation of Project-Based Learning
- Tyler's (1949) Three Principles of Learning
- Plan of Action
- Planning With the End in Mind
- Frequently Asked Questions
- Philosophical and Psychological Rationale
- Fidelity to +1P

  o +1P Diagram—12 Essential Components

- Professional Development

2

NAVIGATING THE ROAD

+1 Pedagogy necessitates thoughtful planning and a strategic guide for implementation. Just as you would need a map to plan a road trip, the same concept applies to this framework. To ensure sustainable outcomes, this next chapter provides a guide for navigating four of the twelve essential components—standards, big ideas, universal concepts, and essential questions. While it is imperative to plan for all twelve components, these four components require strategic planning to jumpstart the process. As a whole, the +1P experience can be grouped into seven interrelated checkpoints that include the twelve essential components. These checkpoints will be addressed in Chapters 2, 3, and 5. Figure 2.1 clarifies which intersections and chapters include checkpoints, while Figure 2.2 provides a template for +1P planning. For consistency, you will notice that Figure 2.2 includes the same twelve components as the +1P Diagram (Figure 1.3).

This comprehensive planning template was specifically designed to support teachers as they engage in the +1P process. To foster cohesive planning, each of the twelve components from the +1P Diagram (Figure 1.3) has a designated space in Figure 2.2. The template is conveniently one page, which saves on paper and time. Teachers can complete the template within a day, or less. Of course, some teachers may still need more space and time to plan, which is perfectly okay. More importantly, this planning template is accessible to students. It can be easily e-mailed, sent home, posted in the classroom, or posted

Figure 2.1   +1P Checkpoints

INTERSECTION 1—Planning
CHAPTER 2
Checkpoint 1: +1P Planning Rubric and Standards **Checkpoint 2:** Topic Selection and Big Ideas **Checkpoint 3:** Universal Concepts and Essential Questions
INTERSECTION 2—Managing
CHAPTER 3
Checkpoint 4: Project Objective **Checkpoint 5:** Focused Inquiry, Learning Activities, and Investigation (Research)
INTERSECTION 3—Assessing
CHAPTER 5
Checkpoint 6: Recommendations and Presentation **Checkpoint 7:** Writing Assessment, Reflection, and Commitment

Figure 2.2   +1P Planning Template

Teacher's Name: **+1P Topic:**   **Date:**

Big Ideas		Universal Concepts		Essential Questions			
Standards	Project Objective						Writing Assessment
	Focused Inquiry	Learning Activities	Investigation Research	Recommendations	Presentation		
							Reflection and Commitment

on a teacher's website to serve as a visual reminder of the unit plan for a topic of study. Figure 2.2 will be used to create two model unit plans as you read—my unit plan and your unit plan. As I create a model unit, you will simultaneously create your own unit. This is the "I do, you do" approach to learning. A proponent of this type of modeling, I truly believe that you cannot draw a rainbow if you do not know what a rainbow looks like. As a result, I am providing a "model rainbow" for you. Our students function the same way. Some, more than others, need models of what we expect them to know and do. By the end of this book, you will have your own completed unit plan, my completed unit plan, and additional models to review in Appendix B. The remaining sections and chapters focus on building your capacity to plan a +1P unit.

CHECKPOINT 1: +1P PLANNING RUBRIC AND STANDARDS

The general purpose of a rubric is to provide a standard of performance for all learners. Regarding +1P, there are performance expectations for each of the twelve components. Teachers need a rubric to gauge mastery and effectiveness of implementation. Without a rubric, it is harder to measure performance outcomes. With a rubric, teachers are more cognizant of how and what to plan during the process.

Figure 2.1 is a planning rubric designed to provide clarity of expectations for the twelve components of +1P. There are three levels of competency—*beginning*, *emerging*, and *outstanding*. Since teachers may exhibit varying levels of readiness with +1P, the planning rubric honors different stages of implementation. Due to individual learning curves, it may take more practice and time to reach the higher levels on the rubric. The key is starting from where you are, but not stopping there. Teachers need to initiate the process before they can get better at the process. With time and repetition, planning becomes smoother and easier.

Figure 2.3 is specific to +1P. You may find other rubrics with similar components, but it is highly recommended that teachers use this particular rubric when planning. To experience the +1P framework in its entirety, teachers need a rubric that includes the twelve essential components.

STANDARDS

Standards establish guidelines and expectations for various content areas. The skills and concepts addressed in standards are

Figure 2.3   +1P Planning Rubric

+1P Components	Beginning	Emerging	Outstanding
Standards	One English, Math, Science, History/Social Studies, Art, or Physical Education (PE) standard that clarifies what students should know and be able to do.	Two or more discipline-specific standards that clarify what students should know and be able to do.	Integration of multiple standards that clarify what students should know and be able to do, including reading, writing, listening, speaking and language standards.
Big Ideas	General ideas related to the topic of study.	General and specific ideas related to the topic of study.	Ideas large in scope, specific, interdisciplinary, and related to the topic of study.
Universal Concepts	Broad statements related to big ideas and the topic of study.	Broad statements thematic in nature and related to big ideas and the topic of study.	Broad statements thematic in nature and deepen conceptual understanding of big ideas and the topic of study. Applicable within and across disciplines.
Essential Questions	Open-ended questions that are related to the topic of study and include big ideas.	Overarching questions that include big ideas and contextualize the topic of study.	Overarching questions that are transferrable, debatable, generate more inquiry, and interdisciplinary. Questions include big ideas and contextualize the topic of study.
Project Objective	A call to action that includes what students should know and do.	A call to action that includes what students should know, do, and produce.	A call to action that encompasses thinking skills (*think*), content (*know*), resources (*source*), and a product (*do*).
Focused Inquiry	General questions related to big ideas and the topic of study.	General and specific questions related to big ideas and the topic of study.	A cycle of inquiry that includes general, specific, elaborate, and sourcing questions related to big ideas and the topic of study.
Learning Activities	Tasks related to the topic of study that include a low level of cognitive demand (*remembering*).	Tasks related to the topic of study that include low and mid levels of cognitive demand (*remembering, understanding, and applying*).	Multifaceted tasks that contextualize the topic of study through all levels of cognitive demand (*remembering, understanding, applying, analyzing, evaluating, and creating*).

+1P Components	Beginning	Emerging	Outstanding
Investigation (Research)	Sources of information are researched to contextualize the topic of study.	Credible primary and secondary sources of information are researched to contextualize the topic of study.	Credible primary and secondary sources of information contextualize the topic of study. Research also includes "Look Fours" (*trends over time, multiple perspectives, technological advances, and forecasting*).
Recommendations	Recommendations are related to the project.	Recommendations are supported by evidence from the research and related to the project.	Recommendations are supported by evidence from the research, include an explanation of benefits, and are related to the project.
Presentation	Presentation is related to the topic of study, includes findings from research, and considers some elements of PEACES (projection, eye contact, attire, confidence, engagement and succinctness).	Presentation is related to the topic of study, includes findings from research, provides answers to focused inquiry, and considers elements of PEACES and EPL (ethos, pathos, logos).	Presentation is related to the topic of study, includes findings from research, provides answers to focused inquiry, considers PEACES and EPL, and connects to universal concepts and essential questions.
Writing Assessment	Short essay that is research-based and aligned to writing standards.	Short essay that is research-based, aligned to standards, and includes academic vocabulary.	Short essay that is aligned to standards, research-based, includes academic vocabulary, and answers three questions from PBL template.
Reflection and Commitment	Perspectives reflect understanding about the topic.	Perspectives reflect understanding of 21st Century Skills (21st CS), big ideas, universal concepts, and essential questions. Considerations are made for what could be done differently the next time.	Perspectives reflect understanding of 21st CS, big ideas, universal concepts, and essential questions; considerations are made for what could be done differently the next time; commitments are made to extend and share the project with others in the community.

designed to prepare students for the next grade level, which eventually leads to preparation for college. In terms of +1P, standards provide additional specificity around what students should know and be able to do throughout a project. Teachers must be acutely aware of which standards to emphasize in order to plan accordingly, and students must be acutely aware of which standards to master in order to meet certain learning targets. We cannot expect students to reach learning targets if they are unaware of the requisite knowledge and skills to achieve mastery. For this reason, standards are an essential part of the +1P process.

One question still remains: What do you do if your discipline or college course does not have standards? In this case, it is strongly advised that you incorporate literacy standards outlined in this chapter. College professors may consider embedding language from the College and Career Ready (CCR) Anchor Standards into their course objectives. If students are going to achieve success in college and compete globally, they must be literate. Most jobs and careers involve some form of reading, comprehending, listening, and speaking. Although some jobs and careers require less writing than others, most, if not all, K–12 classrooms and college courses involve writing. Even mathematics courses and technical subjects contain some elements of writing, especially when students are asked to explain their reasoning or justify their answers. It is imperative that students learn to use language effectively, which includes skills in reading, writing, listening, and speaking. Literacy is also paramount to successful implementation of +1P. Teachers and students cannot engage in the process without oral, written, and digital communication.

COMMON CORE STATE STANDARDS

The impact of the new Common Core State Standards (CCSS) can be felt nationwide. On one hand, the CCSS are viewed as political, debatable, and controversial. On the other hand, the CCSS are viewed as accessible, feasible, and equitable. For the purposes of this book, neither side will be debated. Instead, we will take what is relevant from the CCSS and apply it to the +1P process. If your school does not use the CCSS, you may still apply the standards mentioned in this section or use content standards and achievement measures pertinent to your school.

Broadly defined, the CCSS are nationalized standards in English and mathematics that participating states have adopted. Formal adoption of these standards has already taken place in over forty of the fifty United States. Similar to 21st Century Skills, the new CCSS prepare students to be college and career ready by teaching them to go deeper for conceptual knowledge. Students are equipped with the ability to (Fletcher, 2010):

- Demonstrate independence
- Build content knowledge
- Respond to varying demands of audience, task purpose, and discipline
- Comprehend as well as critique
- Value evidence
- Use technology and digital media strategically and capably
- Come to understand other perspectives and cultures

According to Trilling and Fadel (2009), in order to be productive contributors to society in the twenty-first century, students need to quickly learn core content "while also mastering a broad portfolio of essentials in learning, innovation, technology, and career skills needed for work and life" (p. 16). These "essentials" are highlighted in the CCSS. Learning experiences supported by the CCSS encourage transfer and application of knowledge, thus contributing to students' ability to compete locally and globally—an important goal of +1P.

Stated in the previous chapter, +1P is designed to supplement an already existing curriculum. Grade-specific standards can be mastered through the everyday curriculum, while general standards can be mastered through +1P projects. For example, general standards may be more aligned to projects on homelessness, global warming, or transportation. For these projects, general standards within English, math, science, history, physical education, and/or art might be more applicable than grade-specific standards. General standards may include the following:

- College and Career Readiness (CCR) Anchor Standards
- Standards for Mathematical Practices (MPs)
- Science and Engineering Practices (Next Generation Science Standards)
- Historical and Social Science Analysis Skills
- Physical Education Overarching Standards
- Visual and Performing Arts Standards

For courses that do not have content standards, it is recommended that teachers pull standards from the CCR Anchor Standards

Figure 2.4 College and Career Readiness Anchor Standards

Common Core State Standards - English Language Arts

READING

Key Ideas and Details

1. Read closely to determine what the text says explicitly and to make logical inferences from it; cite specific textual evidence when writing or speaking to support conclusions drawn from the text.

2. Determine central ideas or themes of a text and analyze their development; summarize the key supporting details and ideas.

3. Analyze how and why individuals, events, and ideas develop and interact over the course of a text.

Craft and Structure

4. Interpret words and phrases as they are used in a text, including determining technical, connotative, and figurative meanings, and analyze how specific word choices shape meaning or tone.

WRITING

Text Types and Purposes

1. Write arguments to support claims in an analysis of substantive topics or texts using valid reasoning and relevant and sufficient evidence.

2. Write informative/explanatory texts to examine and convey complex ideas and information clearly and accurately though the effective selection, organization, and analysis of content.

3. Write narratives to develop real or imagined experiences or events using effective technique, well-chosen details, and well-structured event sequences.

Distribution of Writing

4. Produce clear and coherent writing in which the development, organization, and style are appropriate to task, purpose, and audience.

SPEAKING & LISTENING

Comprehension and Collaboration

1. Prepare for and participate effectively in a range of conversations and collaborations with diverse partners, building on others' ideas and expressing their own ideas clearly and persuasively.

2. Integrate and evaluate information presented in diverse media and formats, including visually, quantitatively, and orally.

3. Evaluate a speaker's point of view, reasoning, and use of evidence and rhetoric.

Presentation of Knowledge and Ideas

4. Present information, findings, and supporting evidence such that listeners can follow the line of reasoning and the organization, development, and style are appropriate to task, purpose, and audience.

5. Make strategic use of digital media and visual displays of data to express information and enhance understanding of presentations.

LANGUAGE

Conventions

1. Demonstrate command of the conventions of standard English grammar and usage when writing or speaking.

2. Demonstrate command of the conventions of standard English capitalization, punctuation, and spelling when writing.

Language

3. Apply knowledge of language to understand how language functions in different contexts, to make effective choices for meaning or style, and to comprehend more fully when reading or listening.

Vocabulary Acquisition and Use

4. Determine or clarify the meaning of unknown and multiple-meaning words and phrases by using context clues, analyzing meaningful word parts, and consulting general and specialized reference materials, as appropriate.

Reading Anchor Standards

Craft and Structure

5. Analyze the structure of texts, including how specific sentences, paragraphs, and larger portions of the text (e.g., a section, chapter, scene, or stanza) relate to each other and the whole.
6. Assess how point of view or purpose shapes the content and style of a text.

Integration of Knowledge

7. Integrate and evaluate content presented in diverse media and formats, including visually and quantitatively, as well as in words.
8. Delineate and evaluate the argument and specific claims in a text, including the validity of the reasoning as well as the relevance and sufficiency of the evidence.
9. Analyze how two or more texts address similar themes or topics in order to build knowledge or to compare the approaches the authors take.

Complexity

10. Read and comprehend complex literary and informational texts independently and proficiently.

Writing Anchor Standards

Distribution of Writing

5. Develop and strengthen writing as needed by planning, revising, editing, rewriting, or trying a new approach.
6. Use technology, including the Internet, to produce and publish writing and to interact and collaborate with others.

Research to Present Knowledge

7. Conduct short as well as more sustained research projects based on focused questions demonstrating understanding of the subject under investigation.
8. Gather relevant information from multiple print and digital sources, assess the credibility and accuracy of each source, and integrate the information while avoiding plagiarism.
9. Draw evidence from literary or informational texts to support analysis, reflection, and research.

Range

10. Write routinely over extended time frames (time for research, reflection, and revision) and shorter time frames (a single sitting or a day or two) for a range of tasks, purposes, and audience.

Speaking and Listening Anchor Standards

Presentation of Knowledge and Ideas

6. Adapt speech to a variety of contexts and communicative tasks, demonstrating command of formal English when indicated or appropriate.

Language Anchor Standards

Vocabulary Acquisition and Use

5. Demonstrate understanding of word relationships and nuances in word meanings.
6. Acquire and use accurately a range of general academic and domain-specific words and phrases sufficient for reading, writing, speaking, and listening at the college and career readiness level; demonstrate independence in gathering vocabulary knowledge when encountering an unknown term important to comprehension or expression.

Key

	Organizing Elements (gray boxes)
10	Reading Anchor Standards
10	Writing Anchor Standards
6	Speaking and Listening Anchor Standards
6	Language Anchor Standards
32	Total Anchor Standards

Adapted from Veronica Gonzalez, PhD, LAUSD, 2014.

when planning for +1P. Anchor standards are interdisciplinary, support literacy development for all students, and are applicable to any project. When planning, college professors can reference the CCR Anchor Standards as well. Referencing these standards would promote coherency and transfer from K–12 to college.

Notice the language domain included in Figure 2.4. Language anchor standards address conventions, language use, and vocabulary acquisition. These skills are particularly important for college and career readiness. At the college level, students are expected to express and articulate ideas using academic vocabulary and to know conventions in grammar and syntax. Students must possess these skills prior to enrolling in college and/or starting a career.

Some anchor standards lend themselves more to planning than others, but all four domains—reading, writing, speaking and listening, and language—are critical to +1P implementation. Consider the following anchor standards (AS) when planning your unit:

- **Reading AS 7:** Integrate and evaluate content presented in diverse media and formats, including visually and quantitatively, as well as in words.
- **Reading AS 9:** Analyze how two or more texts address similar themes or topics in order to build knowledge or to compare the approaches the authors take.
- **Writing AS 6:** Use technology, including the Internet, to produce and publish writing and to interact and collaborate with others.
- **Writing AS 7:** Conduct short as well as more sustained research projects based on focused questions demonstrating understanding of the subject under investigation.
- **Speaking and Listening AS 1:** Prepare for and participate effectively in a range of conversations with diverse partners, building on others' ideas and expressing their own clearly and persuasively.
- **Speaking and Listening AS 4:** Present information, findings, and supporting evidence such that listeners can follow the line of reasoning and the organization, development, and style are appropriate to task, purpose, and audience.
- **Language AS 1:** Demonstrate command of the conventions of Standard English grammar and usage when writing or speaking.
- **Language AS 4:** Determine or clarify the meaning of unknown and multiple-meaning words and phrases by using context clues, analyzing meaningful word parts, and consulting general and specialized reference materials, as appropriate.

Planning with these anchor standards is highly recommended. Many of the concepts would already be taught in a unit. What matters most is that teachers consider all four domains.

The Standards for Mathematical Practice are general principles of good math instruction. According to the Common Core State Standards Initiative (2015), mathematical practices (MPs) "describe varieties of expertise that mathematics educators at all levels should seek to develop in their students. These practices rest on important 'processes and proficiencies' with longstanding importance in mathematics education." Students are better prepared for college and a career when they develop these competencies in math. Everette (2013) explains MPs as a way to approach teaching so that students develop a mathematical mindset that allows them to see math in the world around them. +1P projects are centered on authentic, real-world tasks that heighten student awareness about the world around them. As such, MPs are applicable and useful for projects related to math. The eight mathematical practices are (Common Core State Standards Initiative, 2015):

MP1: *Make sense of problems and persevere in solving them.*

- ✓ Mathematically proficient students start by explaining to themselves the meaning of a problem and looking for entry points to its solution.

MP2: *Reason abstractly and quantitatively.*

- ✓ Mathematically proficient students make sense of quantities and their relationships in problem situations.

MP3: *Construct viable arguments and critique the reasoning of others.*

- ✓ Mathematically proficient students understand and use stated assumptions, definitions, and previously established results in constructing arguments.

MP4: *Model with mathematics.*

- ✓ Mathematically proficient students can apply the mathematics they know to solve problems arising in everyday life, society, and the workplace.

MP5: *Use appropriate tools strategically.*

- ✓ Mathematically proficient students consider the available tools when solving a mathematical problem.

MP6: *Attend to precision.*

✓ Mathematically proficient students try to communicate precisely to others.

MP7: *Look for and make use of structure.*

✓ Mathematically proficient students look closely to discern a pattern or structure.

MP8: *Look for and express regularity in repeated reasoning.*

✓ Mathematically proficient students notice if calculations are repeated and look both for general methods and for shortcuts.

Teachers may use additional English Language Arts (ELA) and math standards when planning. The aforementioned standards are listed as suggestions for a +1P unit. They represent a snapshot of the K–12 CCSS in ELA and math. The CCSS also provide literacy standards in history/social studies, science, and technical subjects. These standards focus on teaching key ideas and details, craft and structure, and integration of knowledge within a discipline. Literacy standards also address skills in organizing ideas, sourcing, reasoning, stating claims and counterclaims, drawing evidence from text, analysis, and conducting research—applicable concepts to +1P. Overall, it is important to remember that student success is predicated on standards that are (Common Core State Standards Initiative, 2015):

- Research and evidence based
- Clear, understandable, and consistent
- Aligned with college and career expectations
- Based on rigorous content and the application of knowledge through higher-order thinking skills
- Built upon the strengths and lessons of current state standards
- Informed by other top-performing countries to prepare all students for success in our global economy and society

NEXT GENERATION SCIENCE STANDARDS

The National Research Council (NRC) of the National Academy of Sciences was instrumental in creating the Next Generation Science Standards (NGSS) and developing *A Framework for K–12 Science Education*. Included in the framework are eight practices of science and engineering that are identified as essential for all students to learn.

Chapter 3 of the framework describes the eight practices of science and engineering and presents the following rationale for why they are essential (National Research Council, 2012, p. 42):

> Engaging in the practices of science helps students understand how scientific knowledge develops; such direct involvement gives them an appreciation of the wide range of approaches that are used to investigate, model, and explain the world. Engaging in the practices of engineering likewise helps students understand the work of engineers, as well as the links between engineering and science. Participation in these practices also helps students form an understanding of the crosscutting concepts and disciplinary ideas of science and engineering; moreover, it makes students' knowledge more meaningful and embeds it more deeply into their worldview.

Consider the significance of these eight practices and how they can be applied to your planning:

Practice #1: *Asking questions (for science) and defining problems (for engineering)*

- ✓ Students at any grade level should be able to ask questions of each other about the texts they read, the features of the phenomena they observe, and the conclusions they draw from their models or scientific investigations. For engineering, they should ask questions to define the problem to be solved and to elicit ideas that lead to the constraints and specifications for its solution (National Research Council, 2012, p. 56).

Practice #2: *Developing and using models*

- ✓ Modeling can begin in the earliest grades, with students' models progressing from concrete "pictures" and/or physical scale models (e.g., a toy car) to more abstract representations of relevant relationships in later grades, such as a diagram representing forces on a particular object in a system (National Research Council, 2012, p. 58).

Practice #3: *Planning and carrying out investigations*

- ✓ Students should have opportunities to plan and carry out several different kinds of investigations during their K–12 years. At all levels, they should engage in investigations that range from those structured by the teacher—in order to expose an issue or question that they would be unlikely to explore on their own (e.g., measuring specific properties of materials)—to those that emerge from students' own questions (National Research Council, 2012, p. 61).

Practice #4: *Analyzing and interpreting data*

✓ Once collected, data must be presented in a form that can reveal any patterns and relationships and that allows results to be communicated to others. Because raw data as such have little meaning, a major practice of scientists is to organize and interpret data through tabulating, graphing, or statistical analysis. Such analysis can bring out the meaning of data—and their relevance—so that they may be used as evidence.

✓ Engineers, too, make decisions based on evidence that a given design will work; they rarely rely on trial and error. Engineers often analyze a design by creating a model or prototype and collecting extensive data on how it performs, including under extreme conditions. Analysis of this kind of data not only informs design decisions and enables the prediction or assessment of performance but also helps define or clarify problems, determine economic feasibility, evaluate alternatives, and investigate failures (National Research Council, 2012, pp. 61–62).

Practice #5: *Using mathematics and computational thinking*

✓ Although there are differences in how mathematics and computational thinking are applied in science and in engineering, mathematics often brings these two fields together by enabling engineers to apply the mathematical form of scientific theories and by enabling scientists to use powerful information technologies designed by engineers. Both kinds of professionals can thereby accomplish investigations and analyses and build complex models, which might otherwise be out of the question (National Research Council, 2012, p. 65).

Practice #6: *Constructing explanations (science) and designing solutions (engineering)*

✓ The goal of science is the construction of theories that provide explanatory accounts of the world. A theory becomes accepted when it has multiple lines of empirical evidence and greater explanatory power of phenomena than previous theories (National Research Council, 2012, p. 52).

Practice #7: *Engaging in argument from evidence*

✓ The study of science and engineering should produce a sense of the process of argument necessary for advancing and defending a new idea or an explanation of a phenomenon and the norms for conducting such arguments. In that spirit, students should argue for the explanations they construct, defend their interpretations of the associated data, and advocate for the designs they propose (National Research Council, 2012, p. 73).

Practice #8: *Obtaining, evaluating, and communicating information*

✓ Any education in science and engineering needs to develop students' ability to read and produce domain-specific text. As such, every science or engineering lesson is in part a language lesson, particularly reading and producing the genres of texts that are intrinsic to science and engineering (National Research Council, 2012, p. 76).

The eight science and engineering practices are applicable to the +1P process. Those practices that emphasize inquiry, investigation, making models, and analyzing data are particularly relevant. In support of an integrated model of literacy, Practice #8 (communicating information) indicates "every science or engineering lesson is in part a language lesson . . . " (National Research Council, 2012, p. 76). This statement could not be further from the truth. All lessons, regardless of subject matter, are language lessons. Students are required to read, write, speak and listen, and use language as they learn. For this reason, all disciplines should embrace literacy as a key component of their instructional practices, which calls for intentional planning around the four domains of literacy.

HISTORY/SOCIAL STUDIES STANDARDS

Every state has content standards for history/social studies. While I cannot reference each state's standards, California's history/social studies standards can serve as a general guide when planning for +1P. These standards include similar themes to CCSS and NGSS. In addition to grade-specific standards, the standards include a "Historical and Social Sciences Analysis Skills" section for Grades

K–5 and for Grades 6–12. They are designed to teach intellectual reasoning, reflection, and research skills. The general standards in history/social studies are applicable to +1P projects and equally transferrable outside of California. The Historical and Social Sciences Analysis Skills for Grades K–5 include (California Department of Education, 2015):

Chronological and Spatial Thinking

1. Students place key events and people of the historical era they are studying in a chronological sequence and within a spatial context; they interpret timelines.

2. Students correctly apply terms related to time, including *past, present, future, decade, century,* and *generation.*

3. Students explain how the present is connected to the past, identifying both similarities and differences between the two, and how some things change over time and some things stay the same.

4. Students use map and globe skills to determine the absolute locations of places and interpret information available through a map's or globe's legend, scale, and symbolic representations.

5. Students judge the significance of the relative location of a place (e.g., proximity to a harbor, on trade routes) and analyze how relative advantages or disadvantages can change over time.

Research, Evidence, and Point of View

1. Students differentiate between primary and secondary sources.

2. Students pose relevant questions about events they encounter in historical documents, eyewitness accounts, oral histories, letters, diaries, artifacts, photographs, maps, artworks, and architecture.

3. Students distinguish fact from fiction by comparing documentary sources on historical figures and events with fictionalized characters and events.

Historical Interpretation

1. Students summarize the key events of the era they are studying and explain the historical contexts of those events.

2. Students identify the human and physical characteristics of the places they are studying and explain how those features form the unique character of those places.

3. Students identify and interpret the multiple causes and effects of historical events.

4. Students conduct cost-benefit analyses of historical and current events.

The Historical and Social Sciences Analysis Skills for Grades 6–12 include (California Department of Education, 2015):

Chronological and Spatial Thinking

1. Students explain how major events are related to one another in time.

2. Students construct various timelines of key events, people, and periods of the historical era they are studying.

3. Students use a variety of maps and documents to identify physical and cultural features of neighborhoods, cities, states, and countries and to explain the historical migration of people, expansion and disintegration of empires, and the growth of economic systems.

Research, Evidence, and Point of View

1. Students frame questions that can be answered by historical study and research.

2. Students distinguish fact from opinion in historical narratives and stories.

3. Students distinguish relevant from irrelevant information, essential from incidental information, and verifiable from unverifiable information in historical narratives and stories.

4. Students assess the credibility of primary and secondary sources and draw sound conclusions from them.

5. Students detect the different historical points of view on historical events and determine the context in which the historical statements were made (the questions asked, sources used, author's perspectives).

Historical Interpretation

1. Students explain the central issues and problems from the past, placing people and events in a matrix of time and place.

2. Students understand and distinguish cause, effect, sequence, and correlation in historical events, including the long- and short-term causal relations.

3. Students explain the sources of historical continuity and how the combination of ideas and events explains the emergence of new patterns.

4. Students recognize the role of chance, oversight, and error in history.

5. Students recognize that interpretations of history are subject to change as new information is uncovered.

6. Students interpret basic indicators of economic performance and conduct cost-benefit analyses of economic and political issues.

To reiterate, the aforementioned standards in ELA, math, science, and history/social studies represent a snapshot of the K–12 core content standards. However, teachers should be noting correlations between the CCR Anchor Standards, Mathematical Practices, NGSS Science and Engineering Practices, and the Historical and Social Sciences Analysis Skills. Repetitive themes in these general standards include, but are not limited to:

- Inquiry/Questions
- Research/Investigation
- Evidence
- Sources (primary and secondary)
- Models
- Analysis
- Reasoning
- Argument
- Factual knowledge
- Procedural knowledge
- Conceptual knowledge
- Problem Solving
- Communicating
- Critical Thinking

These skills and recursive themes are evident throughout the +1P process. For this reason, standards are not only essential to planning, but also complementary. Moreover, standards ensure that students learn the requisite skills and knowledge necessary for success in college, career, and life.

PHYSICAL EDUCATION STANDARDS

Academic standards in physical education (PE) are applicable to +1P projects as well. Once again, each state has its own PE standards. Congruent themes of movement, physical fitness, and health are present in most PE standards. Teachers have the option of using their own state standards for PE or California's general PE standards for elementary, middle, and high school students (California Department of Education, 2015):

Elementary and Middle School

> **Standard 1:** Students demonstrate the motor skills and movement patterns needed to perform a variety of physical activities.

> **Standard 2:** Students demonstrate knowledge of movement concepts, principles, and strategies that apply to the learning and performance of physical activities.

> **Standard 3:** Students assess and maintain a level of physical fitness to improve health and performance.

> **Standard 4:** Students demonstrate knowledge of physical fitness concepts, principles, and strategies to improve health and performance.

> **Standard 5:** Students demonstrate and utilize knowledge of psychological and sociological concepts, principles, and strategies that apply to the learning and performance of physical activity.

High School

> **Standard 1:** Students demonstrate knowledge of and competency in motor skills, movement patterns, and strategies needed to perform a variety of physical activities.

> **Standard 2:** Students achieve a level of physical fitness for health and performance while demonstrating knowledge of fitness concepts, principles, and strategies.

Standard 3: Students demonstrate knowledge of psychological and sociological concepts, principles, and strategies that apply to the learning and performance of physical activity.

The interdisciplinary nature of +1P supports projects that integrate PE standards. For example, students could launch an investigative study on Pilates, yoga, training camps for professional athletes, diet, or physical fitness. These topics align with elementary and middle school Standard 4 (knowledge of physical fitness concepts, principles, and strategies to improve health and performance) and high school Standard 3 (psychological and sociological concepts, principles, and strategies that apply to the learning and performance of physical activity). Other topics related to PE standards can also be explored.

VISUAL AND PERFORMING ARTS STANDARDS

Artistic expression and performing arts are deeply rooted in our society. A famous quote by Michelangelo states, "I saw the angel in the marble and carved until I set him free." In a sense, it is incumbent upon educators to see the potential in their students and carve an educational pathway that leads to their future success. Through the arts, students can master skills that prepare them for college, career, and life. Most states have adopted visual and performing arts (VAPA) standards for Grades K–12. Teachers have the option of planning with their own VAPA standards or California's VAPA standards. Five overarching strands, followed by general standards, are used to organize the standards for dance, music, theatre, and visual arts. Stated below is an example of how the strands and general standards are organized for visual arts. See Appendix A for general standards in dance, music, and theatre.

1. **Artistic Expression**

   ✓ Processing, Analyzing, and Responding to Sensory Information Through the Language and Skills Unique to the Visual Arts

   ✓ Students perceive and respond to works of art, objects in nature, events, and the environment. They also use the vocabulary of the visual arts to express their observations.

2. **Creative Expression**

   ✓ Creating, Performing, and Participating in the Visual Arts

✓ Students apply artistic processes and skills using a variety of media to communicate meaning and intent in original works of art.

3. **Historical and Cultural Context**

   ✓ Understanding the Historical Contributions and Cultural Dimensions of the Visual Arts

   ✓ Students analyze the role and development of the visual arts in past and present cultures throughout the world, noting human diversity as it relates to the visual arts and artists.

4. **Aesthetic Valuing**

   ✓ Responding to, Analyzing, and Making Judgments About Works in the Visual Arts

   ✓ Students analyze, assess, and derive meaning from works of art, including their own, according to the elements of art, the principles of design, and aesthetic qualities.

5. **Connections, Relationships, Applications**

   ✓ Connecting and Applying What Is Learned in the Visual Arts to Other Art Forms and Subject Areas and to Careers

   ✓ Students apply what they learn in the visual arts across subject areas. They develop competencies and creative skills in problem solving, communication, and management of time and resources that contribute to lifelong learning and career skills. They also learn about careers in and related to the visual arts.

This overview of general standards across the disciplines will help me decide which ones to use for my sample unit plan. Even without knowing my topic of study, I am certain that students will read, write, speak, listen, and use language. As a result, I will start by choosing CCR Anchor Standards. Standards can also be deleted or added throughout the planning process.

Notice that the anchor standards in Figure 2.5 relate to any topic of study. For this reason, you can easily choose the same standards for your unit plan. These anchor standards are also comprehensible for

Figure 2.5   Standards for Sample +1P Unit

Standards

Common Core State Standards:

College and Career Readiness (CCR) Anchor Standards (AS)

Reading AS 7:

Integrate and evaluate content presented in diverse media and formats, including visually and quantitatively, as well as in words.

Writing AS 6:

Use technology, including the Internet, to produce and publish writing and to interact and collaborate with others.

Writing AS 7:

Conduct short as well as more sustained research projects based on focused questions demonstrating understanding of the subject under investigation.

Speaking and Listening AS 4:

Present information, findings, and supporting evidence such that listeners can follow the line of reasoning and the organization, development, and style are appropriate to task, purpose, and audience.

Language AS 1:

Demonstrate command of the conventions of standard English grammar and usage when writing or speaking.

---

both teachers and students. The standards in Figure 2.5 are directly aligned to +1P goals and expectations:

- **Reading AS 7:** Evaluate content from <u>diverse media</u>
- **Writing AS 6:** Use <u>technology</u> to <u>communicate and collaborate</u>
- **Writing AS 7:** Conduct <u>research projects</u> using <u>focused questions</u>
- **Speaking and Listening AS 4:** <u>Present</u> information supported by <u>evidence</u>
- **Language AS 1:** Apply <u>standard English conventions</u> when <u>writing and speaking</u>

YOUR TURN TO PRACTICE

What standards would you consider using for your sample unit? Please note that you do not need to know the topic of study just yet. This is your time to practice and familiarize yourself with applicable standards for the project. Write your standards in the table provided:

Standards

Stated earlier, +1P includes a cycle of inquiry and investigation around projects that incorporate rigor, technology, real-world application, and 21st Century Skills. As students engage in the process, they develop skills that prepare them for college, career, and life. The +1P planning rubric and general content standards set expectations for meeting these goals. The comprehensive list of standards provided in this section enabled me to complete the standards component of the planning template without having to search the Internet or browse through hundreds of standards across multiple disciplines. I used the standards section to create *all* sample units within this book. The purpose of this book is to provide a turnkey model that includes everything you need in one package. Keep this in mind as you continue to plan.

Think about rubrics and standards that you have used (or currently use) for planning. How have these tools influenced performance outcomes and expectations? How might you transfer knowledge about the +1P planning rubric and general content standards back to your district, school, or classroom?

CHECKPOINT 2: TOPIC SELECTION AND BIG IDEAS

According to Zimmerman (1989), learning is not something that happens *to* students, it is something that happens *by* students.

Furthermore, learning that happens *by* students involves student interest. Engaging student interest is important for maximizing student potential. Just as adults show more interest in activities of their choosing (sports, leisure reading, traveling, social outings, etc.), students show more excitement when they are engaged in an activity of interest. This is not to say that students who are not interested cannot learn. Although learning may still take place for "disinterested" students, engagement and participation is enhanced with student interest. Tyler (1949) asserts that education is seen as an active process that involves the active efforts of the learner himself. Where interests are desirable ones, they can serve as the focus of educational attention. Tyler (1949) goes on to state that learning experiences designed to develop interests give students the opportunity to explore and to have *satisfying* results from these explorations.

Every teacher, regardless of geographic location and classroom demographics, teaches a rainbow of diverse learners. By diverse learners, I mean student personalities and various ethnic, cultural, socioeconomic, religious, and educational backgrounds. Inevitably, diverse students will have diverse interests. That being said, +1P accommodates the eclectic range of student interests through topic selection. Students are given an opportunity to choose a topic that is of particular interest to them, thus raising the level of engagement and excitement around learning.

TOPIC SELECTION

There are many different approaches to choosing a topic of study. Teachers can either brainstorm random topics with students or brainstorm topics related to a current theme that students are studying. Neither approach supersedes the other. Topics will vary depending on grade level and age of students. Figure 2.6 provides a sample list of topics that students can explore for their project. Students are not confined to this list; the sandbox for topics of study is massive. However, you will find that many of the suggested topics are not highlighted in state-/district-/school-adopted textbooks and curriculums. The topics in Figure 2.6 have real-world application, which makes learning about them more interesting and meaningful. Real-world application prepares students for college, career, and life, as they are better equipped to transfer and apply knowledge across disciplines and in their personal lives. +1P is strategically designed to meet these outcomes.

Figure 2.6   +1P Sample Topics

+1P Sample Topics	
• Animal Rights • Animals/Insects • Natural Disasters (e.g., earthquakes, tornadoes, hurricanes) • Rain Forests • Droughts • Water/Water Conservation • Geometric Shapes in Society • Diamond Industry • Oil and Natural Gas Industry • Fashion • Hollywood/Celebrities • Wealth (e.g., inherited or acquired, assets, privilege, network) • Media/Social Media • Bullying • Prisons • Artistic Design (e.g., architecture, paintings, pottery, statues) • Famous Artists • Cultural Foods, Art, Customs, and Celebrations • Languages (e.g., dialects, culture, formal and informal) • Archeology • Space Exploration • Engineering (e.g., civil, electrical, chemical, computer) • Science (e.g., earth, physical, life) • Science, Technology, Engineering, Art, and Mathematics • Health (e.g., diseases, food consumption, diets) • Inventions (e.g., patents, trademarks, prototypes) • Technology (e.g., robots, coding/programming, digital devices) • Buying a Car or Buying a House • Modes of Transportation • Owning or Starting a Business • Poverty (e.g., rural, urban, socioeconomic status) • Oceanography	• Stock Market (e.g., supply and demand, investing) • Marketing • Schools • Math (e.g., formulas, blueprints, finances, statistics) • Politics • Political Figures • Military Branches • Maritime Industry (e.g., vessels, cargo, ports, crew) • Graphic Arts Design • Global Warming • History (e.g., timelines, societies, people, religions) • Historical Figures • Governments • Wars • Civil Rights • Revolutions • Genocide • Heroes • Sheroes • Folktales • Modes of Communication • Sports (e.g., MLB, NFL, NBA, WNBA, NHL, MLS) • Athletes • Humanities • Structures • Homelessness • Colleges (e.g., private, state, university, community) • Careers (e.g., white collar, blue collar, pink collar) • Places to Live • Gender • Laws (e.g., federal, state, and local) • Contracts (e.g., government, state, corporate)

Since many of the topics listed in Figure 2.6 are general, teachers may want to assist their students in choosing a subtopic that is related to the general topic. For example, students could study baseball, which is a subtopic of sports. To study every sport would be cumbersome and overwhelming. For this reason, a subtopic focuses the project around one component of a general topic, allowing students go more in-depth. To foster career readiness, students can also study a career for their +1P project. Oftentimes, students aspire to have a career in a particular area, but they may not know what that career entails. For instance, students may want to be a doctor or an attorney, but they may not understand the full scope of that profession. +1P can expose students to more details about a certain profession. See Appendix B for sample +1P unit plans.

For my topic of study, I chose Vessel Operations, which is a subtopic of the maritime industry. I chose this topic because I live in a port town and vessels have always intrigued me. I also know several people in the maritime industry—maritime officers, sailors, engineers, superintendents, managers, and longshoremen. More importantly, I feel obligated to study the universal impact and pervasive influence of Vessel Operations on everyday life. Nearly everything from food, clothes, and furniture to digital devices, books, and cars is transported on a ship. Most of the items in our schools and classrooms—desks, chairs, tables, computers and laptops, LCD projectors, Elmos, SMART boards, paper, pencils, pens, books, crayons, food, etc.—are transported on a vessel before reaching our schools/classrooms. Vessel Operations is an example of a real-world topic that may not exist in a textbook or school curriculum.

YOUR TURN TO PRACTICE

Given the list of sample +1P topics, what might your students be interested in exploring? Write down three to five topics that your students can use to engage in a cycle of inquiry and investigation. Use the table to write your ideas below:

+1P Topics to Consider
1.
2.
3.
4.
5.

MOTIVATION

What role does motivation play in student learning? Contextually, the Latin root of the word "motivation" means "to move"; hence, the study of motivation is the study of action (Eccles & Wigfield, 2002, p. 110). Once teachers spark student interest, students must be motivated to act and persevere. It is not enough to just be interested. Students need to be interested *and* motivated. Pintrich (2003) contends that learning and motivation are reciprocal. It can be argued that the more motivated students are, the more they are willing to learn. Our responsibility as educators is to optimize instructional environments that promote student interest, meaningful learning, and academic motivation. To guide planning around motivation, teachers can use the five conceptions of how academic motivation works—*interest, beliefs, attributions, goals,* and *partnership* (Mayer, 2011). A description of each conception is provided, along with student examples related to +1P (Mayer, 2011, p. 41):

- **Interest:** Students work harder to learn material that has personal value to them.

  - *+1P example:* I am interested in this project and I will strive to do my best.

- **Beliefs:** Students work harder to learn when they believe their hard work will pay off.

  - *+1P example:* I will excel at this project because I know that it will prepare me for college and a career.

- **Attributions:** Students work harder to learn when they attribute their successes and failures to effort.

  - *+1P example:* The effort that I put into my project will determine my success or failure.

- **Goals:** Students work harder to learn when their goal is to master the material.

  - *+1P example:* I want to achieve mastery as I learn about my topic of study.

- **Partnership:** Students work harder to learn when they view the instructor as a social partner.

  - *+1P example:* My teacher and I are collaborating and building capacity together.

These indicators may help teachers gauge student motivation during the +1P process. We want students to be interested in their topic of study *and* motivated to complete the project. Outside of +1P, students may not have as many opportunities to study topics that are of particular interest to them. For this reason, teachers and students should take advantage of the varied topics of interest that students can study. There is one caveat to consider when planning. While we honor student interest, we need to be aware that "students don't know what they don't know." In some cases, students may not be interested in a topic that is unfamiliar to them. For instance, a teacher might brainstorm topics related to engineering and find that his or her students only take interest in mechanics and design. However, we know that engineering encompasses more than just mechanics and design. Other types of engineering include electrical, civil, computer science, and chemical. If students have no prior knowledge of the different types of engineering, this does not mean they are not interested in studying them. Teachers just need to be mindful of these discrepancies when they brainstorm different topics for student projects.

BIG IDEAS

Big ideas are terms and concepts related to a topic, discipline, or project. They can be broad in scope, as in interdisciplinary, or specific to a topic or discipline. Big ideas are mainly used as focal points for an investigative study. The purpose of generating big ideas is to build a student's repertoire of related terms and concepts for a topic of study. Students need to understand that ideas and concepts do not exist in isolation; they are generally connected to other ideas and concepts. Big ideas help students make these connections, thus avoiding confusion from fragmented and disjointed ideas. For the purpose of +1P, big ideas are single words related to a topic of study, principle, and universal concept. The correlation between big ideas and universal concepts is further explored in Checkpoint 3, which explains universal concepts and essential questions.

As a teacher, you want students to quickly generate big ideas for their topic of study. Big ideas are not intended to be complex, confusing, and confounding. The key is to determine why big ideas are important to a topic of study and to decide which big ideas merit deeper exploration. Deeper exploration of specific big ideas, as opposed to all big ideas, will help students acquire and maintain conceptual knowledge. There is nothing worse than spending hours teaching a concept that students will forget within weeks or days. If we expect student learning to be applicable and transferrable, students must retain the information

Figure 2.7   Big Ideas for Sample +1P Unit

Big Ideas
transportation, **vessel operations**, **cargo** (imported and exported), **systems**, **container ports**, **technology**, **trade** (national and international), rules, safety, contracts, **supply and demand**, and labor/unions

they learn. Retention of knowledge is heightened when we engage student interest and teach with the "inch deep" versus "mile wide" approach. See the example big ideas for the Vessel Operations unit.

It is necessary to brainstorm several big ideas so that students have options to choose from when conducting their research. Notice that some of the big ideas in Figure 2.7 are bolded. The bolded words represent ideas that will be further explored in the Vessel Operations unit. Remember, students may not have time to research all big ideas. You might still ask, "Why keep big ideas on the list that will not be explicitly taught or researched?" Students may discover that some big ideas on the list, not originally intended for deeper exploration, are appearing in their research. For this reason, it is important to keep all big ideas on the list. Students can still engage in conversation about these big ideas and possibly add them to their investigative study.

YOUR TURN TO PRACTICE

Choose one of the topics from the list that you previously generated. Generate five to ten big ideas related to your topic of study. Remember to use the +1P rubric to assist you in this process. When you are finished with your list of big ideas, it may help to circle or underline those big ideas that you would like for students to explore further. Write your big ideas below.

+1P Topic of Study: _____

Big Ideas	
1.	6.
2.	7.
3.	8.
4.	9.
5.	10.

Note: For consistency, keep the same topic of study as you construct your sample +1P unit.

Now that we have covered the purpose of engaging student interest and motivation and chosen a topic of study and big ideas, we are ready to explore universal concepts and essential questions.

Think about ways you have fostered student interest and motivation. Why does student interest and motivation matter? How might you transfer knowledge about student interest, motivation, topic selection, and big ideas back to your district, school, or classroom?

CHECKPOINT 3: UNIVERSAL CONCEPTS AND ESSENTIAL QUESTIONS

Universal concepts are broad statements that are thematic in nature and designed to deepen conceptual understanding of a topic. They are applicable within and across disciplines, they include big ideas, and they are intended to stimulate and stretch student thinking.

UNIVERSAL CONCEPTS

Universal concepts prompt students to think critically about the bigger picture and broader meaning for a topic of study. Essentially, universal concepts represent subsets of big ideas that increase breadth and depth of understanding for a project. They relate to many facts and can be used as organizing elements, or focal points, for a unit of study. According to Tyler (1949), organization greatly influences efficiency and desired outcomes. Similarly, "when learning is organized in logical steps—rather than disconnected episodes—students are able to construct their own deep knowledge and understanding" about a topic, concept, or discipline (Tomlinson, Kaplan, Purcell, Leppien, Burns, & Strickland, 2005, p. 58). The +1P process is organized in a way to illicit deeper understanding from big ideas and universal concepts and to provide coherency across checkpoints. As each checkpoint is further examined, coherency will become more apparent.

Big Ideas and Universal Concepts

PARADIGM SHIFTS
- Paradigm shifts are unavoidable
- Paradigm shifts can be positive or negative
- Paradigm shifts are needed for societies to progress
- Paradigm shifts have causes and effects
- Paradigm shifts require flexibility

DIVERSITY
- Societies should embrace diversity
- Diversity can lead to conflict
- Diversity allows for enriched conversations
- Diversity is needed for progress
- Diversity has costs and benefits

SOCIAL JUSTICE
- Social justice places value on equal rights
- Social justice is the result of human failure
- Social justice is a utopian concept
- Social justice considers individual and joint rights
- Social justice protects disenfranchised members of society

CULTURE
- Culture is complex
- Culture is controlled by society
- Culture changes over time
- Culture is passed down from one generation to another
- Cultural identity can be abused
- Cultures can be inclusive and exclusive

SYSTEMS
- Systems include interdependent parts
- Systems suggest organization
- Systems require relationships
- Systems are influenced by other systems
- Systems can be disturbed
- Systems are dependent upon rules

TECHNOLOGY
- Technology allows for increased production
- Technology meets human needs and wants
- Technology requires innovation
- Technology has costs and benefits
- Technology shapes the future
- Technology influences how people act and interact

COMMUNITY
- Community requires unity
- Community has structure and laws
- Communities are supported by their members
- The larger a community, the stronger it is
- Community is cooperation

COURAGE
- Courage requires sacrifice
- Courageous people are wise
- Courage is defined by society
- Courage requires trials
- Courage depends on the environment (individual, group, society, friendship, family, work, peers, school, public speaking, travel, sports, etc.)

COMPETITION
- Competition advances an economy
- Competition is universal
- Competition has consequences
- Competition requires boundaries
- Competition takes on different forms (sports, schools, politics, religion, business, media, etc.)

SURVIVAL
- Survival requires will power
- Survival is not giving up
- Survival requires faith
- Survivors live to tell the story
- Survivor's remorse is conditional

CONTROL
- If you have control, you have power; if you have power, you have control
- Control has costs and benefits
- Control brings order to groups and societies
- Control may be used or abused
- No control, no order—no order, no control

INNOVATION
- Innovation is dynamic
- Innovation is healthy for an economy
- Innovation advances a society
- Innovation requires creativity
- Innovation requires law and order

(Continued)

Figure 2.8 (Continued)

Big Ideas and Universal Concepts

EDUCATION
- Education is defined by culture and society
- Education reveals successes and failures
- Education has costs and benefits
- Education is knowledge and knowledge is power
- Education is timeless

PATTERNS
- Patterns follow a repetitive structure
- Patterns have order
- Human behavior follows patterns
- Patterns are predictable and spontaneous
- Patterns take on different forms (numbers, shapes, lines, symbols, trends, data, etc.)

TRUTH
- The truth can set you free
- Truth is debatable
- Truth is what can and cannot be proven
- Truth has a price
- Truth requires evidence

BEAUTY
- Beauty is defined by culture and society
- Beauty is subjective
- Beauty may be internal and external
- Beauty is in the eyes of the beholder
- Beauty is marketable
- Beauty can be mistaken for vanity

NUTRITION
- A healthy diet is subjective
- Nutrition and exercise are interdependent
- Nutrition and diet has costs and benefits
- Nutrition is influenced by geographic region and money
- Nutrition is defined by culture and society
- Nutrition requires consistency

FRIENDSHIP
- Friendship is voluntary
- Friendship is defined by sacrifices
- Friendship is unconditional
- Friendship has consequences
- Friendship has no time limit
- Friendship is mutual

LOYALTY
- Loyalty can be unethical
- Loyalty is commitment and dedication
- Loyalty is enduring
- Loyalty requires boundaries
- Loyalty takes on different forms (political, religious, organizational, relational, career, marriage, friendship, parents, offspring, etc.)

RELATIONSHIPS
- Relationships are voluntary and involuntary
- Relationships change over time
- Relationships are influenced by values and beliefs
- Status dictates relationships
- Relationships take on different forms (humans, adults, kids, business, animals, marriages, staff, supervisor–employee, families, siblings, etc.)

MEDIA
- Media provides a means of communication
- Media is biased and partial
- Media controls the discourse in a society
- Media is inclusive and exclusive
- Media takes on different forms (TV, Internet, magazine, music, newspaper, radio, social media, advertising, commercials, etc.)

FAMILY
- Family is defined by culture and society
- Family may be biological or social
- Family values are subjective
- Families have customs and traditions
- Family comes first

SERVICE
- Service is giving back
- Service requires commitment and dedication
- Service requires sacrifice
- Service is influenced by values and beliefs
- Service is personal

JUSTICE
- Justice has costs and benefits
- Justice is human-made and human-destroyed
- Justice is conditional
- Justice requires action
- Justice ignored has consequences

Figure 2.8 includes two separate templates with sample big ideas and universal concepts. These samples are recommended to enhance your planning. The more examples you have at your disposal, the less anxiety you will have when planning your sample unit. Please note that the big ideas and universal concepts listed can be expanded to include others. Big ideas not mentioned are fear, grief, love, tragedy, happiness, perseverance, resilience, and many others. Use the examples provided in Figure 2.8 to enhance your efficacy in generating big ideas and universal concepts.

The universal concepts listed in Figure 2.8 are broad, interdisciplinary, and connected to big ideas. They are also thematic, thought provoking, and stimulating. For my sample unit, I used two big ideas listed in Figure 2.7—*systems* and *technology*—to generate universal concepts. To do this, I used Figure 2.8 to connect my big ideas (*systems* and *technology*) to universal concepts that were pertinent to Vessel Operations.

Figure 2.9   Big Ideas and Universal Concepts for Sample +1P Unit

Big Ideas	Universal Concepts
transportation, **vessel operations**, **cargo** (imported and exported), **systems**, **container ports**, **technology**, **trade**, rules, safety, contracts, **supply and demand**, and labor/unions	**Systems** include interdependent parts. **Technology** allows for increased production.

The big ideas within the universal concepts are bolded to show continuity and consistency. Ideas and concepts that are explicitly connected lead to more clarity and less confusion. As much as possible, teachers should ensure that the essential components of +1P are coherent, connected, and reinforced throughout the unit.

YOUR TURN TO PRACTICE

First, choose one or two big ideas from the list that you generated earlier. Next, using the templates from Figure 2.8, find one or two universal concepts that relate to your big ideas. You also have the option of creating your own universal concepts. Remember to use the +1P rubric to assist you in determining the quality of your planning. To highlight the correlations, it may help to circle or underline the big ideas within your universal concepts. Write your universal concepts below:

+1P Topic of Study: _____

Universal Concepts
1.
2.

Note: You may go back and adapt the tasks in "Your Turn to Practice" at any time, as long as you maintain consistency with your topic of study. For example, if you find that you would like to add more standards, big ideas, or universal concepts, please feel free to do so.

At this point, your knowledge of big ideas and universal concepts should be clearer. If you already have expertise in these areas, assist a colleague who may benefit from knowledge. The last part of this chapter addresses essential questions. Your understanding of essential questions will enhance your planning and +1P journey.

ESSENTIAL QUESTIONS

Essential questions are overarching questions that frame a topic of study. They can be discipline specific or interdisciplinary. Essential questions are also transferable, debatable, and generate more inquiry. According to McTighe and Wiggins (2013), they are questions that are "not answerable with finality in a single lesson or a brief sentence" (p. 3). Students must critically think about an essential question before providing an answer. Notably, essential questions are designed to stimulate thought beyond what a student may already know. McTighe and Wiggins (2013) assert that "by tackling such questions, learners are engaged in *uncovering* the depth and richness of a topic that might otherwise be obscured by simply *covering* it" (p. 3). To assist you in determining what makes a question "essential," McTighe and Wiggins (2013) provide seven defining characteristics of a good essential question (p. 3):

1. *Open-ended*; that is, it typically will not have a single, final and correct answer.

2. *Thought-provoking* and *intellectually engaging*, often sparking discussion and debate.

3. Calls for *higher-order thinking*, such as analysis, inference, evaluation, prediction. It cannot be effectively answered by recall alone.

4. Points toward *important, transferable ideas* within (and sometimes across) disciplines.

5. Raises *additional questions* and sparks further inquiry.

6. Requires *support* and *justification*, not just an answer.

7. *Recurs* over time; that is, the question can and should be revisited again and again.

Since +1P is designed to incorporate learning activities that are intellectually challenging, essential questions are one avenue for achieving such rigor. We want students to walk away from their projects feeling enlightened, academically stimulated, and able to think critically. To build your repertoire of essential questions, sample questions are provided. The first template in Figure 2.10 offers suggestions for interdisciplinary essential questions, while the second template offers suggestions for topic-specific essential questions. A question you might ask is, "What is the difference between a discipline-specific essential question and a topic-specific essential question?" Not all topics lend themselves to a specific discipline. For example, Figure 2.6 (sample +1P topics) lists topics such as animal rights, modes of transportation, and homelessness. These three topics cannot be defined by a specific discipline, such as English, math, science, or history. Although there may be elements of English, math, science, and history within these topics, they are not defined by one particular discipline. For this reason, I have provided sample essential questions that are discipline-specific *and* topic-specific. Use Figure 2.10 to generate essential questions for your sample unit.

The essential questions listed in Figure 2.10 are transferrable, debatable, and they generate more inquiry. This still holds true for those questions that start with "Do," "Does," "Is," "Can," and "Should." Although these question starters may generate yes and no answers, they still require an explanation, evidence, and reasoning. For example, the essential questions, "Is literacy a gatekeeper?" and "Should people buy new cars?" are debatable and require evidence. In other words, there is no right or wrong answer to the latter questions. If a student answers "yes" or "no" to these questions, his or her answer should be justified with an explanation that includes evidence and reasoning. The examples in Figure 2.10 are suggestions to guide your planning.

For the sample unit on Vessel Operations, I used one essential question from Figure 2.10 (under the category of Vessel Operations). My second essential question is related to *technology* and *systems*,

Figure 2.10 Sample Essential Questions

Discipline-Specific Essential Questions

ENGLISH

- Is literacy a gatekeeper?
- Do you have to be literate to be successful?
- How does reading connect us to the world?

HISTORY

- Whose "story" is this?
- Why does my story matter?
- Why do some ethnic groups get more attention (e.g., media, articles, history text books, etc.) than others?

MATH

- Is math a gatekeeper?
- Why do some countries perform better in math than others?
- What does it take to become an expert in math?

SCIENCE

- Is scientific evidence based on truth?
- Can all theories be tested?
- Why does science involve inquiry and research?

COMPUTERS/TECHNOLOGY

- How are we impacted by computer technology?
- Should students be required to take a typing class in grade school?
- How does technology help and harm a society?

PHYSICAL EDUCATION (PE)

- How does physical fitness change our lives?
- What does it take to be physically fit?
- Should physical education be mandated in schools?

FOREIGN LANGUAGE

- Does society benefit from bilingual citizens?
- Why do we study foreign languages?
- What makes a foreign language foreign?

HUMANITIES

- How do cultures gain respect?
- Should we inspire communication across cultures?
- How does one culture influence another?

ART

- What defines art?
- Who determines the value of art?
- Why is some art worth more than others?

YEARBOOK/NEWSPAPER

- Should we preserve our memories?
- What constitutes a worthy article for the yearbook/newspaper?
- What influence does technology have on a yearbook/newspaper?

ENGINEERING

- Can society advance without engineers?
- What does it take to become an expert in engineering?
- Does engineering require more theory or practice?

MUSIC

- How is music cross-cultural?
- What defines music?
- How does music influence human behavior?

DANCE

- Does dance require rhythm?
- What constitutes a good dancer?
- Should all forms of dance be treated with the same respect?

THEATRE

- How is theatre realistic?
- What constitutes good acting?
- How has technology influenced theatre?

LEADERSHIP

- What defines leadership?
- How does money influence leadership?
- Does status matter in leadership?

Topic-Specific Essential Questions

VESSEL OPERATIONS

- What are the costs and benefits of trade?
- How does technology impact production?

STOCK MARKET

- Why do stock markets exist?
- What makes a company's stock attractive?

HOLLYWOOD

- What defines a good movie?
- How does technology influence Hollywood?

WATER

- Why do some societies conserve water?
- Who controls the rights of water?

CARS

- What makes a car attractive?
- Should people buy new cars?

BUYING A HOUSE

- What are the costs and benefits of buying a house?
- How does a person prepare for buying a house?

GLOBAL WARMING

- How is global warming defined?
- Should societies address climate change?

BULLYING

- What causes a person to be a bully?
- Should bullying be a crime?

WARS

- How do we justify war?
- What constitutes victory in a war?

FASHION

- What makes a person fashionable?
- Who determines fashion trends?

HOMELESSNESS

- How does a person become homeless?
- Should societies end homelessness?

INSURANCE

- Why do people have insurance?
- What are the costs and benefits of having, or not having, insurance?

ANIMAL RIGHTS

- Why do animals have rights?
- Why do some animals have more rights than others?

SPACE EXPLORATION

- Why do we study space?
- How does technology impact space exploration?

HEROES

- What makes a hero?
- Should heroes be rewarded?

CAREER

- What are the costs and benefits of having a career?
- How does a person prepare for a career?

HEALTH

- What makes a healthy person?
- How do genetics supersede a poor diet?

RELIGION

- Why do people practice religion?
- What is faith?

which are big ideas stated in my universal concepts. For consistency, I used these big ideas to create my second essential question. Figure 2.11 illustrates congruencies within big ideas, universal concepts, and essential questions.

Figure 2.11   Essential Questions for Sample +1P Unit

Big Ideas	Universal Concepts	Essential Questions
transportation, **vessel operations**, **cargo** (imported and exported), **systems**, **container ports**, **technology**, **trade**, rules, safety, contracts, **supply and demand**, and labor/unions	**Systems** include interdependent parts. **Technology** allows for increased production.	What are the costs and benefits of **trade**? Can a **system** advance without **technology**?

By now, you are cognizant of the purpose and characteristics of essential questions, in addition to *how* essential questions relate to big ideas and universal concepts. Figure 2.11 illustrates these correlations. Ideally, you want to plan your sample unit around explicit connections that deepen conceptual understanding for a topic of study.

YOUR TURN TO PRACTICE

Choose one or two essential questions from Figure 2.10 that relate to your topic of study. If your topic or discipline is not represented in Figure 2.10, you have the option of creating your own essential questions. Remember to use the +1P rubric to assist you in this process. To highlight connections, it may help to circle, underline, or bold the big ideas within your essential questions. Write your essential questions below:

+1P Topic of Study: _____

Essential Questions
1.
2.

Congratulations! Now that you have practiced generating essential questions, you are ready to proceed. Before we advance to the next intersection, which addresses management, take a moment to reflect on the process thus far.

Think about ways you have referenced or taught universal concepts and essential questions. How would the samples provided assist or influence your instructional planning? How might you transfer knowledge about universal concepts and essential questions back to your district, school, or classroom?

SUMMARY

The four essential components addressed in this chapter—standards, big ideas, universal concepts, and essential questions—necessitate rigor, critical thinking, and correlations across concepts. Equally imperative is student interest and motivation. Our charge as educators is to cultivate environments that accelerate achievement, stimulate cognition, and increase student motivation. The +1P framework reinforces these principles of learning. The user-friendly templates and practical strategies provided in this chapter are designed to foster planning and efficacy around standards, big ideas, universal concepts, and essential questions.

Most importantly, this chapter extends the discourse on rigor and its purpose in learning. Teachers cannot accelerate achievement without the presence of cognitive demand. +1P builds on habits of mind that include rigor, elevating student consciousness, accelerating achievement through 21st Century Skills, and preparing students to compete in a global economy. Students can and will achieve these outcomes if they are exposed to learning opportunities that stimulate growth and development. +1P is one avenue for promoting these outcomes. Your expanded skills in +1P planning will support your exploration of four additional checkpoints. These checkpoints address project management through objectives, focused inquiry, learning activities, and investigation (research).

================= MICs =================

MOST IMPORTANT CONCEPTS

- Seven Checkpoints of +1P
- +1P Planning Rubric
- Standards

  o Common Core ELA/Literacy
  o Common Core Mathematics
  o Next Generation Science Standards (Science and Engineering Practices)
  o History/Social Studies
  o Physical Education
  o Visual and Performing Arts

- Topic Selection

  o Student Interest
  o Motivation

- Big Ideas
- Universal Concepts
- Essential Questions

INTERSECTION 2

MANAGING

"There are three secrets to managing. The first secret is have patience. The second is be patient. And the third most important secret is patience."

—Chuck Tanner

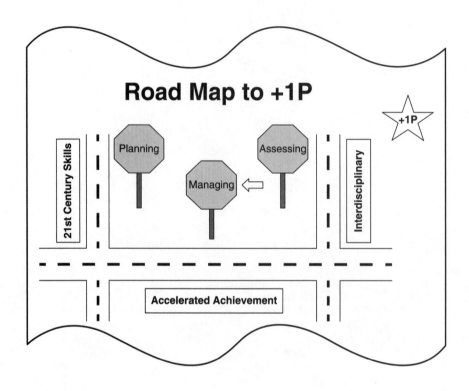

3

ROUTE TO PROJECT MANAGEMENT

B roadly defined, project management is the act of planning, organizing, executing, and monitoring (POEM) a project to achieve a desired goal. Every +1P project requires these characteristics for successful management and implementation. The POEM strategy guides student application of all four steps during the process. The following table defines each characteristic of POEM in further detail.

Students need skills and expertise in all levels of POEM as they manage their own acquisition of learning. The latter is achieved when teachers *facilitate* the process, as opposed to dominating the process. In other words, we need to teach students how to use the POEM strategy by modeling, providing scaffolds, and assisting where needed—and then we need to let go. The more we facilitate and provide opportunities for students to take initiative and problem solve, the better prepared they will be for college, career, and life. These are critical principles espoused by the +1P framework. Last but not least, implementation requires patience and perseverance. Some things may not go as planned, resulting in unanticipated challenges. Despite these challenges, it is essential for students and teachers to remain optimistic and patient. As educators, we need to embrace room for improvement, flexibility, and revisions to original plans. Those who finish what they start exemplify resilience and perseverance. That being

Figure 3.1　POEM Guide for Project Management

Plan	Students understand that planning is essential to project management: • Think about the purpose and desired goals/outcomes of your project. • Establish a plan of action that includes activities to meet your goals. • List specific steps for your plan of action.
Organize	Students understand that organization is essential to project management: • Gather resources and research about your project. • Be conscious of project deadlines by prioritizing your time and setting calendar dates. • Create a checklist for accountability.
Execute	Students understand that execution is essential to project management: • Put your plan into action. • Adhere to your project deadlines. • Finish what you started.
Monitor	Students understand that monitoring is essential to project management: • Stay focused on the desired goals/outcomes. • Check your progress by matching your results to your desired goals/outcomes. • Make changes and revisions as necessary.

said, the purpose of this chapter is to closely examine Checkpoint 4 (project objective) and Checkpoint 5 (focused inquiry, learning activities, and investigation/research). Strategies and templates are provided to bolster planning and project management.

CHECKPOINT 4: PROJECT OBJECTIVE

Instructional practices are sustained by objectives that express what students should know, do, and produce. Objectives define the overall purpose for a given task, assignment, or project. Without objectives, teachers and students can lose sight of the intended outcomes for a particular assignment. Project objectives are imperative to the success of +1P implementation. They are needed to guide the process and serve as reminders about expectations and outcomes. All +1P projects require an objective. One model that teachers can use to enhance depth and complexity of objectives is the +1P Objectives Organizer. Four categories included in the model are *think*, *know*, *source*, and *do*. The *think* category relates to thinking skills, *know* relates to content knowledge, *source* relates to evidence, and *do* relates to the product. Each category includes a unique list of characteristics pertinent to utilization. The +1P Objectives Organizer is a comprehensive model that promotes cognitive development and engagement in students. This model is highly recommended for generating objectives.

Figure 3.2   +1P Objectives Organizer

Think	Know	Source	Do
Identify and Describe (recognize and explain)	**Technological Advances** (development and progress)	**Internet** (website, blog, podcast, webinar, etc.)	**Writing** (essay, brochure, newsletter, story, etc.)
Compare (relate one thing to another)	**Theory** (scientific, mathematical, educational, etc.)	**Qualitative Data** (interviews and observations)	**Flow Chart or Concept Map** (diagram process/steps *or* diagram relationships)
Contrast (differentiate one thing from another)	**Cause and Effect** (roots and impact)	**Quantitative Data** (surveys and statistics)	**Build a Model** (blocks, paper, clay, popsicle sticks, straws, foil, metal, plastic, wood, etc.)
Analyze (study and investigate)	**Trends Over Time** (patterns and dates)	**Field Trip** (museum, science center, college, business, nature, theatre, concert, theme park, library, waterfront/ port, etc.)	**Digital Project** (website, graphic arts, movie, app, game, library, etc.)
Prove With Evidence (test and determine)	**Purpose and Function** (what, why, how)	**Visual Text** (videos, pictures, charts, graphs, tables, etc.)	**Illustration or Performance** (collage, drawings, pictures, graphs, pictures, poster, storyboard, etc. *or* dance, play, skit, concert, debate, etc.)
Evaluate (examine and judge)	**Laws** (rules, decrees, principles, legislation, divine law, etc.)	**Informational Text** (magazines, eMagazines, newspapers, eNewspapers, books, eBooks, articles, journals, eJournals, etc.)	**Digital Presentation** (PowerPoint, Prezi, video, music, Google Presentation, etc.)

Figure 3.3   Project Objective for Sample +1P Unit

Project Objective

Students will **identify and describe** the **purpose and function** of Vessel Operations. They will gather information from the **Internet, observations (field trip to the port)**, and **videos**. Students will present their findings to their classmates in a **presentation**, write a **short essay** about their topic of study, and reflect on the process.

When writing a project objective, it is important to include language from all four categories to ensure what students should *think, know, source,* and *do* for their project. The topic of study should also be included in the objective. Once again, these are suggestions to guide your planning. To generate an objective for the sample unit on Vessel Operations, I used the +1P Objectives Organizer.

Figure 3.3 highlights the gist of student expectations for the project on Vessel Operations. The bolded language shows how specific characteristics from the +1P Objectives Organizer are represented. Of course, students may demonstrate knowledge, skills, and products other than what is stated in the project objective. The purpose of having the project objective is to provide a snapshot of project outcomes; it is not intended to be an extensive list of what students will do throughout the entire project. Project objectives should be no more than a few sentences. They should be concise and to the point. At any time during the project, students can refer to the project objective to keep them focused and on track. It is recommended that teachers and/ or students post the project objective someplace visible (classroom wall, student binder, teacher's website, white board, etc.) to serve as a reminder of project expectations and outcomes.

YOUR TURN TO PRACTICE

Use the language from Figure 3.2 to determine the *think, know, source,* and *do* for your project objective. You may borrow exact language from Figure 3.3 when generating your objective. For consistency, it may help to circle, underline, or bold the characteristics related to the four categories. You also have the option of creating a project objective without the +1P Objectives Organizer (but I highly suggest that you give it a try!). Remember to use the +1P rubric to assist you in this process. Write your project objective in the template provided:

+1P Topic of Study: _____

Project Objective

The purpose and rationale for project objectives should be clearer for you. Now that you have practiced writing your own objective, we can advance to Checkpoint 5. Get ready to apply your knowledge of big ideas, universal concepts, essential questions, and the project objective as we delve into focused inquiry, learning activities, and investigation (research).

Think about strategies you have used to create objectives for a particular unit, lesson, or project. What is the purpose of including the *think, know, source,* and *do* within an objective? How might you transfer knowledge about the +1P Objectives Organizer back to your district, school, or classroom?

CHECKPOINT 5: FOCUSED INQUIRY, LEARNING ACTIVITIES, AND INVESTIGATION (RESEARCH)

In a nutshell, inquiry-based learning places inquiry at the center of student learning. Inquiry learning is a student-centered approach that allows students to construct knowledge and understanding through exploration, discovery, reflection, and critical thinking (Santrock, 2001). These underlying concepts of inquiry-based learning are essential to successful implementation of +1P. In terms of inquiry and investigation, one cannot occur without the other. In other words, investigation and inquiry complement each other. Inquiry fosters student awareness and curiosity before, during, and after an investigation. According to Slavin (2006), inquiry learning arouses students' curiosities and motivates students to continue to seek until they find answers. Inquisitive students are typically more driven and motivated to find answers related to a topic of study. Their inquisitive nature promotes independent thinking and learning. As educators, it is important to foster this type of passion and desire for learning, all of which is championed by +1P.

FOCUSED INQUIRY

Focused inquiry relates to a cohesive experience where students investigate a series of questions related to their topic of study. Students are "focused" on the questions and task in front of them, a skill they need to develop as researchers. Conducting research is often like traveling to a new place. You know where you want to go, but getting there can pose a challenge. In terms of research, having a set of questions to focus the investigation mitigates confusion and guides the process along. Focused inquiry is derived from big ideas that are related to a project. Teachers use the +1P Questioning Technique to focus inquiry around big ideas. This technique includes a series of questions related to big ideas (teacher and/or students decide on which big ideas to investigate). There are four levels that build on each other—*general*, *specific*, *elaborate*, and *sourcing*. Each level is defined by specific characteristics.

+1P necessitates effective questioning for successful implementation. By sequencing various types of questions, students build a base of factual information that they can use to answer deeper and more complex questions (Marzano & Simms, 2014). As students progress through the series of questions within the +1P Questioning Technique, the level of cognitive demand increases. Teachers can use this model to foster questioning experiences that allow students to acquire basic and conceptual knowledge of a topic. Student learning is enhanced because factual questions lead to more complex questions about big ideas and perspectives. For this reason, focused inquiry is an essential component of the +1P diagram. The term "focused" intentionally precedes the term "inquiry" because inquiry is not a haphazard process. The more focused students are with inquiry, the easier it is to launch an investigation around a topic of study.

As seen in Figure 3.4, the +1P Questioning Technique follows a progression of questions that would work for any project. This strategy prompts students to answer a range of questions that require lower and higher levels of cognitive demand. Students are given opportunities to extend their factual knowledge of big ideas to conceptual knowledge of big ideas, the main purpose of the questioning

Figure 3.4   +1P Questioning Technique

General Questions	Specific Questions	Elaborate Questions	Sourcing Questions
Definition:	**Definition:**	**Definition:**	**Definition:**
Questions derived from big ideas that are broad in scope and related to the topic of study	Questions derived from big ideas that are specific to the topic of study	Questions derived from big ideas that elaborate on specific questions related to the topic of study	Questions that identify sources (evidence) to all questions related to the topic of study
Purpose:	**Purpose:**	**Purpose:**	**Purpose:**
Generate prior knowledge and provide overarching information about a topic of study.	Highlight details about one or more big ideas related to the topic of study.	Extend the complexity of specific questions that highlight big ideas (i.e., why/how/what if).	Determine access to sources, type of sources, and credibility of sources.
EXAMPLE	EXAMPLE	EXAMPLE	EXAMPLE
Topic:	**Topic:**	**Topic:**	**Topic:**
Animal Rights	Animal Rights	Animal Rights	Animal Rights
Big Ideas:	**Big Ideas:**	**Big Ideas:**	**Big Ideas:**
animals, endangered species, laws, animal shelters, furs, skin, hunting	animals, endangered species, laws, animal shelters, furs, skin, hunting	animals, endangered species, laws, animal shelters, furs, skin, hunting	animals, endangered species, laws, animal shelters, furs, skin, hunting
General Questions:	**Specific Questions:**	**Elaborate Questions:**	**Sourcing Questions:**
What are animal rights? What is an endangered species?	What types of animals have rights? What specific animals are endangered species?	Why do animals have rights? What would happen if some animals were not endangered species?	How will you access your information and what sources will you use? How will you determine the credibility of your sources?

technique. Because students experience a progression of questions related to big ideas, their comprehension and ability to make connections is enhanced. Of course, teachers have the option of including more than two questions for each level. Figure 3.4 is a resource to support your planning around the focused inquiry component of +1P. I used the same template to formulate questions for the Vessel Operations unit and sample units in the appendix. This technique helped "focus my inquiry" around big ideas related to Vessel Operations.

Teachers can also use the +1P Questioning Technique to do a "questioning storm" with students. For this activity, the teacher would have students write their topic of study on a blank piece of paper (students could also do this on a computer). Students would have three minutes to write as many questions as possible about their topic of study. After three minutes, students can categorize their questions into the four levels (general, specific, elaborate, and sourcing). This helps teachers and students assess which categories have more questions than others. Students could then add questions to those categories that need more questions. The purpose of a questioning storm is to help balance the number of questions within each category.

Notice that the big ideas in Figure 3.5 are bolded in three of the four levels in the +1P Questioning Technique. Focused inquiry should not be generated without big ideas. The bolded big ideas represent academic terms that warrant further exploration and investigation. They also show relevance to the topic of study, which is important for consistency and coherency. Keep in mind that focused inquiry is not the same as essential questions. Remember, essential questions are

Figure 3.5   Focused Inquiry for Sample +1P Unit

Big Ideas	Focused Inquiry
transportation, **vessel operations**, **cargo** (imported and exported), **systems**, **container ports**, **technology**, **trade**, rules, safety, contracts, **supply and demand**, and labor/unions	*General Questions:* What modes of **transportation** are used to transport goods? What cities have major **ports** (inside and outside of the United States)? What is a **system**? *Specific Questions:* ***Vessels:*** What are some specific types of vessels? ***Technology:*** What type of technology is used on vessels and within the ports? ***Cargo:*** What are specific types of cargo? What types of cargo does the US import and export? ***Trade:*** What is trade? *Elaborate Questions:* ***Vessels:*** What purpose and function do vessels serve? ***Technology:*** How does technology improve vessel operations? ***Cargo:*** Why do countries import and export goods? ***Trade:*** How does **supply and demand** impact trade? *Sourcing Questions:* How will you access your information? What sources will you use? What makes your sources credible?

overarching questions that frame the *entire* project. That is not the purpose of focused inquiry, hence the word "focused." These questions are intended to guide the cycle of inquiry and investigation for a project. Students will use focused inquiry to launch their investigation and enhance their conceptual knowledge of big ideas related to the topic of study.

YOUR TURN TO PRACTICE

Choose at least two big ideas (or more) from your sample unit and use the +1P Questioning Technique to create questions for each big idea. Include your topic of study and big ideas in the practice template below. Remember to use the +1P rubric to assist you in this process and to circle, underline, or bold the big ideas for each question. Write your questions in the template provided:

General Questions	Specific Questions	Elaborate Questions	Sourcing Questions
Definition: Questions derived from big ideas that are broad in scope and related to the topic of study	**Definition:** Questions derived from big ideas that are specific to the topic of study	**Definition:** Questions derived from big ideas that elaborate on specific questions related to the topic of study	**Definition:** Questions that identify sources (evidence) to all questions related to the topic of study
Purpose: Generate prior knowledge and provide overarching information about a topic of study.	**Purpose:** Highlight details about one or more big ideas related to the topic of study.	**Purpose:** Extend the complexity of specific questions that highlight big ideas (i.e., why/how/what if).	**Purpose:** Determine access to sources, type of sources, and credibility of sources.
YOUR EXAMPLE	YOUR EXAMPLE	YOUR EXAMPLE	YOUR EXAMPLE
Topic:	**Topic:**	**Topic:**	**Topic:**

(Continued)

(Continued)

General Questions	Specific Questions	Elaborate Questions	Sourcing Questions
Big Ideas:	Big Ideas:	Big Ideas:	Big Ideas:
General Questions	Specific Questions:	Elaborate Questions:	Sourcing Questions:

It is highly recommended that students generate questions using the +1P Questioning Technique. After all, inquiry-based learning includes the learner. Students need multiple opportunities to actively engage in formulating questions that span all levels. Like adults, they will only get better at asking questions with more practice. Students can work in groups to generate questions, or they can write them independently. They can also use the questioning technique to formulate questions with their teacher or classmates. This technique is also applicable to units/lessons outside of +1P. The key is getting students to independently generate a sequence of questions related to their topic of study.

By now, you should be feeling pretty adept at composing questions using the +1P Questioning Technique. The purpose and benefits of inquiry-based learning should be clearer as well. The next section of this chapter addresses learning activities.

Figure 3.6   Student Template for +1P Questioning Technique

General Questions	Specific Questions	Elaborate Questions	Sourcing Questions
Teacher Example	*Teacher Example*	*Teacher Example*	*Teacher Example*
Topic:	Topic:	Topic:	Topic:
Big Ideas:	Big Ideas:	Big Ideas:	Big Ideas:
General Questions:	Specific Questions:	Elaborate Questions:	Sourcing Questions:
STUDENT EXAMPLE	STUDENT EXAMPLE	STUDENT EXAMPLE	STUDENT EXAMPLE
+1P Topic:	+1P Topic:	+1P Topic:	+1P Topic:
Big Ideas:	Big Ideas:	Big Ideas:	Big Ideas:
General Questions:	Specific Questions:	Elaborate Questions:	Sourcing Questions:

LEARNING ACTIVITIES

Learning activities involve cognitive processes, also known as thinking skills. Students use a range of cognitive processes as they engage in interdisciplinary tasks. Bloom (1984) created a framework for classifying knowledge and skills into educational objectives. The framework, referred to as Bloom's taxonomy, has since been adapted for leveling questions and learning activities. Bloom's taxonomy includes six hierarchical levels: 1) *Knowledge*, 2) *Comprehension*, 3) *Application*, 4) *Analysis*, 5) *Synthesis*, and 6) *Evaluation*. The first level—*Knowledge*—emphasizes basic recall of facts, while the remaining five levels emphasize conceptual understanding and transfer. Conceptual understanding is needed for students to transfer knowledge to new situations. A student's ability to transfer knowledge is a clear indication of understanding, retention, and mastery. Students are less likely to transfer and retain knowledge if they do not understand the content/materials being taught. A primary goal of the +1P process is to advance students' conceptual knowledge of a topic and their ability to transfer this knowledge to other situations.

Educators around the world utilize Bloom's taxonomy for various reasons. One major purpose for its use in schools is to ensure that learning activities and assessments include a range of all levels. Bloom's taxonomy provides a useful frame for planning tasks that engage students at multiple levels. Anderson and Krathwohl (2001) have further revised Bloom's taxonomy into a framework called The Cognitive Process Dimension. In addition to renaming some of the cognitive skills listed in Bloom's taxonomy, their taxonomy categorizes actions (verbs) instead of skills (nouns). Figure 3.7 highlights these differences.

Figure 3.7   Bloom's Taxonomy and the Adapted Taxonomy

Bloom's Taxonomy (nouns)	Adapted Taxonomy (verbs)
Knowledge	Remember
Comprehension	Understand
Application	Apply
Analysis	Analyze
Synthesis	Evaluate
Evaluation	Create

According to Anderson and Krathwohl (2001), if educators wish to expand and examine ways to foster and assess meaningful learning, we need to examine processes that go beyond remembering. A focus on meaningful learning is consistent with a constructivist approach to learning, where students gain knowledge through exploration and active learning. As students construct knowledge, they are also making meaning, which goes beyond factual knowledge and simple recall (Anderson & Krathwohl, 2001). +1P is predicated on learning experiences that result in meaningful learning. The essential components are designed to aid students in making sense of their learning experiences. Anderson and Krathwohl (2001) contend that meaningful learning provides students with the knowledge and cognitive processes (thinking skills) needed for successful transfer. Teachers can refer to Figure 3.7 as they plan learning activities for their students. Cognitive processes for each category, with alternate names in parenthesis, are as follows (Anderson & Krathwohl, 2001, pp. 67–68):

1. **Remember:** recognizing (identifying) and recalling (retrieving)

2. **Understand:** interpreting (clarifying, paraphrasing, representing, translating), exemplifying (illustrating, instantiating), classifying (categorizing, subsuming), summarizing (abstracting, generalizing), inferring (concluding, extrapolating, interpolating, predicting), comparing (contrasting, mapping, matching), and explaining (constructing models)

3. **Apply:** executing (carrying out) and implementing (using)

4. **Analyze:** differentiating (discriminating, distinguishing, focusing, selecting), organizing (finding coherence, integrating, outlining, parsing, structuring), and attributing (deconstructing)

5. **Evaluate:** checking (coordinating, detecting, monitoring, testing) and critiquing (judging)

6. **Create:** generating (hypothesizing), planning (designing), and producing (constructing)

The cognitive processes represent a continuum of increasing cognitive complexity for any discipline. Because some thinking skills require less cognitive demand and others require more, it is essential to include a range of cognitive processes when planning learning activities. Keep in mind that too much cognitive demand may cause stress and anxiety, while too little cognitive demand prevents students from reaching their full potential. For this reason, it is better to balance the thinking skills required for your learning activities. Important to note is the difference between complexity and difficulty. According to Sousa (2006), complexity refers to the thought process that the brain uses to decipher information, while difficulty refers to the amount of effort that a learner expends to accomplish an activity/task. An example of difficulty within the Vessel Operations unit would be asking students to name and describe the uses for every type of maritime vessel, an activity that falls under the *remember* category. While the latter activity is relevant and necessary, it requires more effort than complexity. To engage students in more cognitive processing, the teacher could ask students to compare and analyze three or four different vessels using multiple sources, an activity that falls within the *understand, apply,* and *analyze* categories. This activity requires a higher level of cognitive demand and is more complex than naming and describing vessels. However, *both* activities are fundamental to contextualizing student learning around Vessel Operations and *both* can be taught in this unit. Lastly, notice that many of the categories and cognitive processes are stated in the +1P Objectives Organizer under the *think* column (see Figure 3.2). The purpose of combining concepts from the objectives organizer and cognitive processes is to encourage consistency, coherency, and transfer. Moreover, transfer is an indication of one's conceptual understanding and mastery.

I considered the different cognitive processes to determine learning activities for the Vessel Operations unit. This information helped to ensure that I was incorporating learning activities with a range of cognitive demand. Teachers cannot accelerate student achievement without higher levels of cognitive demand and rigor. Students must engage in rigorous learning activities and experiences if they are expected to compete globally. Without some level of academic challenge and complexity, mediocrity becomes the norm. It is better to raise the bar on norms for student achievement than to lower it. For your review, a list of learning activities for the sample unit on Vessel Operations is provided.

Figure 3.8 represents an exhaustive list of learning activities that may or may not come to fruition. It is always better to overplan than to underplan. Note that the learning activities in Figure 3.8 include a range of cognitive processes, some requiring higher levels of cognitive demand than others. A range and plethora of learning activities will assist you in meeting the cognitive demands of your students.

YOUR TURN TO PRACTICE

Generate a list of five to ten learning activities that you would consider implementing for your unit. Refer to the aforementioned

Figure 3.8 Learning Activities for Sample +1P Unit

Learning Activities
1. Dialogue and Discussion
2. Journal/Diary/Log [paper or digital]
3. Create a Timeline
4. Field Trips
5. Online Collaboration [Google Drive, Facebook, E-mail, Padlet, Blogs, TodaysMeet, Twitter, etc.]
6. Create a Blog
7. Interviews or Surveys
8. Build a Model
9. Display Board
10. Debate
11. Socratic Seminar
12. Quizzes [paper or digital]
13. Academic Games
14. Vocabulary Placemat
15. Venn Diagram
16. Collage

cognitive processes and Figure 3.8 as a model of learning activities that include a range of cognitive processes. Be creative and remember to use the +1P rubric to assist you in this process. Write your learning activities in the template provided:

+1P Topic of Study: _____

Learning Activities	
1.	6.
2.	7.
3.	8.
4.	9.
5.	10.

PROJECT MANAGEMENT

Once the learning activities have been decided, teachers need to determine how students will come to understand and "own" the knowledge. In other words, consider how students will process their knowledge. One example of how students can process knowledge is through student teaming. Students can be teamed for their project, or they can work individually. It is highly recommended that students work in teams to develop their skills in collaborating, communicating, and cooperating with other classmates. By design, +1P is a very involved and demanding process. It may be easier for students to bounce ideas off of other classmates and share resources, as opposed to going through the process alone. Interdependence is a skill that students need to develop to prepare for college, career, and life. Varied possibilities for student teaming include, but are not limited to:

- **Whole Team** (all students)
- **Whole Team** with a different class (all students)
  - switch teacher or students
- **Small Team**—same ability (3–5 students)
- **Small Team**—mixed ability (3–5 students)
- **Paired Team**—same ability (2 students)
- **Paired Team**—mixed ability (2 students)
- **Triad Team**—same ability (3 students)
- **Triad Team**—mixed ability (3 students)
- **Intervention Team** (2–5 students)
  - students who may require additional support for various reasons
- **Interest Team** (3–5 students)
  - students who share the same interest in topic of study

For clarity purposes, "same ability" means students who exhibit similar academic skills and competencies, while "mixed ability" means students with a range of academic skills and competencies. Due to myriad ways in which students can be teamed, there is no right or wrong way to team students. Teachers would have to determine the best possible situation for their students. For the purposes of this book, the sample unit on Vessel Operations is intended for small teams. The term "team" is preferred over "group." If we want students to take ownership of the project, they need to feel as if they are part of a team. Once teachers have determined the types of teams their students will be placed in, students need to know their roles and responsibilities. Different roles can include project manager, assistant manager, resources manager, recording manager, and time manager. Teachers would decide on the interchangeability of roles. Teams with four students would not have an assistant manager.

Once student roles and responsibilities have been determined, it is highly recommended that students sign a "+1P Team Agreement." The agreement, also known as a contract, serves two purposes: 1) Ensure that all team members agree to collaborate, communicate, cooperate, and complete the project, and 2) Define roles and responsibilities of each team member. A sample agreement is provided in Figure 3.10. Although this agreement is highly recommended for use with +1P, teachers have the option of creating their own agreement.

As team roles change, a new agreement must be signed. The term "agreement" is preferred over the term "contract" to create a

Figure 3.9   +1P Team Roles and Responsibilities

Team Members, Roles, and Responsibilities		
Team Member Names	**Role**	**Responsibilities**
1.	Project Manager	Team leader; guides, supports, and facilitates; keeps the team focused; spokesperson for the team; delegates; talks daily with the teacher; inspires the team.
2.	Assistant Manager	Commits to the same responsibilities as the Project Manager; fills in for absent team members; lightens the workload of the Project Manager.
3.	Resources Manager	Gathers resources for the team; delegates which team members are responsible for specific resources; logs and keeps track of project resources.
4.	Recording Manager	Records (written or digital) data, information, notes and questions pertaining to the project; sends out and receives communications; shares updates with the team.
5.	Time Manager	Informs team of deadlines and time constraints; sets a timer for specific activities; warns/signals the team when time is almost up; ensures punctuality of the team.

Note: If the team has five members, but one team member is absent, the Project Manager fills in for that member.

Figure 3.10   Sample +1P Team Agreement

+1P Team Agreement
School: _____ **Teacher/Period**: _____ **Date:** _____

Project Topic:
_____

Big Ideas:
_____
_____

Universal Concepts:
_____
_____

Essential Questions:
_____
_____

Project Objective:
_____
_____

Terms of Agreement: We agree to collaborate, communicate, cooperate, and complete the +1P project as a team. We agree to maintain our assigned (or chosen) role and responsibilities. We agree to follow the **Seven Norms of Collaboration** as a team at all times (Garmston & Wellman, 2009): 1) *Pausing*, 2) *Paraphrasing*, 3) *Posing Questions*, 4) *Putting Ideas on the Table*, 5) *Providing Data*, 6) *Paying Attention to Self and Others*, and 7) *Presuming Positive Intentions*.

Team Members, Roles, and Responsibilities		
Team Member Names and Signatures	**Role**	**Responsibilities**
1.	Project Manager	Team leader; guides, supports, and facilitates; keeps the team focused; spokesperson for the team; delegates; talks daily with the teacher; inspires the team.
2.	Assistant Manager	Commits to the same responsibilities as the Project Manager; fills in for absent team members; lightens the workload of the Project Manager.

Team Member Names and Signatures	Role	Responsibilities
3.	Resources Manager	Gathers resources for the team; delegates which team members are responsible for specific resources; logs and keeps track of project resources.
4.	Recording Manager	Records (written or digital) data, information, notes and questions pertaining to the project; sends out and receives communications; shares updates with the team.
5.	Time Manager	Informs team of deadlines and time constraints; sets a timer for specific activities; warns/signals the team when time is almost up; ensures punctuality of the team.

*Failure to meet the terms of this agreement may result in removal from your team.

spirit of "we-ness" and ownership. The word "contract" can sometimes come across as harsh and punitive. To circumvent a negative connotation and reaction, the term "agreement" is more favorable. You will notice that the Seven Norms of Collaboration are stated within the contract. Garmston and Wellman (2009) define the norms as essential capacities and skills for high-performing groups. The purpose of norms is to help teams develop shared meaning and collaborative decisions. These skills are critical to establishing productive teams that get along with each other and fostering skills in project management. More about the norms can be accessed through the following website: **http://www.thinkingcollaborative.com/norms-collaboration-toolkit/**

When team roles and responsibilities have been defined and the team agreement is signed, students are ready for project management. For starters, students need to be cognizant of all learning activities and due dates. Without this knowledge, students can get lost in the process. Awareness of learning activities and due dates will help keep students focused and on track. A handout that helps students keep track of their assignments and progress is helpful.

Teachers can also refer students to the POEM strategy (Figure 3.1) for additional guidance with project management. Once project management has been established, students are ready to start their investigative research. At this point, students have concrete strategies for project management, they know their team roles and expectations, they have signed the team agreement, they have their focused inquiry questions, and they have been given specific learning activities—all they need is the green light to start their research.

Figure 3.11   Sample Learning Activities Template

Learning Activities	Due Date	Completed (write yes, no, or in progress)

Note: Students should add to their list of learning activities throughout their +1P project.

INVESTIGATION (RESEARCH)

Investigation and research involve the active pursuit of new information and discovery. The purpose of investigation and research is to advance prior or existing knowledge about a topic, subject, or discipline. Regarding funds of knowledge, never assume that students come to school as empty vessels; just assume that their vessels need additional "water" from time to time. Whatever knowledge students (and teachers!) possess, there is always room for more. Since we can never know it all, research keeps us informed and up to speed on the latest news. Investigation and research also contextualize teaching and learning around a topic of study.

A specific way to contextualize learning about a topic of study is through text sets. With the advent of Common Core State Standards, the word "text" has been redefined to go beyond printed text. According to Cappiello and Dawes (2012), text includes *literature* (fiction and nonfiction), *periodicals* (newspapers and magazines), *primary sources* (documents, photographs, and artifacts), and *multimodal digital text* (webcasts, podcasts, websites, blogs, songs, reports, and art). It is important to note that primary sources are first-hand accounts of an event. An example would be a letter written directly by a soldier from the war, as opposed to a letter written about a soldier in the war. The letter written about a soldier constitutes a secondary source, because the author of the letter did not actually experience the war. That being said, text sets are primary and secondary sources of different reading levels, genre, and media that offer perspectives on a theme or topic of study (Cappiello & Dawes, 2012). Within text sets, teachers can add voices and perspectives to the study of any complex issue or topic. Text sets allow educators to use multiple sources (stimuli) to build background knowledge, foster critical thinking, and stimulate learning in more meaningful ways. Among many other benefits, text sets help to (Cappiello & Dawes, 2012, p. 30):

- Capture student interest and cultivate engagement
- Prompt inquiry
- Provide opportunities to read for multiple perspectives
- Build prior knowledge on a topic
- Encourage authentic student writing practices
- Support vocabulary development

Text sets are compilations of primary and secondary sources that can be stored digitally, manually, or both. Text sets also focus resources around a topic of study. As students engage in +1P, they must decide which print and digital resources to use for their topic of study. The next step is conducting research around their topic of study. Without a text set to guide the investigative process, students may get lost in a haystack of information. Advances in technology allow students to be as creative as possible with text sets. Access to the Internet allows students to generate text sets from home. Teachers and students do not need to wait until they reach the investigation phase to create a text set. The process of collecting artifacts and sources related to a topic of study can start at any time. Teaching with text sets stimulates student interest and motivation as well. Students have a choice in what resources to select for their topic of study, thus enhancing their academic engagement (Cappiello & Dawes, 2012). In other words, students take ownership of their learning experiences when they are interested and included in the process. Refer to these websites to help build text sets around a project: **http://www.slideshare.net**, **http://watchknowlearn.org**, and **http://readingandwritingproject.org/resources/text-sets**

Through text sets, students learn to interpret, analyze, and critique pertinent resources related to their topic of study. Resources collected for a text set can be revisited or used during the presentation phase of +1P. Text sets are evidence of information and data collected during research, so it is critical for students to save what is collected. Students can also create a visual text set of their primary and secondary sources. For example, students could manually or digitally select certain images and documents to insert into a collage. Students are encouraged to exercise their creative energy when designing and showcasing their visual text set. The collage serves two purposes: 1) contextualizing the topic of study and 2) providing a visual text set that can be used for the presentation. Below is a visual text set for the Vessel Operations unit.

A helpful technique for analyzing pictures and other visual text is called the Visual Thinking Strategy (VTS). The Museum of Contemporary Art (MOCA) in Los Angeles, CA, introduced the strategy in the early 1990s. VTS involves extensive analysis of art/visual text to help students find meaning in what they see. The guiding questions within VTS can be used for any visual text:

1. What is going on in this picture?

2. What do you see that makes you say that?

3. What more can we find?

Figure 3.12   Visual Text Set for Sample +1P Unit

Strategies such as VTS deepen contextual knowledge about a topic or theme and generate more inquiry. Students develop a deeper understanding of visual text because they are prompted to substantiate their claims with evidence. The guiding questions from VTS could start a compelling conversation about the images depicted in Figure 3.12. Teachers (or students) could use VTS to gauge prior knowledge about Vessel Operations and generate additional questions about the images. The +1P Questioning Technique can also be used to generate questions. Making these connections enhances application and transfer of concepts related to a project.

Another critical aspect of investigation and research is self-directedness. +1P is not intended for teachers to project manage everyone's research. Students must develop their own skills in taking initiative and being proactive about project management. As student teams progress through their investigation, the POEM strategy (Figure 3.1) should be revisited. Conducting research and managing a project requires planning, organizing, executing, and monitoring. The more self-directed students are, the smoother the research process for everyone involved. Dembo and Eaton (2000) assert that an important component of academic success is students' ability to take responsibility for their own learning. Taking responsibility for academic performance starts with teaching students how to become self-regulated learners. In return, students develop an increased sense of efficacy and pride in their work (Dembo & Eaton, 2000).

Self-directed learners use metacognitive skills to sharpen their performance. Ambrose et al. (2010) define metacognition as a process of reflecting on and directing one's thinking. Students use metacognitive skills when they ask, "What did I do and how did I do it?" or "What am I doing and how am I doing it?" These questions prompt self-reflection and ownership. When students reflect on their learning process, they make strides to improve their performance. Similarly, when students take ownership of their learning process, they become responsible for their actions and they are less likely to blame others when problems occur. Two general strategies are recommended to promote metacognition (Ambrose et al., 2010):

1. **Model your metacognitive processes**—Teachers need to show students how they would approach a task; "talk out loud" when describing how you would tackle a task.

2. **Scaffold students in their metacognitive processes**—Ask students to explain their thinking; encourage students to ask questions like

a. "What am I learning from this project?"

b. "How am I going to accomplish this task?"

c. "How can I better assist my team?"

d. "What will I do differently next time?"

As teachers, we want our students to possess strong metacognitive skills. This requires explicitly stating the steps in a process and modeling to students. Even if it feels like we are stating the obvious when explaining a task, students (especially novice learners) need metacognitive guidance from an expert. The POEM strategy (Figure 3.1) is exponentially enhanced with self-directed learners. These learners are not only cognizant of their roles and responsibilities, but they also adopt a mindset of personal accountability. +1P develops students' competence and metacognitive skills through focused inquiry, learning activities, project management, and investigation/research. When we provide opportunities for students to practice and perfect their metacognitive skills, we prepare them for college, career, and life.

You might still be asking, "What exactly are students investigating and researching?" The +1P Questioning Technique is intended to guide the investigative process. These are questions that were generated during the focused inquiry phase (refer back to Figure 3.4 and Figure 3.5). Teachers and students may add to the questioning sequence at any time, but you want to ensure that students answer the original questions. Students are also encouraged to revisit the essential questions as they conduct their research. The essential questions frame the entire project and should be referenced throughout the +1P process. Students can record answers to their questions manually or digitally. It is highly recommended that students utilize a paper or digital journal to document their experiences. Students need to record the date on all documents, correspondences, and learning activities. Incorporating dates will help students organize their work and remember what data is gathered on which day. Use the aforementioned strategies for collecting, analyzing, and managing data to accelerate learning as students conduct research.

Another strategy for deepening conceptual knowledge of a topic is called Look Fours (L4s). The four tenets of L4s are trends over time, multiple perspectives, technological advances, and forecasting. L4s increase the complexity and rigor of research as students go deeper for content knowledge. Without L4s, students might not consider the depth of their topic of study. For example, students may not think about the impact of technological advances when they

Figure 3.13 Look Fours Strategy

Look Fours (L4s) in Research	
Trends Over Time • Explore patterns in the data • Connect the past with the present	**Multiple Perspectives** • Acknowledge multiple viewpoints • Determine pros and cons
Technological Advances • Examine the impact of technology • Specify what, when, and how	**Forecasting** • Predict the future • Extend the conversation

conduct research, yet technology has influenced nearly every aspect of our lives, from food and clothes to cell phones and cars. L4s bring these critical elements to the investigative process. The benefit of using L4s is that they are interdisciplinary and applicable to any topic of study.

Students can use L4s symbols as visual aids when conducting research for their project. They can relate the symbols to certain themes throughout their research or reference them in their journals. It is imperative that teachers scaffold the investigative process with multiple strategies. Symbols and graphic organizers provide a more interesting way to connect themes and document findings during the investigative process.

There are two final considerations to make as students conduct research—credibility and citations. Critiquing the credibility of a source and citing where you obtained it is vital to the research process. Without a strategy to gauge credibility, students might accept whatever they read and discover as legitimate. Not all sources and facts are credible. As students acquire information from their investigative study, they need to distinguish facts from opinions. The Credibility 4 (C4) strategy is useful for assessing the credibility of sources. C4 is applicable to articles and websites. The four steps are as follows:

1. **Check the credibility of the author:**
   a. Is the author of the article/website an expert in the field?
      (e.g., evidence of certification and/or credentials)
   b. Does the author belong to an accredited institution or publishing house?
      (e.g., college/university, state or federal agency, media organization, established newspaper or magazine—Time, Newsweek, Wall Street Journal)

2. **Check the credibility of the content:**
   a. What is the purpose of the content (persuade, inform, or entertain)?
   b. What evidence is used to support the author's claims?

3. **Check the credibility of the dates:**
   a. When was the article/website written or published?
   b. Is the information relevant to today?

4. **Check the credibility of the author's sources:**
   a. Does the author reference outside experts?
   b. How many additional experts are cited?

Strategies such as C4 help students authenticate their research. To avoid plagiarism, students must also substantiate their information by citing the sources. They also need to know the ramifications of not using citations when quoting or copying someone else's words/work. These skills will prepare students for college as well.

For the sample unit on Vessel Operations, I generated a list of sources that students can use to collect data/information. The list includes multiple sources at a teacher's disposal, in addition to sources that students can access outside the classroom. It is important to note that multiple sources provide multiple perspectives on a topic of study.

NOTE TO PRIMARY TEACHERS

Teachers who teach Grades K–2 may need to adapt the research component for their students. A suggestion would be to model the research process with the whole class. You may need to utilize more scaffolds, such as realia, visuals, and graphic organizers.

Figure 3.14   Investigation/Research Sources for Sample +1P Unit

---

Investigation (Research)

Text Set: primary and secondary sources of information that are credible and contextualize learning for a topic of study

Optional Sources

Internet

Newspapers

Magazines/Articles

Journals

Books

School or Public Library

Videos

Television

Movies

Documentaries

Pictures

Charts and Graphs

Statistics/Data/Surveys

Personal Accounts

Interviews

Observation

Field Trip

Museums

Science Centers

Look Fours (L4s) in Research:

1) Trends Over Time

2) Multiple Perspectives

3) Technological Advances

4) Forecasting

Credibility 4 (sourcing)

YOUR TURN TO PRACTICE

Make a list of five to ten potential sources that your students could use for their research. You may borrow ideas from the sample unit on Vessel Operations (Figure 3.14). It is highly recommended you include L4s in your planning. Remember to use the +1P rubric to assist you in this process. Once your list has been generated, circle the top three sources that students can access. Write your sources below:

+1P Topic of Study: _____

Investigation (Research)	
1.	6.
2.	7.
3.	8.
4.	9.
5.	10.

Your toolkit for +1P implementation is almost full. Use the plethora of strategies, techniques, and samples in this chapter to jump-start project management. The next chapter explores different ways to manage content using the Internet.

Think about strategies you have used to promote student inquiry and investigation. How would the +1P Questioning Technique, text sets, Look Fours, and/or Credibility 4 assist students as they conduct research? How might you transfer knowledge about these particular strategies, and others discussed in this chapter, back to your district, school, or classroom?

Figure 3.15 is a visual reminder of where we are in our +1P journey. Take pride in knowing that we are two-thirds of the way there. Feel free to give yourself or colleague a pat on the back.

Big Ideas	Universal Concepts	Essential Questions
transportation, vessel operations, cargo (imported and exported), **systems, container ports, technology, trade,** rules, safety, contracts, **supply and demand,** and labor/unions	**Systems** include interdependent parts. **Technology** allows for increased production.	What are the costs and benefits of **trade**? Can a **system** advance without **technology**?

Standards	Project Objective		Writing Assessment
	Students will **identify and describe** the **purpose and function** of Vessel Operations. They will gather information from the **Internet, observations (field trip to the port),** and **videos.** Students will present their findings to their classmates in a presentation, write a **short essay** about their topic of study, and reflect on the process.		

	Focused Inquiry	Learning Activities	Investigation (Research)	Recommendations	Presentation	Reflection and Commitment
Common Core State Standards: College and Career Readiness (CCR) Anchor Standards (AS)	**General Questions:** What modes of **transportation** are used to transport goods? What countries have **container ports**? What is a **system**?	*Optional Activities* → 1) Dialogue and Discussion	**Text Set:** primary and secondary sources of information that are credible and contextualize learning for a topic of study			
Reading AS 7: Integrate and evaluate content presented in diverse media and formats, including visually and quantitatively, as well as in words.	**Specific Questions:** **Vessels:** What are some specific types of vessels?	2) Journal/Diary/Log [paper or digital] 3) Create a Timeline 4) Field Trips 5) Online Collaboration [Google Drive, Facebook, E-mail, Padlet, Blogs, Twitter, TodaysMeet, & Skype]	*Optional Sources* → Internet Newspapers Magazines/Articles Journals Books			
Writing AS 6: Use technology, including the Internet, to produce and publish writing and to interact and collaborate with others.	**Technology:** What type of technology is used on vessels and within the container ports?	6) Create a Blog 7) Interviews or Surveys 8) Build a Model 9) Display Board	School or Public Library Videos Television Movies			

(Continued)

Figure 3.15 (Continued)

Writing AS 7: Conduct short as well as more sustained research projects based on focused questions demonstrating understanding of the subject under investigation. **Speaking and Listening AS 4:** Present information, findings, and supporting evidence such that listeners can follow the line of reasoning and the organization, development, and style are appropriate to task, purpose, and audience. **Language AS 1:** Demonstrate command of the conventions of standard English grammar and usage when writing or speaking.	**Cargo:** What are specific types of cargo? What types of cargo does the United States **import and export?** **Trade:** What is trade? **Elaborate Questions:** **Vessels:** What purpose and function do vessels serve? **Technology:** How does technology impact vessel operations? **Cargo:** Why do countries import and export goods? **Trade:** How does **supply and demand** impact trade? **Sourcing Questions:** How will you access your information? What sources will you use? What makes your sources credible? (i.e., www.aapaports.org and www.worldshipping.org)	10) Debate 11) Socratic Seminar 12) Quizzes [paper or digital] 13) Academic Games 14) Vocabulary Placemat 15) Venn Diagram 16) Collage	Documentaries Pictures Charts and Graphs Statistics/Data/Surveys Personal Accounts Interviews Observation Field Trip Museums Science Centers **Look Fours (L4s) in Research:** 1) Trends Over Time 2) Multiple Perspectives 3) Technological Advances 4) Forecasting **Credibility 4** (sourcing)		

SUMMARY

Checkpoints 4 (project objective) and 5 (focused inquiry, learning activities, and investigation/research) are the "GPS" of +1P projects. These checkpoints guide teachers as they facilitate the process, and they guide students as they engage in the process. This chapter emphasizes the importance of having a project objective that captures the essence of a project. Focused inquiry and investigation are equally imperative to the process. If students do not understand what they are inquiring about, they will not understand what to investigate. Checkpoints 4 and 5 are also paramount to establishing rigor, cognitive demand, and project management—all of which prepare students for college, career, and life. These checkpoints are directly aligned to several CCR Anchor Standards. For example, Writing AS 7 states, "Conduct short as well as more sustained research projects based on focused questions demonstrating understanding of the subject under investigation," and Writing AS 8 states, "Gather relevant information from multiple print and digital resources, assess the credibility and accuracy of each source, and integrate the information while avoiding plagiarism." Both standards, in addition to many others, are explicitly addressed throughout this chapter.

Checkpoints 4 and 5 serve to enhance students' factual, procedural, conceptual, and metacognitive knowledge. As educators, we need to be aware that making learning *easier* for students makes it *harder* for them to compete locally and globally. For this reason, Chapter 3 provides concrete strategies and examples of how project objectives, focused inquiry, learning activities, and investigation/research can be meaningfully applied in classrooms. A range of cognitive processes (thinking skills) and learning activities is also essential. The next chapter addresses the vital role of technology and its application to the +1P process.

━━━━━━━━━━━━━━━━━━━ MICs ━━━━━━━━━━━━━━━━━━━

MOST IMPORTANT CONCEPTS

- Project Management
  - POEM Strategy
- Project Objective
  - +1P Objectives Organizer

- Focused Inquiry
  - +1P Questioning Technique
- Learning Activities
  - Bloom's Taxonomy
  - Cognitive Processes (Thinking Skills)
- Project Management
  - Student Teams
  - Roles and Responsibilities
  - Team Agreement
  - Managing Learning Activities
- Investigation (Research)
  - Text Sets, Look Fours, Credibility 4
- Self-directed Learners (Metacognition)

4

CROSSROADS OF TECHNOLOGY AND +1 PEDAGOGY

When technology meets the classroom, anything is possible. Computer-mediated technology in the twenty-first century has created a virtual shift in education. This virtual shift calls for greater technology usage and application in the classroom. Students can use technology to access information, communicate beyond the classroom, and experience diverse forms of digital media for authentic purposes. Technology, specifically in the form of computers and the Internet, has become a major focus of education policy and reform. National, state, and local initiatives have provided schools with computer hardware and software, allowed schools and classrooms to connect to the Internet, and supported technology-focused professional development opportunities for teachers (Coley, 1997). Despite these efforts to equip schools and prepare teachers, technology usage during instructional time is not as prevalent as one may expect.

According to the U.S. Department of Education, National Center for Education Statistics (NCES), only 40% of K–12 teachers reported that they or their students regularly use computers in the classroom during instructional time, yet 97% of teachers reported having one or more working computers located in the classroom for everyday use (NCES, 2010). Statistically, the majority of K–12 teachers nationwide do not incorporate computer technology during instructional time.

These statistics are not intended to chastise teachers for limited use of computer technology during instructional time, especially if digital devices are not readily available to their students. More importantly, the data represent a clear rationale for enhancing computer-mediated technology during instructional time, especially as it relates to +1 Pedagogy. This framework builds essential skill sets for students in the twenty-first century, with technology at the forefront. Students must use technology to effectively engage in the +1P process. For this reason, technology is an indispensable part of +1P. In order to prepare students for twenty-first century learning and college, teachers must find ways to integrate technology into their instructional practices.

SAMR MODEL

Teaching and learning with technology requires criteria for gauging effectiveness. While there are many rubrics and methods for assessing technology, Puentedura (2006) provides a comprehensive model for assessing different levels of student engagement with technology. The SAMR model—substitution, augmentation, modification, and redefinition—is a guide for transforming technology

Figure 4.1   SAMR Model With +1P Examples

Redefinition: Technology allows for the creation of new tasks, previously inconceivable.

+1P Example: Create a Google Presentation, PowerPoint, or website on a topic of study.

Modification: Technology allows for significant task redesign.

+1P Example: Use the Internet or software program to conduct research, upload images and videos, and construct knowledge about a topic of study.

Augmentation: Technology acts as a direct tool substitute, with functional improvement.

+1P Example: Highlight and make comments when reading a digital document related to a topic of study.

Substitution: Technology acts as a direct tool substitute, with no functional change.

+1P Example: Use a digital device to take notes about a topic of study instead of paper.

use in the classroom (Puentedura, 2006). Teachers can use the SAMR model to measure progression and exemplary use of technology during +1P instruction.

The bottom levels of SAMR (substitution and augmentation) represent technological enhancement, while the top levels (modification and redefinition) represent technological transformation (Puentedura, 2006). Figure 4.1 illustrates that as computer-mediated technology moves up the continuum, craftsmanship in applying technology to assignments/projects is enhanced. The SAMR model helps define technology outcomes in the classroom. Teachers and students must engage at each level of SAMR to become efficient at integrating technology during instruction. To develop automaticity with technology, they must also go beyond the substitution level. For more resources on the SAMR model, visit this link: **http://www.schrockguide.net/samr.html**.

To access multimedia and digital support, including other technology rubrics, you may go to the following link: **http://www.schrockguide.net/assessment-and-rubrics.html**

The SAMR model is purposeful in redefining our notion of technology integration in the classroom. There are many teachers who have their students use technology on a daily basis, but the greater question is *how* students are interacting with technology. A rubric/criterion that measures lower and higher levels of technology implementation heightens awareness for teachers and students. It can be argued that the SAMR model prevents technological mediocrity. Figure 4.1 gives explicit examples of how educators can facilitate higher levels of computer-mediated technology in the classroom. Increased exposure to technology prepares students for twenty-first century learning and enables them to compete for jobs/careers that require technological skills.

Think   Question   Transfer

Think about ways you have integrated technology in the classroom. How would you use the SAMR model to enhance computer-mediated technology in your classroom? How might you transfer knowledge about the SAMR model back to your district, school, or classroom?

DIGITAL PEDAGOGY

Digital pedagogy is the use of electronic elements that are designed to enhance educational experiences for students, in addition to covering a wide spectrum of online learning opportunities. Familiar digital pedagogies include eLearning (also known as virtual and distance learning) and blended learning systems (combined face-to-face classroom methods with computer-mediated activities). Interest in online learning/eLearning has grown enormously since 1990, and currently, almost every post-secondary institution offers courses using information technologies (Schrum, 2005). eLearning initiatives, such as cyberschools and online teaching/testing, are also changing traditional notions of how K–12 education is provided. According to Bushweller (2002), Florida Virtual School (FVS) is the nation's most prominent state-sponsored online high school. FVS is a public high school that offers courses to students on a one-course basis or as an entire curriculum. There are other institutions that offer complete online degree programs and courses, such as the University of Phoenix and National University. These educational institutions, among many others, prepare students for twenty-first century learning in a technological era.

Another purpose of eLearning programs is to reach learners who cannot readily access courses they need due to illness, disability, learning challenges, geographic location, or other personal circumstances (Schrum, 2005). Face-to-face classroom instruction has limitations for certain students, including minors and adult learners. In addition to diversifying the learning experience, eLearning is conducive, equitable, and accessible to *all* students. Other common reasons for engaging in eLearning include making up credits, earning extra credit to graduate early, the convenience of accessing a course from home or any place outside of school, and mitigating limited financial resources (Schrum, 2005). In terms of college tuition, students may find online courses less expensive than enrolling full time at an educational institution. All of these factors substantiate reasons for investing in digital pedagogy.

Digital pedagogy also includes blended learning, a learning style that incorporates traditional classroom methods with computer technology. The terms "blended learning," "hybrid learning," "technology-mediated instruction," "web-enhanced instruction," "and mixed-mode instruction" are often used interchangeably in current research literature (Martyn, 2003). However, researchers in the United States tend to use the term "blended learning" with more regularity. Blended learning is an integrated approach to learning that includes mobile learning, online learning, and classroom learning. An analysis by the U.S. Department of Education found that blended learning environments are more effective than just online learning or just face-to-face learning (Means, Toyama, Murphy, Bakia, & Jones, 2010). Blended learning uses technology to facilitate learning activities that can occur with or without the teacher.

The University of Southern California's (USC) Hybrid High School is one example of a blended learning program. Their curriculum includes digital courses that are used by students when they are in school, doing research, and participating in community service projects. Students also check out laptops every day, which are used to access digital courseware, web content, and complete writing and multimedia assignments (USC Hybrid High School, 2013). Proponents argue that the blended learning methodology gives students unprecedented access to academic material that is engaging, challenging, and multifaceted (Bushweller, 2002). +1P is another type of blended learning. Students have face-to-face interactions with their teacher and peers in a classroom setting while engaging in computer-mediated technologies to conduct research, collaborate through digital media, upload content, complete learning activities, and prepare presentations for their project. The latter represents an integrated approach to twenty-first century teaching and learning.

+1 PEDAGOGY AND DIGITAL PEDAGOGY

Digital pedagogy at its core is a discipline but only in the most dynamic sense of the word. Stommel (2013) asserts that we become experts in digital pedagogy by devoting our lives to researching, practicing, presenting, facilitating, and teaching learning activities that are embedded in technology and collaboration. Our expertise in digital pedagogy stems from taking an institution or instructional practice that was once inspired by postindustrial machines and redrawing it inside the machines of the digital age (Stommel, 2013). Rheingold (2007) shares a similar perspective and further defines digital pedagogy as a participative instructional method assisted by digital media and networks that focus on catalyzing, inspiring, nourishing, facilitating, and guiding learning that is essential to individual and collective life in the twenty-first century. This participatory instructional method includes, but is not limited to, blogs, wikis, tagging and social bookmarking, music-photo-video sharing, podcasts, digital storytelling, virtual communities, social networking services, virtual environments, and video blogs. These distinctly different media share common, interrelated characteristics of social networking and connectivity through a network, all of which can be used to implement +1P. Computer-mediated technology enables students to experiment with different technologies for various components of +1P. For example, learning activities, research, presentations, writing assessments, discussions, and files can be managed with technology.

Students in the twenty-first century have the opportunity to use computer technology in very advanced ways. Bell (2010) contends that authentic use of technology is highly engaging to students because it taps into their fluency with computers. Moreover, when technology is integrated into instructional practices, students are more likely to build on what they learn from technological skills because their existing knowledge is made central to the learning process (ChanLin, 2008). In other words, digital pedagogy empowers students because they learn to manage and enhance their acquisition of technological skills. As students participate in online research for their projects, they become more adept at navigating other sources of digital media (i.e., wikis, blogs, videos, images/pictures, and audio), sharing information with other students, and troubleshooting when needed. In the presentation phase of +1P, students may use various forms of technology to display their learning (more on this in Chapter 5). Overall, digital pedagogy delivers twenty-first century instruction that is innovative, collaborative, and communicative. Students advance these skills when they are given opportunities to practice them inside and outside of school.

Think about an educational experience that was enhanced through technology. How does digital pedagogy prepare students for twenty-first century learning? How might you transfer knowledge about integrating computer-mediated technology back to your district, school, or classroom?

CLOUD MANAGEMENT SYSTEMS

Authentic forms of learning through technology are necessary to support the +1P process. The interactive nature of gathering research to find answers, collaborating and communicating inside and outside of the classroom, and organizing data necessitates computer-mediated technology during implementation. When technology accommodates instructional practices, teachers and students are less dependent on worksheets and lectures (Ullman, 2013). While fewer worksheets save on paper, fewer lectures allow students to take a more active role in their education. One approach to utilizing technology during +1P is through cloud management technology. Networked projects require a place to store and manage content. Cloud-based platforms allow students to digitally interact with their peers, in addition to uploading and storing content.

Online technology helps maximize implementation and 21st Century Skills. Students are given opportunities to engage in critical thinking from Internet sources, collaborate with peers, adapt to diverse media, practice self-directedness, communicate digitally, and access and analyze information as they delve into their projects. Cloud Management Systems (CMSs) offer creative solutions for storing content, increasing technology use during instruction, and enhancing formal and informal communication skills. A CMS is a computer program that organizes information/content from one central interface, such as a website. The management of information is exhibited through creating, editing, publishing, and archiving content (White, 2005). CMSs facilitate collaborative content creation, video media, and other assignments that involve data collection or storage (Roebuck, 2011).

The core functions of a CMS are threefold: 1) present information on a website, 2) store information on a website, and 3) operate as a collaborative tool for users. To circumvent the paper load for projects, it is highly recommended to invest in digital ways to organize and store student work. A CMS is one solution for collaborative management of content. Teachers can use a CMS to store and manage classroom data from assignments and assessments as well. They can also use a CMS to foster student collaboration and engagement through digital communication. Even if students work independently on a project, they still need to collaborate with their teacher and peers. As stated in Figure 1.2, +1P projects require technology and collaboration. Developing skills in technology and collaboration will prepare students for college, career, and life. Most college courses and careers require computer-mediated technology and collaboration, so the earlier students develop technological and interpersonal skills, the better.

Some CMS services are free, accessible, and readily available on any mobile device. This accessibility makes it easier for teachers and students to use a CMS while engaged in the +1P process. More importantly, using a CMS during implementation bolsters teacher and student efficiency in web-based tools and project management. The end result is increased efficacy and competency with an online platform. A CMS also increases long-term implementation of +1P because it leverages resources of teachers, students, and parents. Since websites are easily accessible on smart phones and other digital devices, in schools and the workplace, more stakeholders can be involved in the learning process.

Edmodo is one type of CMS that teachers may find useful as they engage in the +1P process. Established in September 2008, Edmodo is a free social learning platform with over 51,000,000 users (Wikipedia, 2015). The platform, or website, is accessible to any educator, student, or parent with Internet access. Edmodo provides teachers and students with a secure place to connect, collaborate, and share content (Dobler, 2012). Since Edmodo supports online learning, the platform could be used to implement +1P. For example, teachers can post assignments related to students' topics of study. They can also customize specific folders for various topics and student groups. Each folder would contain pertinent information related to inquiry, learning activities, research, and the presentation. Students can use Edmodo to upload assignments and engage in dialogue with their teacher and peers. If you are a secondary teacher, you can create classroom groups to accommodate multiple classes/periods. An excellent resource for learning more about digital tools and platforms for the classroom can be found at this website: **www.educatorstechnology.com** (if you type "Edmodo" into the search engine, several resources will be generated, particularly YouTube tutorials).

One key aspect of Edmodo is its safety. Because the platform is designed for schools and classrooms, it is a controlled environment where teachers and students can collaborate. When teachers create an Edmodo account, they also administer, manage, and control all content. Social networking on Edmodo for students is managed in the following ways (Educational Technology and Mobile Learning, 2014):

- Each Edmodo class group is managed and controlled by the teacher.
- Students need an access code to join the class. If a student shares the code outside the class, the teacher can change it without affecting students already in the group.
- Students can only communicate to the whole class or the teacher—private messages between students are not possible.

- Anonymous posting is not possible.
- Teachers can delete posts.
- If schools upgrade (free) to the institutional feature, the school can audit all teacher and student activity.
- Parental access to their children's posts and to the teacher is an optional feature.

The best way to acclimate yourself with Edmodo is to open an account and start practicing. If you already have an Edmodo account, think of ways that you can use the platform to support implementation. Figure 4.2 provides a snapshot of what an Edmodo page might look like for your classroom. Notice the different groups and other relevant features on the page.

Teachers can use Edmodo to post assignments, create polls for student responses, embed video clips, create learning groups, post quizzes for students to take, and create a calendar of events and assignments. As students upload their project assignments, teachers can also annotate the assignments directly into Edmodo to provide instant feedback. This type of technology supports educators as they

Figure 4.2   Screenshot of Edmodo Page

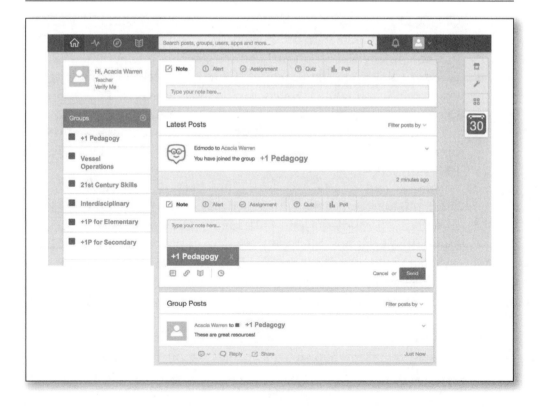

facilitate +1P. Since Edmodo is free, it can be incorporated into any classroom at any time.

Laur (2011) is known for sharing her Edmodo experiences with teachers, schools, and administrators. She allows teachers to use her model as a blueprint for creating their own project-based learning. Laur (2011) describes how she used Edmodo with her high school law class to support a project aimed at understanding how to reduce crime in the United States. First, she posted relevant articles and encouraged her students to discuss them in small groups using Edmodo. Next, students posed essential questions related to the topic. Students then created electronic presentations and shared them with their classmates, allowing them to gather feedback and revise their work in Edmodo. At the end of the project, Laur (2011) posted a poll on Edmodo, asking students to reflect on their research and weigh in on the best method for reducing crime. The integrated features of Edmodo enabled Laur's (2011) students to simultaneously collaborate on their projects and build capacity with technology. This type of engagement reflects twenty-first century learning and prepares students for college, career, and life.

Google Drive, also known as the Google Cloud, is another CMS that can be used to facilitate the +1P process. There are over 240,000,000 Google Drive users worldwide. Created and managed by Google, Google Drive allows users to store documents in a cloud, share files, and edit documents with other users (Wikipedia, 2015). Google Drive files can also be shared publicly on the Internet, a feature that allows account holders and non-account holders to access information. For example, the following public URL (Uniform Resource Locator—also known as a web address) contains a special message for you. You do not need an account to access the link: **https://docs.google.com/ presentation/d/1FSukrppreZSNxkDN6bAJJ4YBOvwpl1VjPQDxuS uSKVw/edit#slide=id.p**.

Notice that this URL is incredibly long. Good news—you can shorten it by copying the entire URL and pasting it into **http://goo.gl** (it will say "Paste your long URL here"). Once you have pasted the long URL in the box, click on the blue tab that says "Shorten URL" and you will see a new, shortened URL (see arrows in Figure 4.3). The new URL is now **http://goo.gl/LVRtwR** (case sensitive).

If you want to get even fancier, you can create a QR (Quick Response) Code. To do this, you would click on the word "Details" (circled in Figure 4.3) and a QR Code will populate. See Figure 4.4 for a visual representation of what comes up on the screen when you click "Details." The little box that says "Total Clicks" monitors how

Figure 4.3   Screenshot of Google URL Shortener

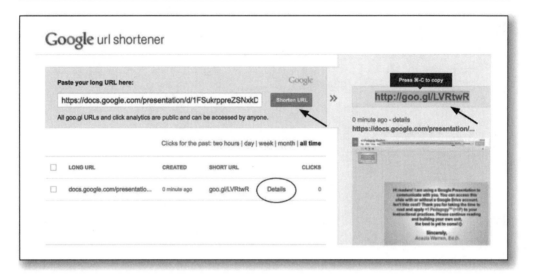

many people have accessed your QR Code. The QR Code in Figure 4.4 is legitimate, meaning that it is ready to scan. Go ahead and try it!

QR Codes provide a "quick" way to access information. They have become more popular in recent years and are generally found on advertisements, flyers, Google Presentations, agendas, websites, and food items (i.e., containers and bags). **Note:** Download the QR app on your cell phone or other digital device, and then scan the QR Code to receive the information. The next time you see a QR Code, scan it and read the information provided. While we are on the topic of URL shorteners, **https://bitly.com** is another great resource for shortening and customizing a URL. If I take my shortened URL from Google, which is **http://goo.gl/LVRtwR**, and paste it onto the bitly website, I can create a new name for the URL. You must create an account with bitly (it is free) to customize the link, but it is worth your time.

Figure 4.4   Screenshot of Google QR Code

Figure 4.5   Screenshot of Bitly URL Shortener

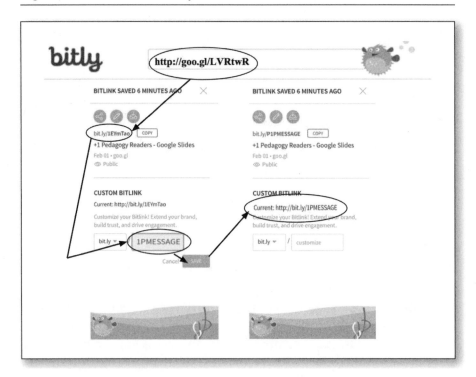

If you follow the arrows in Figure 4.5, you will notice that Google URL was changed into a bitly URL (**http://goo.gl/LVRtwR** became **http://bit.ly/1EYmTao**). I took the bitly URL and customized it to say "1PMESSAGE." Once I typed in my customized URL name, I clicked "SAVE" (see Figure 4.5) and my new URL became **http://bit.ly/1PMESSAGE** (case sensitive). It is important to note that my Google URL still works! So now you can access either URL to read my message. Why did I spend this amount of time taking you through the URL shortening process? It is cumbersome to ask students (and parents) to use a long URL to access information. Why not shorten a URL to make access to a website a little easier? With a shortened URL, teachers and students avoid misspelling a long URL by typing in the wrong letter, number, or symbol. Teachers can use URL shorteners and QR Codes to inform/update students and parents about the progress of a project. Either way, it is hard to argue against using a simpler URL to access information.

In addition to file sharing and storing content, Google Drive has many other attractive features. Specific benefits of Google Drive include:

- Available 24/7
- Reduces paper copies

- Publish student work
- Automatically saves
- Revision history
- Microsoft Office compatible
- Template Gallery

The Google Docs Template Gallery is especially useful for educators. You can use the Template Gallery to access hundreds of templates for Google docs, spreadsheets, presentations, forms, and drawings.

Figure 4.6   Sample Google Drive Features

Grading	Digital Note Taking
<ul><li>Google Forms</li><li>Google Spreadsheets</li><li>Use for planning and informing instruction</li></ul>	<ul><li>Google Docs</li><li>Integrate digital resources and writing tools</li><li>Comment on notes</li></ul>
Templates	**Reader's Workshop**
<ul><li>Google Presentations, Docs, Forms, etc.</li><li>Diverse range of digital templates</li><li>Templates automatically save</li></ul>	<ul><li>Digital articles (scholar article search)</li><li>Hyperlinks to pictures, videos, and resources</li><li>Read, collaborate, share, and publish books</li></ul>
Writer's Workshop	**Multimedia**
<ul><li>Google Docs</li><li>Make comments and use writing supports</li><li>Peer edit, revise (revision history), source</li></ul>	<ul><li>Upload and share videos, pictures, and music</li><li>Link videos and images to Google Presentation</li><li>Modify layout and transitions for presentation</li></ul>
Project-Based Learning	**Vocabulary Builder**
<ul><li>Facilitate student-centered learning</li><li>Create surveys with Google Forms</li><li>Conduct research for any topic of study, cite sources, present, and reflect (Google Docs, Spreadsheets, Forms, Presentations)</li></ul>	<ul><li>Google Docs</li><li>Use videos, images, and dictionary tools</li><li>Create quizzes/vocab. tests with Google Forms</li></ul>
Content Organization and Management	**Brainstorming**
<ul><li>Create, organize, and manage assignments</li><li>Organize content in folders and subfolders</li><li>Organize and manage data in spreadsheets</li></ul>	<ul><li>Collaborative and metacognitive mapping</li><li>Visualize ideas and concepts</li><li>Project planning</li></ul>

This wonderful resource prevents educators from reinventing the wheel. You can access the templates from this site (case sensitive): **http://bit.ly/GOOGLETEMPLATES**.

While Figure 4.6 does not represent all Google Drive features, it highlights those that are particularly useful for +1P. Students can simultaneously record their work, conduct research, download and upload files/images/videos, and communicate with their teacher/ peers. Teachers can check on student progress at any time and post comments about student work. Figure 4.7 illustrates a sample learning activity (learning log) on Google Docs.

There are several things going on in Figure 4.7. Note the drop-down menu from the *Tools* tab. The menu includes Spelling, Research, Define (for dictionary), Word Count, Translate document, Script editor, Preferences, and Personal dictionary (where students can enter and track their vocabulary words). If students click on the *Research* tab, they can conduct research while typing into the Google document. A drop-down menu populates from the *Research* tab as well (see far right side of Figure 4.7). Students can choose to research Everything, Images, Scholar, Quotes, Dictionary, Personal, and Tables. For this particular Google Doc, I chose to research *Images* and typed "cargo vessels" into the search engine. As depicted in Figure 4.7, several images appear under the search engine. To insert these images into the Google Doc, students would click on the image and drag it to the Google Doc, where the image can be resized and moved to a

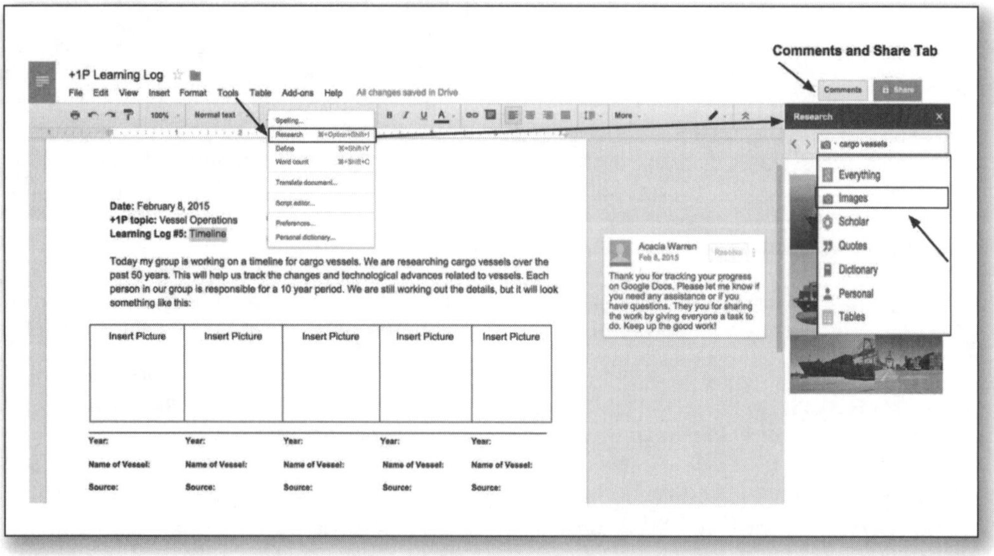

Figure 4.7   Screenshot of Google Docs Learning Activity

desired place in the document. Once the imaged is dragged into the Google Doc, a reference will appear at the bottom of the document. To inhibit plagiarism, references automatically populate when an image is uploaded. Look at the comment made by the teacher (me) in the Google Doc. To make a comment, I clicked on the *Comment* tab in the upper right-hand corner of the page. Teachers can make as many comments on a document as they choose.

Note the *Share* tab at the top right-hand corner of Figure 4.7. This feature allows teachers and students to share documents by entering e-mail addresses of desired participants, which saves on time and e-mail storage. The owner of the document can allot "edit rights" or "view only rights" to shared participants. The owner can also share the web link (click on "Get sharable link"), which gives anyone viewing access, with or without a Google Drive account.

Google Drive's sharing feature is multifaceted. Users can create and share folders, presentations, spreadsheets, forms (surveys), drawings, and maps. These features greatly enhance computer-mediated technology during the +1P process, while also reducing the paper load for teachers and students. Figure 4.9 illustrates the different features of Google Drive (see arrow).

To access and employ the Google Drive features, also known as Google Apps, teachers need to set up a Gmail account. Although signing up for an account is free, there is one caveat—students need a Gmail account to access the Google Apps as well. This could present some challenges for teachers and students, especially those teachers who teach primary grades. For this reason, Google recently introduced

Figure 4.8   Screenshot of Google Drive Sharing Feature

Figure 4.9   Screenshot of Google Drive Page

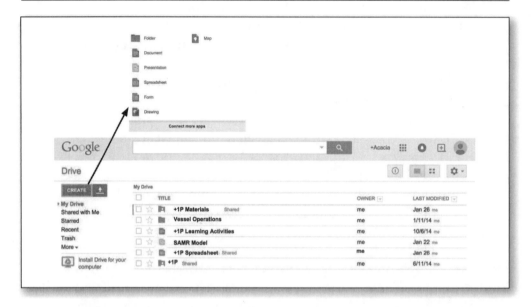

the Google Classroom, a Learning Management System (LMS) that allows teachers to digitally organize, create, assign, and collect student work. Access more Google Drive tips at this site (case sensitive): **http:// bit.ly/100GOOGLEDRIVETIPS**.

I want to take a brief moment to speak about the critical importance of parental involvement in education. Parents are typically very busy and their time is consumed by many variables (family needs, work, etc.). Educators make it easier on parents when they integrate technology for instructional purposes. Parents can monitor their student's work through online platforms, such as Edmodo and Google Drive. They can also access a teacher's website at any time of the day, which still allows them to participate in their student's learning. Generally speaking, parents appreciate the ability to access websites that support their student's learning, especially websites that provide progress reports and updates on current assignments. Face-to-face conferences and meetings to discuss student progress are not always conducive for parents. If parents work two or more jobs, or their job hours conflict with school hours, a face-to-face meeting may not be feasible. I am not advocating for a free pass on face-to-face parent conferences. Instead, I am advocating for accommodations and inclusive ways to involve more parents in their student's education. Websites and emails are alternative ways to communicate with parents and keep them informed about their student's academics.

The diverse features of Edmodo and Google Drive make them invaluable resources for +1P implementation. These platforms are designed to enhance digital collaboration and project management through technology. Teachers also have the option of creating their own website. There are many online supports for designing your own website. Popular platforms for customizing your own website are as follows: Google Sites, Weebly, GoDaddy, WordPress, and Haiku. School websites, if applicable, are additional platforms that support digital communication, storing content, and collaboration around a common purpose.

LEARNING MANAGEMENT SYSTEMS

Learning Management Systems (LMSs) provide another type of interface for managing content. Although an LMS may offer similar features to a CMS, it is specifically designed to manage educational records and track progress through attendance, grades, quizzes, and assignments (Szabo & Flesher, 2002). An LMS is a virtual learning environment that contains actual online courses. LMSs are predominately utilized at the college level. Students can use an LMS platform to enroll in one or more courses, in addition to managing content. A popular LMS used in education is the Moodle website, with nearly 70,000,000 users and over 7,000,000 courses worldwide. The term Moodle stands for Modular Object Oriented Developmental Learning Environment (Moodle, 2013). Moodle is a free web application for producing internet-based courses. Within these courses, students can interact with each other and their teacher/professor via fourteen different activities. The activities include the following (**https://docs .moodle.org/24/en/Activities**):

- **Assignments:** Enable teachers to grade and give comments on uploaded files and assignments created on- and off-line
- **Chat:** Allows participants to have a real-time synchronous discussion
- **Choice:** Allows teachers to ask questions and specify a choice of multiple responses.
- **Database:** Enables participants to create, maintain, and search a bank of record entries
- **External tool:** Allows participants to interact with LTI-compliant learning resources and activities on other websites
- **Feedback:** For creating and conducting surveys to collect feedback

- **Forum:** Allows participants to have asynchronous discussions
- **Glossary:** Enables participants to create and maintain a list of definitions, like a dictionary
- **Lesson:** For delivering content in flexible ways
- **Quiz:** Allows the teacher to design and set quiz tests, which may be automatically marked and feedback and/or correct answers shown
- **SCORM:** Enables Sharable Content Object Reference Model (SCORM—standards and specifications for web-based learning content) packages to be included as course content
- **Survey:** For gathering data from students to help teachers learn about their class and reflect on their own teaching
- **Wiki:** A collection of web pages that anyone can add to or edit
- **Workshop:** Enables peer assessment

Schools and districts can customize their own Moodle sites and courses. Moodle's popularity relates to its convenience and accessibility to all users with Internet access, in addition to no fees for creating an account. Other Moodle features include calendars, discussion forums, and assignment submission. Schools can use Moodle to manage content, establish online communication with teachers and students, and create additional courses if necessary. For a more prominent list and explanation of Moodle's digital features, visit this website: **https://docs.moodle.org/20/en/Features**.

Another ubiquitous LMS is Blackboard Learn, also known as Blackboard, which is owned and operated by Blackboard Inc. Approximately 17,000 schools and 100 countries worldwide utilize their services, including 75% of U.S. colleges and universities and more than half of the K–12 districts in the U.S. (Wikipedia, 2015). Blackboard functions as a course management system with numerous features that support online learning. The platform is known for adding online elements to face-to-face courses, especially in college. For example, you could take an on-campus college course on Mondays and Wednesdays and still access Blackboard's discussion board, assignments, and other features outside of class. Blackboard is not a free platform; schools must pay for services. However, Blackboard does have a newer platform called CourseSites that allows schools to create up to five courses for free.

Two statements posted on Blackboard's website are "On a mission to reimagine education" and "Solutions for a new generation of learners." Both statements are applicable to twenty-first century learning and digital pedagogy. Our world is quickly changing and adapting to new technologies every day. For this reason, it is incumbent upon educators to prepare students for the digital age. We can start by integrating more computer-mediated technology into our classrooms.

Think about ways that you have used Edmodo, Google Drive, Moodle, Blackboard, or other CMSs not mentioned above. How would a CMS support implementation of +1P? How might you transfer knowledge about CMSs and LMSs back to your district, school, or classroom?

SOCIAL MEDIA

Computer-mediated technology supports the unlimited exploration of concepts and ideas through creativity, critical thinking, collaboration, and research. Social media is another form of digital technology that allows people to create and share content in virtual communities (Facebook, Twitter, Instagram, Pinterest, Snapchat, etc.). Virtual communities exist for the purpose of social networking and gathering information about people, ideas, and/or topics. Students mainly use social media for digital communication among peers. Many of our students are highly competent with social media. Some students even communicate more through social media than in the actual classroom. These are realities that educators cannot afford to ignore. Have you ever caught a student using social media during instructional time? If you are a secondary teacher, your answer is most likely yes. Social media can be added to the laundry list of things that divert a student's attention away from instruction. Let's face it; social media can be fun, engaging, enticing, and addictive. That being said, how do we flip the script and get students to use social media for educational purposes?

First, we have to be intentional about integrating social media into our classroom practices (e.g., creating a Facebook account for school-related purposes). If we are not intentional about this process, less action will be taken to leverage social media use in the classroom. Second, we need to solicit support from other stakeholders, namely parents. Parent advocacy is critical, especially for promoting instructional practices that embed 21st Century Skills, technology, and global competitiveness. Third, we need to establish a plan of action that includes guidelines for what social media looks and sounds like in the classroom. This plan includes rules, regulations, and expectations. We are well aware that social media can be used inappropriately, and establishing protocols is the best way to circumvent problems/issues that may arise. Teachers can support the responsible use of social media and the Internet, both inside and outside of the classroom, through Digital Citizenship (DC). DC sets norms and expectations for appropriate use of technology in a digital world. According to Mike Ribble (2015), the nine elements of DC are as follows: 1) Digital Access, 2) Digital Commerce, 3) Digital Communication, 4) Digital Literacy, 5) Digital Etiquette, 6) Digital Law, 7) Digital Rights and Responsibilities, 8) Digital Health and Wellness, and 9) Digital Security. Teachers can access more information and lessons about DC at the following website: www.digitalciti zenship.net Finally, we test our plan by incorporating educational uses of social media inside and outside of the classroom. For example, teachers and students could use Twitter/Facebook to engage in dialogue or share research related to +1P projects. This can occur during class, in the evening, or over the weekend. If we provide a structure for academic engagement through social media and computer-mediated technology, we can enhance appropriate uses of technology during instructional time.

Educators may also benefit from allowing *structured* cell phone use in the classroom. Many schools nationally and internationally are not equipped with one-to-one digital devices for students. Chances are, there are more smartphones in a classroom than digital devices. Moreover, there are many classrooms that still have less than five working computers/laptops/digital devices. This presents a challenge for integrating technology, especially if you have 35–45 students per classroom (or period). Considering these facts, do we ban cell phone use in the classroom, or do we find ways to make it work? As long as cell phones are used appropriately for instructional purposes, such as conducting research and collaborating on projects, there is less reason to oppose their use in the classroom. Of course, there would be concerns about safety, firewalls, and monitoring cell phone activities within the classroom. While I understand the need to be concerned, I also know that when expectations, clear guidelines, and consequences are outlined for students, they are generally compliant. For those students who choose to "bend the rules," they can be dealt with accordingly. I am mainly suggesting the strategic use of cell phones in the classroom, as opposed to a complete ban on cell phone use altogether. We are not doing our students any favors by denying them opportunities before they get a chance to prove otherwise. It is also important to note that not all classroom activities/lessons/tasks warrant cell phone usage. Teachers would determine the appropriate time to incorporate cell phone use for an activity, project, or task.

Back to the topic of social media and digital collaboration, there are numerous platforms that teachers and students can use for +1P. In addition to those listed above, other platforms include iChat, Google +, Skype, blogs, wikis, TodaysMeet, and Padlet. Regardless of which platform is utilized, the purpose of highlighting these resources is to start a conversation about integrating digital communication and collaboration tools. Two user-friendly platforms that teachers and students could use are TodaysMeet (**www.todaysmeet.com**) and Padlet (**www.padlet.com**). Both websites function as "chat rooms" that enable digital communication among users. Teachers and students can access the platforms during school and outside of school. TodaysMeet is free and does not require users to sign up for an account. However, setting up an account gives teachers additional benefits, such as creating a room for longer periods of time. Teachers can log onto the website and name their room (make sure there are no spaces in the name you choose). Once you name your room, you will see a URL in the search engine that can be shared with students to generate a conversation around their projects. Students can access the room without signing up for an account. When they go to the designated URL, they will be prompted to create a "nickname." Similar to naming the room, nicknames cannot include any spaces. For example, "JessicaDavis or JessicaD" would work, but "Jessica Davis" would not because of the space in between the name. When students enter the room, they will see the number "140" above the message box. This number stands for the maximum amount of characters allowed per individual message at one time. Note that the dialogue under *Listen* will populate in order from top to bottom, with the most recent message posted on top. See Figure 4.10 for an example of how TodaysMeet can be used to collaborate and share resources during the +1P process.

Since teachers create the TodaysMeet session, they also control the conversation. This is especially convenient for safety purposes and for filtering out superfluous dialogue that may exist in more popular forms of social media (e.g., Twitter and Facebook).

Figure 4.10   Screenshot of TodaysMeet

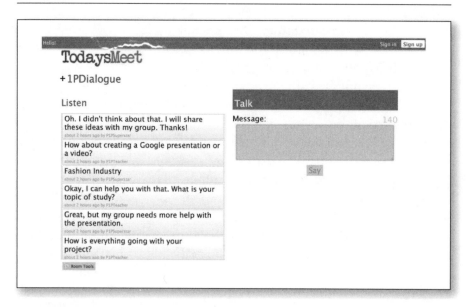

Padlet functions as another virtual medium for communication around a specific topic. The platform is free but requires users to set up an account. Once the account is established, users can create and name their wall, then share the URL with others. Teachers can use Padlet to start a dialogue about any topic of study. They can also customize multiple walls for different purposes. Similar to TodaysMeet, Padlet does not require students to create an account to post on their teacher's wall. Students would just need the web link to access the wall. Once students type the web link into the search engine, they are automatically included in the discussion.

Notice in Figure 4.11 that I created a wall to initiate a conversation about +1P. I chose the map of the world as my background, mainly because +1P promotes global competence, but there are many other backgrounds from which to choose. After creating my room, my next step is to share the URL with my students, which they can access on any digital device (laptop, cell phone, iPad, etc.). Teachers also have the option of sharing the Padlet link with parents. Virtual platforms make it easier to include parents in the process. Figure 4.11 includes an example comment from a parent (look for "Parent of David"). As you can see, Padlet is multifaceted and a great resource for supporting project management. Teachers and students can engage in dialogue, share web links, upload files, take pictures from their webcam, and watch/share videos. These types of virtual communities foster

Figure 4.11   Screenshot of Padlet

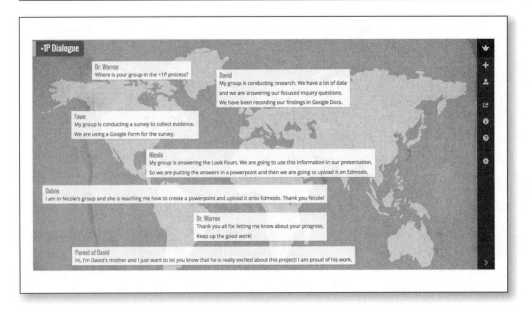

computer-mediated technology in the classroom, student collaboration on projects, exploration/sharing of content and resources, progress monitoring, and constructive feedback—all of which support +1P implementation. Let's start a real dialogue about +1P and implications for our professional practice. Please go to this link to type comments (double-click on the wall to post a comment): **http://bit.ly/ PADLETFOR1P** (case sensitive).

Think about ways you have used social media or digital communication platforms with students and/or adults. Given the platforms listed above, which ones might you use to foster +1P implementation? How might you transfer knowledge about integrating social media/digital communication platforms back to your district, school, or classroom?

APPS

Broadly defined, mobile apps are computer programs designed to run on smartphones, tablets, computers, and other mobile devices. According to Wikipedia (2015), the term "app" is short for application software. The purpose of an app is accessibility anywhere at any time. Most smartphones contain several apps, which are easy and quick to download. Some apps are free, while others require a small fee. Apps can be used to foster project management as well. Teachers and students can download certain apps onto their mobile device(s) to extend a +1P dialogue, assignment, or task. The aforementioned CMSs (Edmodo and Google Drive) and LMSs (Moodle and Blackboard) have apps that teachers and students can download. Since teachers and students can use these apps to access projects at anytime, +1P does not have to end when the bell rings. For more resources about educational web tools, including social networking and apps, visit this website: **http://bit.ly/EDUCWEBTOOLS** (case sensitive).

+1 PEDAGOGY WITHOUT TECHNOLOGY

Implementing +1P without computer-mediated technology can pose several challenges for teachers. Instruction without technology makes it harder to promote digital learning, application of multiple concepts, storing content, and collaboration outside of the classroom (Boss, 2012). There are other methods of storing content, such as Excel spreadsheets and Microsoft Word, but even these methods pale in comparison to the extensive benefits of a CMS, LMS, social media platform, and educational apps. Jimenez-Eliaeson (2010) argues that advanced technology allows teachers to adequately accommodate multiple methods of learning (e.g., local and global collaboration,

Figure 4.12   Screenshot of App Icons for Edmodo, Google Drive, Moodle, and Blackboard

presentation, video conferencing, and researching). These digital methods of learning enhance project management, communication, and collaboration across networks. Alternatively, limited technology forces teachers to rely on paper methods of managing data/content, such as files, hard copies, binders, and folders. This style of managing data/content is time consuming and further compounded with large numbers of students. For this reason, it is recommended that teachers take advantage of educational websites and apps, especially those that are free.

Without an effective means for digital collaboration, organizing and managing content, and enhancing technology use, teachers and students will find it harder to integrate technology during the +1P process. For this reason, it is imperative to research websites and other digital platforms that broaden the scope of +1P. This reality is made possible with computer-mediated technology. Comprehensive platforms, such as those listed above, inspire teachers and students to creatively engage in the process. Educators worldwide are taking advantage of the many CMSs, LMSs, and other digital tools that support twenty-first century learning. The Internet offers many free websites for curriculum and project development. However, websites that require fees and contractual agreements for product use (e.g., Blackboard for K–12 and Project Foundry) can still enrich implementation. Any form of computer-mediated technology that schools and teachers use to facilitate +1P will enhance twenty-first century learning. Students develop a greater sense of preparedness for college, career, and life when they use online technologies to support their learning.

+1P requires that teachers organize and manage content, create digital pathways for student communication, and build student capacity to apply technological tools to projects. Actively engaging in authentic projects requires resourcefulness and planning, new forms of knowledge representation in school, and expanded mechanisms for digital collaboration and communication. Computer-mediated resourcefulness is not only necessary for successful implementation of +1P but also required in the CCR Anchor Standards. Writing AS 6 states, "Use technology, including the Internet, to produce and publish writing and to interact and collaborate with others," while Speaking and Listening AS 5 says, "Make strategic use of digital media and visual displays of data to express information and enhance understanding of presentations." Even if you are the only person in the classroom with a digital device and Internet access, take advantage by exposing students to a world that is waiting to be discovered by them. This chapter, and those preceding it, highlights the correlations between technology, 21st Century Skills, and the Common Core State Standards.

SUMMARY

Computer-mediated technology enhances learning experiences and provides a context for employing digital tools. In addition to outlining key characteristics of digital pedagogy, this chapter examines technology tools that reinforce content management, implementation, and collaboration. Opportunities for exploring and applying digital tools are also provided. +1P presents a compelling case for integrating technology, collaborating inside and outside of school, and enhancing long-term retention of concepts and ideas. This interactive framework promotes teacher and student ownership as knowledge is constructed. The process is as exciting and engaging as you make it. Teaching and learning is accelerated through projects that embed technology, research/investigation, and 21st Century Skills. Most importantly, students are equipped with skills that enable them to compete locally and globally. Remember, start from where you are with integrating computer-mediated technology in the classroom, but do not stop there. The next intersection explores accountability and assessment practices and brings closure to the +1P process. The remaining checkpoints, namely Checkpoints 6 (recommendations and presentation) and 7 (writing assessment, reflection, and commitment), are examined in further detail.

MICs

MOST IMPORTANT CONCEPTS

- SAMR Model
- Digital Pedagogy
  - Blended Learning
- +1P and Digital Pedagogy
- Cloud Management Systems (CMSs)
  - Edmodo
  - Google Drive
- Learning Management Systems (LMSs)
  - Google Classroom
  - Moodle
  - Blackboard
- Social Media and Digital Communication Platforms
  - TodaysMeet and Padlet
- Apps
- +1P Without Technology

INTERSECTION 3

ASSESSING

"When the cook tastes the soup, that's formative; when the guests taste the soup, that's summative."

—Robert Stake

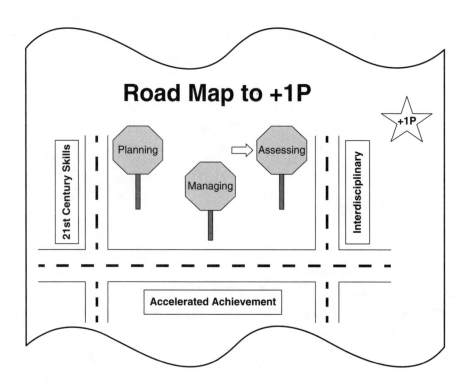

5

EXIT AT ASSESSMENT

Assessments are inevitable in school *and* life. There is no way around them. Literally, assessments are designed to measure mastery of content, concepts, and skills. Symbolically, assessments are designed to gauge competence, resilience, and perseverance. Most indicators of educational outcomes are determined through assessments. Educators use assessments to monitor performance/mastery, identify areas of improvement, and provide a source of feedback for teaching and learning. All assessments, in one way or another, lend themselves to these indicators. The key is using indicators to plan accordingly and prepare students for success in school.

In keeping with our road theme, the Department of Motor Vehicles (DMV) epitomizes the critical importance of assessment. All drivers in the United States must pass a written test *and* a driving test before obtaining a driver's license. Both tests require a certain level of skill and preparation to pass. The same holds true for assessments in education. Students must take numerous assessments before they obtain their high school diploma and even more assessments to obtain a college degree. These tests require skills and preparation to pass. Teachers carry the great responsibility of not only preparing students for assessments but also articulating the purpose of assessments and using assessment data to inform their instructional practices. Assessments are innately connected to accountability as well. Educators, parents, and students are accountable for *what* is assessed and the *results* of assessments. This next chapter highlights important aspects of accountability and the what, why, and how of assessments.

The final checkpoints—Checkpoint 6 (recommendations and presentation) and Checkpoint 7 (writing assessment, reflection, and commitment)—will also be examined. Lastly, this chapter revisits 21st Century Skills and their relevance to accelerating achievement and the +1P process.

ACCOUNTABILITY

Accountability is one of the few constants in education, despite ever-changing demographics, curriculums, personnel, and educational funding. You could even argue that accountability has enduring powers—it will always be there. Aside from accepting responsibility for one's actions, Burke (2004) defines accountability through five questions:

1. *Who* is accountable to whom?

2. For *what* purposes?

3. For *whose* benefit?

4. By *which* means?

5. With *what* consequences?

When we mention accountability in education, it is often tied to student performance. Burke's (2004) questions broaden the scope of accountability beyond student performance. While student performance is a key indicator of success, it should not be the *only* indicator of progress and achievement for schools. Burke's (2004) questions define accountability on many levels. If you are wondering why schools place so much emphasis on accountability, the answer is simple—stakeholders. In education, we are not just accountable to ourselves; we are accountable to parents, students, colleagues, and the community at large. Collectively, we impact learning and achievement, and collectively, we should all be accountable for assessment results. This is especially important to consider when implementing +1P. Everyone is responsible for the achievement outcomes of students. Teachers have a role, students have a role, parents have a role, and administrators have a role in ensuring its success. Without collective accountability, the desired results of the framework are less attainable.

According to Hentschke and Wohlstetter (2004), there are three dimensions of accountability relationships. The first is *values*, which describes what stakeholders care about. When all parties share the same values, accountability relationships work better. +1P necessitates values in elevating consciousness, accelerating achievement through 21st Century Skills, and fostering global competence. The framework is grounded in a philosophical rationale that targets basic values in enhancing the educational program of a school. The second dimension of accountability includes *decision rights*, which requires a certain level of agreement from all stakeholders involved. Due to varying opinions and roles of stakeholders, it is critical to reach some level of consensus between involved parties. Teachers, parents, and administrators benefit from interacting and collaborating on desired outcomes of a school, in this case +1P. For example, teachers may decide to plan projects with colleagues from different grade levels or departments instead of independently. To do this, they need to be supported by an administrative team that fosters collaborative planning. If parents wish to contribute, their input should be considered as well. The final dimension of accountability is *information*, which is needed to clarify objectives and actions. Information is needed to appropriately plan, manage, and assess projects. Schools need as much authentic information as possible for effective implementation. For this reason, +1P is grounded in research, planning, professional development, twelve essential components (see Figure 1.3), practical tools and templates, coherency, and, most importantly, *transfer* in the classroom.

Many professions have accountability systems. These systems are in place to hold members of a profession to high standards of practice (Danielson, 2007). However, high standards of practice are optimized with shared accountability. In addition to the physical, emotional, and cognitive demands, teaching is a multifaceted profession that involves planning, managing, and assessing instruction. Although this profession has its rewards, teaching is very demanding and exhausting. For this reason, teachers need support from parents, administrators, and the community at large in preparing students to be successful in school and life. Teachers cannot carry this weight alone; they need a support system that holds everyone accountable for student achievement.

Professional support and growth for educators is fostered through lesson study and instructional rounds. A description of each strategy and its application to +1P is provided.

The Lesson Study Research Group defines lesson study as follows (Lesson Study Research Group, 2015):

> Lesson study is a professional development process that Japanese teachers engage in to systematically examine their practice, with the goal of becoming more effective. This examination centers on teachers working collaboratively on a small number of "study lessons." Working on these study lessons involves planning, teaching, observing, and critiquing the lessons. To provide focus and direction to this work, the teachers select an overarching goal and related research question that they want to explore. This research question then serves to guide their work on all the study lessons.
>
> While working on a study lesson, teachers jointly draw up a detailed plan for the lesson, which one of the teachers uses to teach the lesson in a real classroom (as other group members observe the lesson). The group then comes together to discuss their observations of the lesson. Often, the group revises the lesson, and another teacher implements it in a second classroom, while group members again look on. The group will come together again to discuss the observed instruction. Finally, the teachers produce a report of what their study lessons have taught them, particularly with respect to their research question.

In a nutshell, lesson study is a collaborative practice that enhances teaching and learning. According to Fernandez and Chokshi (2002), lesson study is an avenue for "creating deep and grounded reflection about the complex activities of teaching" that is shared amongst grade level teams or departments (p. 134). Both authors encourage creative experimentation with lesson study to allow for high-quality learning experiences. In other words, the lesson study model may need to be adapted or situated to better meet the needs of the participating team. Successful implementation of lesson study at one school may not translate to success at another school. It is imperative for grade level teams/departments to develop a common language and understanding for how to use lesson study effectively. The latter may reduce anxiety about implementation.

Educators can easily adapt "study lessons" to include components of the +1P framework. It may be helpful to observe a colleague teach one or more components and reflect on the process afterward. The latter is recommended (if possible) before teachers implement the framework on their own. Lesson study is also feasible across disciplines and different grade levels, meaning that a seventh grade English teacher could observe an eighth grade science teacher implementing one or more components of +1P. Since both teachers would be using the same planning template, the implementation process would be similar. The seventh and eighth grade teachers could also use the same unit plan for a topic of study and observe how +1P is applied in both content areas, which supports the interdisciplinary nature of the framework. Either way, teachers need planning time, a collective commitment by their colleagues, and administrative support to engage in lesson study. Lesson study must be valued at a school site for successful implementation. For more resources on lesson study, visit this website: **http://www.tc.columbia.edu/lesson study/resources.html**.

Instructional rounds are another collaborative process that emphasizes shared accountability. The process has been adapted from the medical rounds that doctors use in hospitals. Teachers use instructional rounds to inform instructional practice, generally around a problem of practice, but it could also be around an instructional goal for a grade level or department. According to Marzano (2011), "The chief benefit of this approach resides in the discussion that takes place among observing teachers at the end of the observation as well as in subsequent self-reflection" (p. 80). Similar to lesson study, one teacher is observed teaching a lesson for about twenty minutes. When the observation is complete, members of the observing team reflect on the experience. Marzano (2011) suggests that teachers watch for strategies of particular interest to them, such as how the teacher uses questioning techniques or graphic organizers. The observation could also have a common focus, such as implementation of district or school instructional objectives. Teachers are encouraged to use instructional rounds as one avenue for observing +1P in practice. They can observe specific components in action, such as focused inquiry, certain learning activities, how students conduct research, student presentations, and other components that they deem necessary. Once again, teachers would need time to plan and implement instructional rounds, in addition to administrative support. For a user-friendly PowerPoint on instructional rounds, visit this website: **http://bit.ly/INSTRUCTIONALROUNDS**.

Think about ways that accountability is emphasized in your setting. What would happen if there was no accountability in our schools? How might you transfer knowledge about Burke's five questions, lesson study, and instructional rounds back to your district, school, or classroom?

FORMATIVE AND SUMMATIVE ASSESSMENTS

Student achievement and performance levels are most often measured by formative and summative assessments. These assessments encompass everything from state tests and district benchmark tests to everyday classroom tests and quizzes. Assessments provide valuable information about student learning, giving us a clearer picture about achievement or where gaps may occur (Garrison & Ehringhaus, 2007). To foster conversations around +1P assessments, it is imperative to articulate differences between formative and summative assessments. According to Stiggins and Chappuis (2005), summative assessments refer to tests administered after learning has occurred to determine whether it did. Because summative assessments occur after instruction, there are few implications for future teaching. Summative assessments are not likely to affect specific day-to-day, week-to-week, or even month-to-month instructional decisions (Stiggins & Chappuis, 2005). They often occur toward the end of a semester or school year. On the other hand, formative assessments are conducted *during* learning, thus helping teachers adjust their instructional decisions along the way to better achieve student success. As a result, formative assessments have several implications for future teaching and adjustments during the learning process. According to Garrison and Ehringhaus (2007), formative assessments inform teachers and students about student understanding at a point when timely adjustments can be made. Garrison and Ehringhaus (2007) assert that in a balanced assessment system, both summative and formative assessments are integral to information gathering.

Formative and summative assessments are essential to the +1P process. Teachers can use formative assessments to gauge student understanding, determine what students know and do not know, and identify learning goals. This allows teachers to reteach certain concepts, adapt specific tasks or learning activities, and monitor progress during instruction. Examples of +1P formative assessments are:

- Student journals and notes
- Quizzes
- Digital dialogue (Padlet, TodaysMeet, Google Drive, etc.)
- Anecdotal notes
- Homework
- Exit tickets
- Observation
- Student/Group conferences with the teacher
- Student inquiry—Are students only generating clarification questions about a specific task or learning activity, or do their questions illustrate deeper understanding and conceptual knowledge about a task learning activity?
- Evidence of application—Can students apply their knowledge to a specific task or learning activity?

The latter formative assessments, among many others that teachers may choose to use, provide information on *what* and *how* students are learning. The more we know about students as they engage in the learning process, the better we can adjust instructional practices to ensure forward movement.

On the contrary, summative assessments help in evaluating mastery of standards, desired outcomes (i.e., project objective), and overall effectiveness of the process. Examples of +1P summative assessments include:

- Project presentation
- Writing assessment
- Reflection and commitment—Do students believe they can change or improve something related to their topic of study?
- Change in behavior—As a result of their learning, are students exhibiting increased motivation and a desire to learn more?

Summative assessments can be used as tools for goal setting and revising the second cycle of implementation. For example, if teachers notice that project presentations are not as thorough and detailed as planned, they can change the presentation criteria for the next cycle. Either way, formative and summative assessments are vital to the successful implementation of +1P.

Think about the different types of formative and summative assessments you have used in your classroom. What are the benefits of using both types of assessments? How might you transfer knowledge about formative and summative assessments back to your district, school, or classroom?

COMMON CORE ASSESSMENTS

The Common Core assessments allow students to be assessed relative to their peers nationwide. Since the standards are nationalized, states share similar expectations of what students should know and be able to do. Prior to Common Core, each individual state assessed students based on their own set of state standards, equating to 50 states with entirely different standards. This system did not allow for congruency, coherency, and consistency across states. As a result, student assessment data across states could not be compared or correlated, making it difficult to determine student "mastery" and proper "ranking" among states.

Four government-funded consortia have begun developing Common Core-aligned assessments (Houghton Mifflin Harcourt, 2015). Two assessments in particular, PARCC (Partnership for Assessment of Readiness for College and Careers) and SBAC (Smarter Balanced Assessment Consortium), have already been piloted with students and implemented with the general population. To date, 12 states and the District of Columbia have adopted the PARCC assessment (**http://www.parcconline.org/parcc-states**), while 18 states and the U.S. Virgin Islands have adopted the SBAC assessment (**http://www.smarterbalanced.org/about/member-states/**). Both the PARCC and SBAC assessments are computer based. The National Center and State Collaborative Partnership (NCSC) and Dynamic Learning Maps (DLM) are developing alternative assessments for students with significant cognitive disabilities.

In addition to end-of-year summative assessments, PARCC and SBAC have formative/interim test materials. The formative assessments are intended to help teachers and parents determine strengths and weaknesses of students throughout the school year. Teachers can use the data to target intervention for specific students before the year is over. Four key components of PARCC for Grades 3–11 are as follows (Houghton Mifflin Harcourt, 2015):

1. Diagnostic assessment administered at the beginning of each school year

2. Mid-year assessment predictive of a student's likely performance by end of year

3. Performance-based assessment in the last quarter of the school year

4. End-of-year summative assessment

The SBAC is administered in Grades 3–8 and again in Grade 11. Three key components of SBAC include (Houghton Mifflin Harcourt, 2015):

1. Computer-adaptive summative assessment that will be administered during the last 12 weeks of the school year

2. Interim assessments that can be used to predict student performance on the summative assessment while also providing feedback on student progress (mandatory)

3. Formative assessment resources to help teachers diagnose and respond to the needs of their students relative to CCSS

The goal of both assessment programs is to add coherence and clarity to the testing process and to assess higher-order thinking skills through performance tasks and technology-enhanced items. Students' familiarity with +1P formative and summative assessments will support them as they navigate the new Common Core assessments.

Other key differences between PARCC and SBAC are (Keany, 2013):

1. PARCC summative assessments will use fixed-form delivery, meaning that students take one of several fixed, equated sets of items and tasks.

2. Smarter Balanced will use computer-adaptive delivery, meaning that students get an individually tailored set of items and tasks depending on their responses as they take the tests. There will also be a retake option for the end-of-year component.

3. PARCC will have one optional diagnostic and one optional midyear computer-based assessment, containing mostly similar tasks to the summative performance-based tasks. PARCC will also have optional K–2 formative performance tasks and a required, nonsummative speaking and listening assessment for Grades 3–8 and high school that is locally scored.

4. Smarter Balanced will have optional interim assessments for Grades 3–12 that are computer adaptive with multiple item types, including performance tasks. The number, timing, and scope will be locally determined.

The new generation of assessments requires skills in computer-mediated technology, irrespective of the type of Common Core assessment each state has adopted (or not adopted). Especially since the PARCC and SBAC assessments are computer based, it is advantageous and forward thinking to integrate technology during the +1P process. Students who routinely practice with technology will be better prepared to take these assessments, in addition to being college and career ready.

CHECKPOINT 6: RECOMMENDATIONS AND PRESENTATION

The general purpose of recommendations is to involve students in making suggestions to a particular audience. Student teams are encouraged to use evidence from their investigation/research to make recommendations, validate their recommendations, and explain the benefits of their recommendations.

RECOMMENDATIONS

This particular component of +1P gives students an opportunity to propose ameliorations related to their topic of study. Students have the option of directing their recommendations to one or more of the following audiences:

- Another classroom
- Another school
- School principal
- Parent/family member/community member
- Association/corporation/business

- Superintendent of Schools
- Mayor
- Congressman/Congresswoman
- State Senator
- President of the United States

Students may also direct their recommendations to audiences outside of this list. The recommendations component of +1P is an inclusive process that enhances students' problem-solving and critical-thinking skills. Student recommendations are not random opinions. Instead, they are based on sophisticated reasoning and evidence from the research. Developing these skills is necessary for preparing students to be college and career ready. Use the template in Figure 5.1 to guide students in generating recommendations.

The recommendations component is not intended to be a lengthy and cumbersome process. Students work together as a team to create two or more general recommendations based on the evidence from their research (can also be done individually). A couple of sentences for each category in Figure 5.1 (recommendation, evidence, and benefits) will suffice. It is important to engage students in stimulating conversations about recommendations, evidence, and benefits. If you teach primary grades, you can brainstorm recommendations as a whole class and then choose the top two from your list. A sample recommendation for the Vessel Operations unit is provided to reinforce your planning.

Notice the brevity of the recommendation in Figure 5.2. This recommendation is concise and to the point. Students must know that recommendations are brief, yet powerful suggestions related to a topic of study. Overall, recommendations help students learn the importance of substantiating a claim with evidence/research. This practice prepares students for research papers, essays, and college writing. Students need multiple opportunities to practice these skills.

YOUR TURN TO PRACTICE

Make a list of potential recommendations for your topic of study and then decide on an audience. You may choose an audience from the list that I generated, or come up with your own. It is highly recommended that you use the model in Figure 5.2 to guide your thinking and planning. Since you have not done research for your topic of study,

Figure 5.1   Recommendations Template

+1P Recommendations
Topic of Study: _____   Audience: _____
Recommendation 1:   _____   _____   _____   Evidence from Investigation/Research: _____   _____   _____   Benefits: _____   _____   _____
Recommendation 2:   _____   _____   _____   Evidence from Investigation/Research: _____   _____   _____   Benefits: _____   _____   _____

you may not have actual evidence. Instead, you could think about the types of evidence that would support your recommendations.

Figure 5.2   Recommendations for Sample +1P Unit

+1P Recommendations
Topic of Study: Vessel Operations
Audience: American Association of Port Authorities (AAPA)
Recommendation 1: To reduce pollution at the port, my group highly recommends that the AAPA fund a project that studies a "zero emissions" vessel. If we can build cars that run on a battery, maybe we can build a vessel that runs on a battery.
Evidence from Investigation/Research: Statistics from our research showed that 40% of port pollution is attributed to vessel emissions. Another source of data indicated that vessel emissions are more toxic than train and truck emissions.
Benefits: Our group agrees that if we reduce port pollution, we will have cleaner air, which means less respiratory problems for adults and students. We could also reduce the number of people who develop lung cancer from polluted air.

+1P Topic of Study: _____

+1P Recommendations
Topic of Study: Audience:
Recommendation 1:   Evidence from Investigation/Research: Benefits:

(Continued)

(Continued)

+1P Recommendations
Recommendation 2:
Evidence from Investigation/Research:
Benefits:

Even though recommendations are intended to be brief, some teachers may still choose to extend this activity. For example, teachers might want students to write a formal letter to their intended audience. This is entirely up to the teacher. Just keep in mind that recommendations are designed to foster evidence-based thinking, critical thinking, and problem-solving skills around a topic of study.

Think about various recommendations you have received or offered as suggestions for improvement. Were these recommendations grounded in evidence or research? Why consider the audience when making recommendations? How might you transfer knowledge about project-based recommendations back to your district, school, or classroom?

PRESENTATION

Oral communication ranks on the top 10 list of essential skills for most jobs and careers. For this reason, students must become adept at communicating effectively. The best communicators are those who possess the power of persuasion and presentation for varied audiences.

Notice that I said persuasion *and* presentation. There are students who use persuasive language in a presentation but lack the skills to deliver their message effectively. The same holds true for presenting. Students may put together a great presentation but lack the skills to persuade their audience effectively. Skills in persuasion and presentation are imperative to +1P projects and college and career readiness. These skills translate across disciplines and they are applicable in multiple contexts. Inevitably, college professors will require students to present information at some point in time. The earlier students develop persuasive and presentation skills, the better. Building student capacity to speak convincingly and present effectively requires a lot of practice. However, before students can practice, they need criteria for *how* to persuade and present to an audience. Teachers can use the following criteria and icons to guide students through a presentation.

Figure 5.3 indicates necessary criteria for advancing an argument or point of view and protocols for presenting that information. In terms of ethos, pathos, and logos (EPL), students are never too young to learn about rhetorical devices—just show them an enticing commercial with something they want and notice their reactions. Rhetoric is also mentioned in CCR Speaking and Listening Anchor Standard 6, which states, "Evaluate a speaker's point of view, reasoning, and use of evidence and rhetoric." Figure 5.3 is directly aligned to this standard. A user-friendly video for teaching ethos, pathos, and logos through advertising can be accessed at the following link (case sensitive): **http:// bit.ly/ETHOSPATHOSLOGOS**.

Students can practice their persuasion and presentation skills through a strategy called PechaKucha. The term PechaKucha is Japanese for "chit chat." Two architects from Tokyo coined this presentation style in 2003 (Reynolds, 2008). PechaKucha presentations are created with presentation software, such as PowerPoint and Prezi. The structure of a PechaKucha is designed to make presentations creative, concise, and compelling. A PechaKucha includes the following:

- 20 slides—each slide is only given 20 seconds of airtime.
- Slides advance automatically after 20 seconds.
- Total presentation time is 6 minutes and 40 seconds.

Students can create a PechaKucha for their topic of study. Reference Figure 5.3 for pointers on what to include in the presentation. If students create a PechaKucha, teachers need to encourage students to use materials from their learning activities, focused inquiry, research, and text sets. The main purpose of a PechaKucha is to get speakers to

Figure 5.3   Persuasion and Presentation Criteria Chart

Persuasion	Presentation
Use Aristotle's rhetorical devices—ethos, pathos, and logos (EPL)—to effectively persuade your audience. EPL can help convince your audience of your point of view.	Consider all of the PEACES—projection, eye contact, attire, confidence, engagement, and succinctness—when putting a presentation together.
Ethos (credibility): 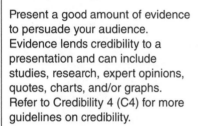	**Projection:**
Present a good amount of evidence to persuade your audience. Evidence lends credibility to a presentation and can include studies, research, expert opinions, quotes, charts, and/or graphs. Refer to Credibility 4 (C4) for more guidelines on credibility.	Make sure your audience can hear your voice. You want to be heard in all corners of the room.
	Eye Contact:
	Look at your audience. If this makes you nervous, focus on an object in the room that is at your eye level (cabinet, poster on the wall, window, etc.)
Pathos (emotions):	**Attire:**
Appeal to the emotions and desires of your audience by using stories, pictures, visuals, and/or music in your presentation. Consider how movies, commercials, and advertisements use these devices to persuade their audience.	Dress appropriately and professionally. If you wear a uniform, make sure it is clean and neat.
	Confidence:
	Trust your expertise on the topic. Be comfortable with yourself and remain calm. You got this!
Logos (logic):	**Engagement:**
Persuade your audience with logic and reasoning through consistency and clarity in the message. Audiences tend to be persuaded by statistics/numbers, compelling facts, and effectiveness of evidence.	Make sure your presentation is engaging and interesting. Incorporate videos, music, movement, and/or visuals.
	Succinctness:
	Timing and organization is everything. Get your point across in the allotted time. Pace yourself and be concise.

Figure 5.4   Organizing Template for a PechaKucha

+1P Topic of Study: _____				
(Each slide is shown for 20 seconds in a PowerPoint, Prezi, Google Presentation, or other platform.)				
Slide 1	Slide 2	Slide 3	Slide 4	Slide 5
Slide 6	Slide 7	Slide 8	Slide 9	Slide 10
Slide 11	Slide 12	Slide 13	Slide 14	Slide 15
Slide 16	Slide 17	Slide 18	Slide 19	Slide 20

Note: Slides can include pictures, images, symbols, charts, graphs, statistics, data, and/or quotes. If a slide includes text, keep it short and concise. Your goal is to compel, inform, and persuade your audience of your point of view in 6 minutes and 40 seconds. The more visuals you include, the better.

do three things: 1) consider the most important components of a topic, 2) think of the best ways to visually represent the ideas, and 3) find the most interactive way to present the material (Atkins-Sayre, 2014). These guidelines orient students to extract the most pertinent information from their research. PechaKuchas follow the concept of "more is less and less is more." Visit **http://www.pechakucha.org** for examples.

An import aspect of presenting is demonstrating what you know about a topic of study. Once students have thoroughly studied their topic and conducted research, they need to present the information to an audience. Presentations hold students accountable for what they learn throughout the +1P process. Students can demonstrate their knowledge through four different presentation styles—kinesthetic, oral, visual, and written. Each presentation style is manifested in various ways.

You will notice that some of the items listed in Figure 5.5 have overlapping characteristics. For example, a play is both oral and kinesthetic, and a PowerPoint/Prezi/Google Presentation is both oral and visual. It is okay for a presentation to have overlapping features.

Figure 5.5   Sample Presentation Styles with Examples

Presentation Styles
Kinesthetic: Concert, Play or Skit, Experiment, Game, Dance, Build a Model
Oral: Debate, PowerPoint/Prezi/Google Presentation, Lecture, Speech, Poem, Webinar
Visual: Website, Poster/Illustration, Video or Short Film, Concept Map, PechaKucha, Collage
Written: Report, Newsletter, Brochure or Pamphlet, Script or Short Story, Blog, Biography

Figure 5.6   Presentation Criteria and Ideas for Sample +1P Unit

---

Presentation

Persuasion:

Ethos (credibility), *Pathos* (emotions), *Logos* (logic)

Presentation:

PEACES (projection, eye contact, attire, confidence, engagement, succinctness)

Optional Presentations

Kinesthetic:

- Music
- Play or Skit
- Experiment
- Board Game

Oral:

- Panel Discussion or Debate
- Video Recording
- PowerPoint/Prezi/Google Presentation
- Lecture

Visual:

- Website
- Poster/Illustration
- Video or Short Film
- Flow Chart or Concept Map

Written:

- Report
- Newsletter
- Brochure or Pamphlet
- Script or Short Story

Teachers are encouraged to add more items to Figure 5.5. This table was created to assist students (and teachers) in planning for their presentation.

The presentation component allows students to be creative and use their imagination as they teach others about their topic of study. Students will also master the art of persuasion through EPL and the art of presenting through PEACES. These are skills that transfer from class to class, grade to grade, discipline to discipline, and most importantly, from college to a career. If we want students to excel in persuading and presenting to an audience, we need to provide them with more learning opportunities to achieve these desired outcomes.

Figure 5.6 highlights essential elements of a presentation, along with sample products to demonstrate mastery of Vessel Operations or any topic of study. Remember, student choice can boost motivation and interest. Students should be engaged and excited about presenting their projects, and letting them choose a presentation style is one way to honor their autonomy. Once students have chosen the type of presentation they want to deliver, they can incorporate information they learned from the previous components—standards, big ideas, universal concepts, essential questions, project objective, focused inquiry, learning activities, research/investigation, and recommendations. Students will have plenty of data to use in their presentations. Please note that there may not be enough time for all teams to present on the actual presentation day. To maximize time, teachers can have student teams present to each other instead of having whole group presentations. Again, use your discretion to determine the structure of the day. If you teach primary grades, you may be the presenter. In this case, you could still blend two or more presentation styles to expose students to different ways of presenting information. For a sample Google Presentation on Vessel Operations, visit the following link (case sensitive, the letter before "Z" is the letter "O" and *not* the number zero) or scan the QR Code:

https://goo.gl/OZMeeX

YOUR TURN TO PRACTICE

Take this time to think about how you would get students to practice using EPL and PEACES in a presentation. You may borrow from any previously stated ideas about persuasion and presentation (e.g., advertising video, PechaKucha, Vessel Operations Google Presentation). Given the various ways that students can demonstrate their knowledge, what presentation styles might you be interested in exploring with your students? This is your chance to process through ideas that prepare students for effective communication. Write your ideas in the space provided.

+1P Topic of Study: _____

Presentation Criteria

Persuasion (ethos, pathos, logos): _____

_____

_____

_____

_____

_____

Presentation (projection, eye contact, attire, confidence, engagement, succinctness):

_____

_____

_____

_____

_____

Presentation Styles	
Kinesthetic:	Oral:
Visual:	Written:

At this point in your +1P journey, you should be cognizant of different ways to build student capacity in communicating strategically and effectively. Oral communication skills are also outlined in the CCR Anchor Standards. For example, Speaking and Listening Anchor Standard 4 states, "Present information, findings, and supporting evidence such that listeners can follow the line of reasoning and the organization, development, and style are appropriate to task, purpose, and audience." The PechaKucha, EPL, and PEACES strategies are aligned to this standard and intentionally designed to meet these expectations. You may still be wondering how to grade student presentations and other components of the framework. Rubrics and grading are addressed after this next section on the writing assessment. Keep up the fabulous work—we are getting closer to the end of our journey.

Think about a time when you participated in a presentation and/or public speaking engagement (besides teaching!). What criteria did you use to prepare for the presentation? What are some benefits of "possessing the power of persuasion and presentation"? How might you transfer knowledge about PechaKuchas, EPL, and PEACES back to your district, school, or classroom?

CHECKPOINT 7: WRITING ASSESSMENT, REFLECTION, AND COMMITMENT

Writing is a challenging task for many students (and adults). In general, if you ask students to rank their top 10 school activities, my guess is that writing would rank toward the bottom (or not the make the list at all). This is especially true for secondary students. The best way to improve writing skills is incessant practice. Students should have multiple writing opportunities across the disciplines and throughout the school day. Edgar Lawrence "E.L." Doctorow, an American author, sums it up best in this quote: "Planning to write is not writing. Outlining, researching, talking to people about what you're doing, none of that is writing. Writing is writing." In other words, people have to engage in the physical act of writing to actually practice writing.

WRITING ASSESSMENT

The writing assessment is critical to the +1P process. If we are truly preparing students to be college and career ready, they need to practice writing in multiple contexts. In college, a good majority of assignments involve writing, regardless of the course content. At minimum, college courses may require students to write a research paper and on-demand essay for the final. Many courses require multiple writing assignments in one semester or quarter. Additionally, the SBAC and PARCC assessments include constructed writing responses (for ELA *and* Math) and analytic essays. Beyond ELA writing standards, there are Common Core Literacy Standards specifically for history/social studies, science, and technical subjects. The literacy standards emphasize the role of argumentative and informative/explanatory writing, with a focus on teaching key ideas and details, craft and structure, and integration of knowledge for discipline-specific texts. These standards also address organizing ideas, sourcing, reasoning, stating claims and counterclaims, drawing evidence from text, analysis, and conducting research. There are writing expectations for math as well. Common Core requires students to explain mathematical concepts and support their reasoning through writing. The teaching of writing is no longer the sole responsibility of English teachers; it is a shared responsibility amongst everyone. If we expect students to develop their craft as writers, writing must be embedded throughout the school day. This speaks to the need for more writing opportunities across content areas, and +1P is one avenue for achieving these outcomes.

Aside from being an evidence-based writing activity, teachers ultimately decide the structure of the +1P writing assessment. Depending on your students' writing levels, you may decide to organize the assessment around an on-demand essay or an extended writing activity where students respond to a writing prompt. The criteria you choose for the writing assessment is entirely up to you. Not giving a writing assessment is not an option. It is imperative that students understand the purpose of writing and establish a positive disposition toward writing. As long as students are in school, writing should be the norm, not the exception. Building student capacity to write like scholars inevitably builds their capacity to think and communicate like scholars.

Notice that the writing task in Figure 5.7 is straightforward and easy to follow. Because this is a culminating activity, students will have a plethora of data from their learning activities, research, recommendations, and presentation. It is highly recommended

Figure 5.7   Writing Assessment Prompt for Sample +1P Unit

Writing Assessment

Students will write a short essay about their topic of study. They will respond to the following questions:

1. Why is this topic important to study (refer to the Universal Concepts and Essential Questions)?

2. What are three major findings from your research?

3. What is the significance of each finding? Support your findings with evidence from your research.

Reminders:

✓ Essay follows the criteria in the rubric
✓ Essay includes a beginning, middle, and end
✓ Essay stays on topic
✓ References are included

---

that students refer to their notes during the writing assessment. This writing assessment is not a "gotcha" activity. You are simply gauging each individual student's +1P experience through the act of writing. The outcome may reveal that students in the same group have differing opinions about their topic of study. What is considered significant to one student may not be the same for another student. Remember, Figure 5.7 is just my example of a writing prompt. You can customize your writing assessment to include what you think is relevant or pertinent to students, as long as students are justifying their answers with evidence from their research. A sample writing assessment for Vessel Operations is illustrated in Figure 5.8.

You will notice that the sample writing assessment in Figure 5.8 has room for revision and enhancement. Teachers can review Figure 5.8 with their students and collectively make any necessary changes. Students can highlight key findings, evidence, transitions, citations, and writing conventions. Mini-lessons could also be created for each of these topics. Primary teachers may choose to have their students draw pictures and explain their reasoning, while secondary teachers may prefer more of an essay format. It may be helpful to have primary students complete a cloze essay, where they plug in words related to their topic of study. Since many of these students are just learning to write, this may be a more feasible option for the writing assessment. A sample cloze essay is depicted in Figure 5.9.

Figure 5.8   Sample Writing Assessment for Vessel Operations

Sample Writing Assessment for Vessel Operations

Vessel Operations occur around the world. We need vessels to supply our food, clothes, and digital devices. Over the past month, I learned about the purpose and function of Vessel Operations. I gathered information from the Internet, a field trip to the port, and lots of videos. This topic is important to study because we need to know where our products and supplies come from. We also need to know how trade and technology impact Vessel Operations.

One important finding from my research is the fact that trade and ports connect the United States to the world. According to the American Association of Port Authorities (AAPA), "Every day, thousands of containers arrive at U.S. seaports from countries all around the world" (AAPA, 2015). The things in these containers include everything from patio furniture from Thailand to shoes from China. This means that things in our homes and environment could be made in other places. It makes me wonder how much stuff is actually made in the United States. Another important fact from the AAPA is that food grown by Iowa farmers could reach the tables of families in Russia and Japan. These are just a few ways that vessels connect us to the world.

I learned from my research that major technology changes are taking place in the ocean shipping that affects ports and services. In the article, *Evolution of Ports in a Competitive World,* I learned that "the ocean transport industry is employing increasing sophisticated information technology (IT) to manage logistics" (Public-Private Infrastructure Advisory Facility, 2015). These new technologies will require shipping companies to pay more money so they can be caught up with everyone else. Ships are also getting larger and it will cost more money to make these bigger ships. All of these things are costs and benefits of trade.

Another important finding is the top 100 ports in the world. According to www.worldshipping .org (2015), Shanghai, China is the number one port in the world. This port has the most cargo volume and container traffic. In other words, more goods are shipped to and from this port than any other port in the world. These facts about China's port means that they employ a lot of people, but they also have to pay a lot of money to run the port. It also means that many interdependent parts help their system work.

I strongly urge people to study things in our society that impact our everyday lives, such as Vessel Operations. I learned so much about cargo ships, trade, ports, and technology. Most importantly, I learned that technology allows for increased production, which means that more things get done at a faster pace because of technology. I feel smarter from this process and I can't wait to share my knowledge with my family members and friends. I am already thinking about the next topic of study.

References:

AAPA, 2015. *From Here to There: Supply Chain Security to the Port of Tacoma.* Retrieved from http://aapa.files.cms-plus.com/PDFs/supply_chain_security_example.pdf?navItem Number=1100

PPIAF, 2015. *The Evolution of Ports in a Competitive World.* Retrieved from http://www.ppiaf .org/sites/ppiaf.org/files/documents/toolkits/Portoolkit/Toolkit/module2/port_dynamics.html

AAPA, 2012. *World Port Rankings (Top 100).* Retrieved from http://aapa.files.cms-plus.com/ Statistics/WORLD%20PORT%20RANKINGS%202012.pdf

World Shipping, 2015. *Ports.* Retrieved from http://www.worldshipping.org/about-the-industry/ global-trade/ports

Figure 5.9　Sample Cloze Essay for Vessel Operations

Cloze Essay

Introduction: We learned about _____ _____. Vessels carry _____.

Finding 1: There are _____ (different, many, lots of, various, etc.) kinds of vessels.

Evidence: Two kinds are _____ and _____.

Finding 2: Things they carry are _____ and _____.

Evidence: A _____ comes from _____ and a _____ comes from _____.

Finding 3: Vessels carry _____ (things, food, goods, stuff, clothes, etc.) in big containers.

Evidence: We saw _____ (pictures, videos, websites, etc.) of containers at the port.

Conclusion: Vessels are important because _____.

Completed Essay

We learned about Vessel Operations. Vessels carry important things we use.

There are different kinds of vessels. Two kinds are an oil tanker and a cargo ship.

Things they carry are cars and toys. A Toyota comes from Japan and my toy (e.g., doll or truck) comes from China.

Vessels carry things in big containers. We saw pictures of containers at the port.

Vessels are important because . . . (student-generated answers by individual or group)

References:

Write or draw—pictures, website, Internet, video, field trip, library, books, guest speaker, etc.

Figure 5.9 is scaffolded with sentence starters and cloze sentences to elicit responses from the students. Because students will be at different writing levels, some may need to trace sentences, some may need to plug in words, and some may be ready to write on their own.

To further scaffold the writing assessment, students could use the following sentence frames:

- This topic is significant because . . .
- One example presented in the article/website/video is . . .
- Studies indicate that . . .

Figure 5.10   Sample Writing Assessment for Vessel Operations (Primary)

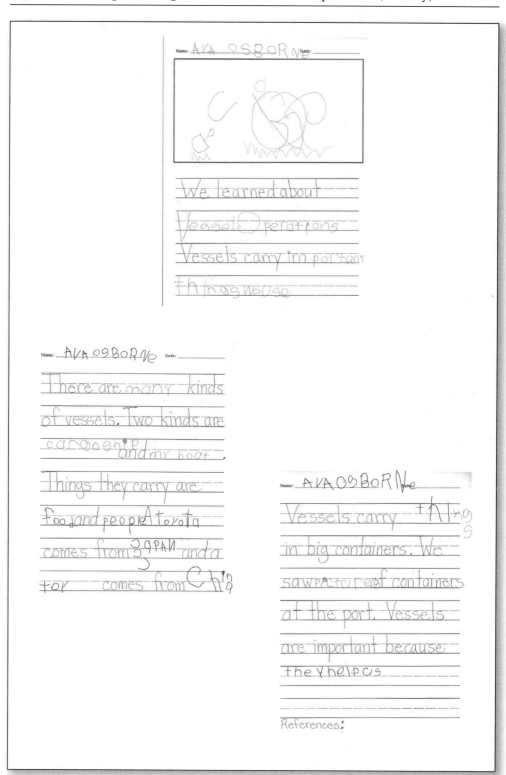

- Our research showed that . . .
- According to _____, . . .
- Another example from the article/website/video is . . .
- An important piece of evidence that we discovered is . . .
- Statistically, . . .

For more sentence starters and frames, visit this website: **http:// bit.ly/SENTENCEFRAMES**.

YOUR TURN TO PRACTICE

Given the sample prompt in Figure 5.7, how might you construct the writing assessment for your students? Feel free to "liberate" ideas from Figure 5.7 or any other ideas that may support your planning. Consider the scaffolds that students may need to effectively communicate in writing. You do not need to provide a detailed lesson plan. Use this time to brainstorm a few ideas for the writing assessment. Write your ideas in the space provided.

+1P Topic of Study: _____

Writing Assessment
Possible writing prompts:
1.
2.
Writing scaffolds (if necessary):
1.
2.

Think about an evidence-based writing assignment or research paper that you wrote in K–12. How did your teacher support you in the writing process? What is the purpose of having students write across the disciplines? How might you transfer knowledge about the writing assessment back to your district, school, or classroom?

RUBRICS AND GRADING

The teaching profession relies heavily on grading systems and rubrics to define performance expectations and content mastery. Grading is an accountability factor in education. Even if we tried, we cannot circumvent grading. Fortunately, many schools and districts have invested in digital grading platforms that make it easier to document assignments and calculate grades. Teachers who engage in the +1P process need a grading system to measure student performance and apply individual grades. It is recommended that teachers and students use a learning log to document all assignments related to the project. Besides displaying grades, learning logs are comprehensive organizers that help teachers and students keep track of assignments. Learning logs can also serve as living documents, meaning that teachers and students can add to the log throughout the unit.

Figure 5.11 is one example of what could be included in a learning log. Teachers would ultimately determine the structure and contents of a learning log. To set expectations ahead of time, assignments and points can be determined before students start their projects. Parents would appreciate viewing their child's learning log as well. They would be informed of their child's assignments, progress, and grades throughout the process. A generic rubric for learning activities and a writing assessment rubric may also help teachers with grading. Remember, you may use your own grading system and rubrics if necessary.

Figure 5.12 can be adapted in multiple ways. Teachers can decide on their own point system, change the language to reflect their current rubrics, or add more details to the descriptors for each letter grade. While this rubric is intended for learning activities and other miscellaneous assignments, the writing assessment rubrics are specific to the writing task (one is for primary and one is for older students). They both clarify expectations for what students should

Figure 5.11   +1P Learning Log

+1P Learning Activities and Dates	Points	Points Earned	Grades
1. *Example:* Student Journal Date: 5/4/2015	50	40/50	80% = B-
2. Survey Date: ___/___/20___	20	___/20	
3. Timeline Date: ___/___/20___	20	___/20	
4. Online Collaboration Date: ___/___/20___	30	___/30	
5. Quiz Date: ___/___/20___	30	___/30	
6. Vocabulary Placemat Date: ___/___/20___	50	___/50	
7. Recommendations Date: ___/___/20___	50	___/50	
8. Presentation Date: ___/___/20___	100	___/100	
9. Writing Assessment Date: ___/___/20___	100	___/100	
10. Reflection and Commitment Date: ___/___/20___	50	___/50	
Total Number of Activities = 10	**Total Points** = 500	**Total Points Earned** = ____/500	**Final Grade** =

know and do for the writing assessment. Notice that the scores for Figure 5.13 are 2, 4, 6, and 8, as opposed to 1, 2, 3, and 4. Writing rubrics that go from 1–4 do not allow flexibility for those students who score "in between" a level. The 2–8 scoring model allows teachers to give a score of 5 if the writing is not quite a 4 or 6. Similarly, scores for the K–2 rubric are 2, 4 and 6, giving teachers more leeway to assign scores that are in the middle (i.e., 1, 3, 5, 7). It is suggested that K–2 teachers start the year in the "On My Way" category before moving up to the next levels. However, if you find

Figure 5.12   +1P Generic Rubric

+1P Rubric for Learning Activities

A = 45–50 points

- Displays excellent effort, neat, creative, outstanding work, no errors in spelling, and no errors in punctuation. Assignment is complete and exceeds the necessary criteria.

B = 40–44 points

- Displays good effort, neat, creative, good work, 1–2 spelling errors, and 1–2 punctuation errors. Assignment is complete and meets the necessary criteria.

C = 35–39 points

- Displays effort, average work, 3 or more spelling errors, and 3 or more punctuation errors. Assignment is complete and meets the necessary criteria.

D = 30–34 points

- Displays little effort, below average work, 4 or more spelling errors, and 4 or more punctuation errors. Assignment is incomplete and only meets some of the necessary criteria.

F = 0 points

- Displays no effort, sloppy work, 5 or more spelling errors, and 5 or more punctuation errors. Assignment is incomplete and does not meet any of the necessary criteria.

Total Points = 50

---

that your students are ready to be assessed using all three levels, you may use the complete rubric.

At first glance, Figures 5.13 and 5.14 might be overwhelming, especially if you are not an English teacher. However, it is better to have a rubric that clearly outlines expectations than a rubric with missing components. There is always room to modify and adapt these rubrics to suit your classroom needs. My goal is to provide concrete models that guide the next steps for teachers and students. It is important for students to reference a criteria list while they are writing. This helps teachers ensure that students are including all of the necessary components in their writing.

The purpose of using a criteria checklist is to hold students accountable for including necessary components within a given assignment. Students are expected to complete the checklist *before* they turn in their final draft. It is recommended that teachers review the checklist with students before the assignment starts. This way,

Figure 5.13 +1P Writing Assessment Rubric

Criteria	Minimal Ability 2	Partial Ability 4	Adequate Ability 6	Exemplary Ability 8	Score
Introduction clearly states why the topic is important to study.	Introduction does not relate to the topic of study.	Includes an introduction, but it is unclear why the topic is important to study.	Includes an introduction that clearly states the importance of the topic of study.	Includes a compelling and creative introduction that clearly states the importance of the topic of study.	__/8
Findings are clearly relevant and significant to the topic of study.	Findings are stated, but they are not relevant to the topic of study.	Includes one finding that is relevant to the topic of study.	Includes two findings that are relevant and significant to the topic of study.	Includes three or more convincing and compelling findings that are relevant and significant to the topic of study.	__/8
Evidence from the research supports the writer's findings.	Evidence from the research does not support findings.	Includes evidence from the research that supports one finding.	Includes convincing evidence from the research to support two findings.	Includes convincing and compelling evidence from the research to support three or more findings.	__/8
Academic vocabulary related to the topic of study is included in the essay.	One academic vocabulary word is used that relates to the topic of study.	Includes two academic vocabulary words that relate to the topic of study.	Includes three academic vocabulary words that relate to the topic of study.	Includes four or more convincing and compelling vocabulary words that relate to the topic of study.	__/8

Criteria	Minimal Ability 2	Partial Ability 4	Adequate Ability 6	Exemplary Ability 8	Score
Transitional words or phrases are used to introduce findings, evidence, or ideas.	One transitional word or phrase is used.	Includes two transitional words or phrases that introduce evidence or an idea.	Includes three transitional words or phrases that introduce evidence or an idea.	Includes a variety of four or more transitional words or phrases that introduce evidence or ideas.	___/8
Conclusion summarizes importance of the study.	Conclusion does not summarize the importance of the study.	Includes a conclusion, but does not summarize the importance of the study.	Includes a conclusion that summarizes the importance of the study.	Includes a convincing and compelling conclusion that summarizes the importance of the study.	___/8
Spelling, Punctuation, and Grammar	Too many errors and writing is not legible.	Writing includes five to six errors.	Writing includes three to four errors.	Writing includes one to two errors.	___/8
References (book, article, website, video, etc.)	One reference is used.	Two references are used.	Three references are used.	Four or more references are used.	___/8

Student: _____ Topic: _____ Date: _____ **Overall Score** ___/64

Grade ___

Figure 5.14   +1P Writing Assessment Rubric for K-2

Criteria	On My Way 2	Getting Closer 4	I Made It 6	Score
Introduction	I have an introductory sentence.	My introductory sentence supports my topic of study.	My introductory sentence clearly states the importance of my topic of study.	__/6
Findings	I have one finding that supports my topic of study.	I have two findings that support my topic of study.	Includes three or more findings that support my topic of study.	__/6
Evidence	I have evidence for one finding.	I have evidence for two findings.	I have evidence for three or more findings.	__/6
Vocabulary	I have one vocabulary word related to the topic of study.	I have two vocabulary words related to the topic of study.	I have three or more vocabulary words related to the topic of study.	__/6
Transitions (use accordingly)	I have a transition that supports evidence or an idea.	I have a transition that supports evidence and ideas.	I have two or more transitions that support evidence and ideas.	__/6
Conclusion	I have a concluding sentence.	My concluding sentence summarizes what I learned.	My concluding sentence summarizes what I learned and includes more information.	__/6
Spelling and Punctuation	I have spelling errors and I did not use capitals and periods.	I have some spelling errors, but I used some capitals and periods (or vise versa).	I have few or no spelling errors and I used capitals and periods.	__/6
References (pictures, websites, articles)	I have one reference that is written or drawn.	I have two references that are written or drawn.	I have three or more references that are written or drawn.	__/6
Student:	**Topic:**	**Date:**	**Overall Score**	__/48
			Grade	__

Figure 5.15 Writing Assessment Rubric for K–2

Student: _____ Topic: _____ Date: _____	Yes/Paragraph #	No
1. Does the **introduction** clearly state why the topic is important to study?		
2. Did you include **two or more findings** that are relevant and significant to the topic of study?		
3. Did you provide **evidence** from the research that supports your findings?		
4. Did you include **three or more academic vocabulary words** related to your topic of study?		
5. Did you include **three or more transitional words/phrases** to introduce findings, evidence, or ideas?		
6. Did you include a **conclusion** that summarizes the importance of the study?		
7. Did you check for **spelling, punctuation,** and **grammar** errors?		
8. Did you include **three or more references** from a book, article, website, or video?		

teachers can address and clarify questions, comments, or concerns prior to the assessment. You may find that some of your students need additional scaffolds for the writing assessment. Stated earlier, writing is difficult and may pose more challenges for certain students. Graphic organizers and sentence starters can mitigate anxiety during the writing assessment. Teacher modeling may also support students as they engage in writing. Two scaffolds in particular that would aid students on the writing assessment are the Boxes and Bullets strategy, coined by Calkins, Hohne, and Gillette (2013), and sentence starters for transitions. While there are many variations of the Boxes and Bullets strategy, it can be used to frontload writing activities and cite evidence. In my past experiences with this strategy, students find it easy to replicate. An example of both scaffolds is provided.

The presentation rubric is also paramount to setting expectations during the +1P process. This interdisciplinary rubric highlights essential components of an effective presentation. It is critical to review the presentation rubric in advance so that students know what and how to prepare. When students are cognizant of expectations before and during an assignment, they are more likely to excel at the task. Teachers have the option of using the presentation rubric or generating their own. There are three categories in the presentation rubric—beginning, approaching, and proficient—each with its own corresponding number (2, 4, or 6). These numbers give teachers

Figure 5.16   Boxes and Bullets Strategy

Introduction (state the significance of the topic of study):
• **Finding 1:** • **Evidence:**
• **Finding 2:** • **Evidence:**
• **Finding 3:** • **Evidence:**
Conclusion (restate the significance of the study in different words):

Figure 5.17   Transitional Words and Sentence Starters

Evidence	Addition	Summary
For example,	In addition,	Finally,
For instance,	Furthermore,	Lastly,
To illustrate,	Moreover,	In conclusion,
In other words,	Besides,	In summary,
As an illustration,	Another reason for _____,	As you can see,
In particular,	Therefore,	Overall,
Specifically,	Likewise,	
Namely,	Similarly,	
According to _____,	In fact,	
To support this finding,	In the same way,	
Research indicates that . . .	With this purpose in mind,	
Statistically,		

flexibility when grading. For example, you may find that a student team is almost proficient with eye contact, but not quite. In this case, you could give the team a 5 instead of a 6. The flexibility of these scores prevents teachers from being "boxed in" when they are grading. This same concept is applied to the writing assessment rubric. A modified version of the presentation rubric is provided for primary teachers that includes icons. Please note that students can still include big ideas, universal concepts, essential questions, and the project objective in their presentation, even though these components are not explicitly stated in the rubric. Use the rubric as an assessment tool to frontload expectations and grading practices.

REFLECTION AND COMMITMENT

Reflection and commitment are additional ways to get students (and adults) to think on critical levels. In order for students to generate purposeful reflections about their project, their reflections must encompass three actions (Yost, Sentner, & Forlenza-Bailey, 2000; Schon, 1987):

1. **Reflection-in-action:** reflecting in the *midst* of action

2. **Reflection-on-action:** reflecting *after* an action is completed

3. **Reflection-for-action:** reflecting to guide *future* actions

Figure 5.18 +1P Presentation Rubric

Criteria	Beginning	Approaching	Proficient		Score
	2	4	6		
Presentation is **organized**. Materials and technology are prepared and ready to go. Team members know their roles.	Little organization, materials are not ready, team members are confused.	Presentation is somewhat organized, materials are ready and team members know their roles.	Presentation and materials are creatively organized and team members excel at their roles.		___/6
Presentation includes **Ethos** (credibility): Evidenced by studies, research, expert opinions, quotes, charts/graphs, etc.	Little evidence is presented to show credibility of the project.	Presentation includes 3 examples of evidence to show credibility of the project.	Presentation includes 4 or more compelling examples of evidence to show credibility of the project.		___/6
Presentation includes **Pathos** (emotions): Stories, pictures, music, and/or questions are used to appeal to the audience's emotions.	Few appeals to the audience's emotions are presented.	Presentation includes 3 appeals to the audience's emotions.	Presentation includes 4 or more compelling appeals to the audience's emotions.		___/6
Presentation includes **Logos** (logic): Evidenced through consistency and clarity in the message and effectiveness of evidence.	Presentation evidence does not follow a logical pattern and is out of order.	Presentation follows a logical pattern, but the message is not clear.	Presentation includes a logical pattern and the message is clear.		___/6

	Criteria	Beginning 2	Approaching 4	Proficient 6	Score
	Projection: presenters are heard in all corners of the room	Not all presenters can be heard.	Presenters can be heard, but it is not consistent throughout the presentation.	Presenters are consistently heard throughout the room.	___/6
	Eye Contact: presenters are facing their audience throughout the presentation	Not all presenters are making eye contact.	Presenters make eye contact, but it is not consistent throughout the presentation.	Presenters make consistent eye contact throughout the presentation.	___/6
	Attire: presenters are dressed appropriately and professionally	Not all presenters are dressed appropriately.	Presenters are dressed appropriately and professionally.	Presenters are dressed appropriately, professionally, and creatively. Attire may coordinated or reflect the topic of study.	___/6
	Confidence: presenters are experts on the topic of study, comfortable, and calm	Not all presenters are comfortable with the content.	Presenters are experts on the topic of study, but uncomfortable in front of an audience.	Presenters are experts on the topic of study, comfortable in front of an audience, and calm.	___/6
	Engagement: presenters keep their audience engaged and interested	Presenters do not keep all audience members engaged.	Presenters keep their audience engaged, but it is not consistent throughout the presentation.	Presenters keep their audience consistently engaged throughout the presentation.	___/6
	Succinctness: presenters are concise and aware of pacing and time	Not all presenters are aware of the time, pacing is off, and presentation is too long or too short.	Presentation is concise, but pacing is not consistent. Some parts are too fast and other parts are too slow.	Presentation is concise, pacing is consistent throughout, and timing is on point.	___/6
					Total: ___/60

Note: Students may include big ideas, universal concepts, essential questions, and project objective in presentation, even though it is not stated in the rubric.

Figure 5.19a   +1P Persuasion Rubric for K–2

Criteria	Beginning 2 points	Approaching 4 points	Proficient 6 points	Score
Organization	Team is almost ready.	Materials are ready, but team is not ready, or team is ready but materials are not ready.	Presentation is neat, interesting, and creative. Materials are ready and everyone on team is ready.	___/6
Ethos (credibility)	Not enough facts for the presentation.	Presentation has 2 facts (quotes, pictures, etc.) to share with audience.	Presentation has 3 or more facts (quotes, pictures, charts) that help the audience understand the project.	___/6
Pathos (emotions)	Not enough to keep the audience interested.	Presentation uses 2 things to keep the audience interested (stories, music, questions, etc.).	Presentation use 3 or more things to keep the audience interested (stories, music, questions, etc.).	___/6
Logos (logic)	The presentation is out of order.	Presentation is sort of in order. The facts, pictures, and stories makes sense, but they are not in the right order.	Presentation is in order. All facts, pictures, and stories make sense because they are in the right order.	**Total Points:** ___/6 ___/24

Note: Students may include big ideas, universal concepts, essential questions, and project objective in presentation, even though it is not stated in the rubric.

Figure 5.19b +1P Presentation Rubric for K–2

Criteria	Beginning 2 points	Approaching 4 points	Proficient 6 points	Score
Projection	Not all presenters can be heard.	Presenters can be heard, but not during the whole presentation.	Presenters are heard in all corners of the room during the whole presentation.	__/6
Eye Contact	Not all presenters are looking at their audience.	Presenters are looking at their audience, but not during the whole presentation.	Presenters are looking at their audience during the whole presentation.	__/6
Attire	Not all presenters are dressed appropriately.	Presenters are dressed appropriately.	Presenters are dressed appropriately and creatively (student teams might wear similar colors or try to wear clothes that match the theme of their project.	__/6
Confidence	Not all presenters are participating.	Presenters are participating, but may be uncomfortable in front of the audience.	Presenters are comfortable in front of the audience and they know their topic.	__/6
Engagement	Presenters do not keep all of their audience interested in the topic.	Presenters keep their audience interested, but not during the whole presentation.	Presenters keep their audience interested during the whole presentation by being creative (student teams might share an item or ask questions to audience).	__/6
Succinctness	Presentation is too long or too short. It is also out of order.	Presentation is in order, but some parts are too long and other parts are too short.	Presentation is in order and the timing is just right.	__/6 **Total Points:** __/36

175

"Action" in this case would represent the student projects. The final phase of +1P mainly focuses on actions two and three. Student reflection "in the midst" would have taken place during the learning activities (e.g., journal entries and digital dialogue/collaboration) and metacognitive moments prompted by students or the teacher (e.g., "What am I learning while doing this project?"). For closure, students are asked to reflect on their learning after the completion of their projects, and make a commitment to future actions. Requiring students to reflect on a deeper level requires teachers to model reflective thinking and provide opportunities for deeper reflection within the school day. The reflection-action model teaches students how to engage in sophisticated levels of reflection. Consider these "reflective actions" as a student's final charge before ending the +1P cycle. Teachers could also use the reflection-action model to gauge how well they facilitated the process for their students.

There are several approaches to addressing this last component on reflection and commitment. The following activities help to initiate a reflective process:

- Answer questions through a writing/journaling activity.
- Create an individual poster (digital or paper).
- Digital response on Padlet, TodaysMeet, Google Docs, Blog, Social Media, etc.
- Write a letter to a family member, community member, teacher, or administrator.
- Write one collective reflection and commitment on a class poster or chart that includes student signatures.

These are just a few ideas to add to your toolkit of strategies. You are invited to personalize this list to meet the specific needs of your students in your classroom. I do want to point out that this component is not intended to consume a lot of instructional minutes. By the

Figure 5.20   Reflection and Commitment for Sample +1P Unit

Reflection and Commitment

1. How did this +1P experience deepen or enhance your knowledge of the topic?

2. What would you do differently next time?

3. What commitment will you make to extend this project and share it with others in your community?

time students get to reflection and commitment, they have already demonstrated mastery of their topic of study. For this reason, it is highly recommended that you limit the time spent on this assignment. In terms of the sample unit on Vessel Operations, these are a few questions to stimulate reflective thinking.

YOUR TURN TO PRACTICE

Stated earlier, there are many different approaches to organizing the reflection and commitment component. Use this time to brainstorm ideas for this particular component. You may borrow from my ideas or create your own. Write your thoughts in the template provided.

+1P Topic of Study: _____

Reflection and Commitment
Possible questions, prompts, or activities: 1.   2.   3.

Congratulations! You just completed a unit that is, plus or minus a few tweaks, ready for immediate implementation. Nine additional unit plans are available to assist your planning—the Vessel Operations unit, five interdisciplinary units, and three career units (see Appendix B). We still have a few more elements to cover, like the sample calendar that breaks down the +1P process within a 20-day cycle (one month). You can adapt this calendar for your current unit and future units. An interdisciplinary chart for the Vessel Operations unit was created for your convenience. The chart can be adapted for any unit of study. Before concluding Chapter 5, we will address differentiation and then bring the conversation back to 21st Century Skills.

Think about a time you used reflection to inform your practice. What commitments did you make after you reflected? Why should students engage in reflective thinking? How might you transfer the three reflective actions (in, on, and for action) back to your district, school, or classroom?

Figure 5.22 is a generic calendar that can be applied to any +1P unit plan. Notice that the 20-day cycle starts with 21st Century Skills and then progresses through all seven checkpoints, which include the 12 essential components of +1P. Teachers can use 21st Century Skills as an entry point to the process and for emphasizing college and career readiness. These skills frame the purpose for engaging in the work and they answer the *why* question. The calendar is intentionally designed to represent a coherent unit that aligns with the +1P framework. This sample calendar is adaptable, but teachers still need to address all 12 components of the framework. You will also notice that technology is referenced in each day of the cycle. Once again, if we are preparing students to complete locally and globally, they need technological skills. Each day includes a *time required* section that may differ across schools and classrooms. Teachers would ultimately determine the best times for teaching the content. Please note that the 20-day cycle is flexible and does not mean 20 consecutive days for all teachers. There is a designated space to write the date for each day. Due to the varied and impacted schedules of teachers, +1P may need to be implemented intermittently throughout a semester or trimester. I do want to caution teachers against too many breaks in the cycle. We

Figure 5.21 Completed Sample Unit on Vessel Operations

Teacher's Name: **+1P Unit Plan – Vessel Operations** **Date:**

Big Ideas	Universal Concepts		Essential Questions
transportation, vessel operations, cargo (imported and exported), **systems, container ports, technology, trade,** rules, safety, contracts, **supply and demand,** and labor/unions	**Systems** include interdependent parts. **Technology** allows for increased production.		What are the costs and benefits of **trade**? Can a **system** advance without **technology**?

Standards	Project Objective			Writing Assessment
	Students will **identify and describe** the **purpose and function** of Vessel Operations. They will gather information from the **Internet, observations (field trip to the port),** and **videos.** Students will present their findings to their classmates in a presentation, write a **short essay** about their topic of study, and reflect on the process.			Students will write a short essay about their topic of study. They will respond to the following questions: 1) Why is this topic important to study (refer to the Universal Concepts and Essential Questions)? 2) What are three or more major findings from your research? 3) What is the significance of each finding?

Standards	Focused Inquiry	Learning Activities	Investigation (Research)	Recommendations	Presentation
Common Core State Standards: **College and Career Readiness (CCR) Anchor Standards (AS)** **Reading AS 7:** Integrate and evaluate content presented in diverse media and formats, including visually and quantitatively, as well as in words. **Writing AS 6:** Use technology, including the Internet, to produce and publish writing and to interact and collaborate with others.	**General Questions:** What modes of **transportation** are used to transport goods? What countries have **container ports?** What is a **system?** **Specific Questions:** **Vessels:** What are some specific types of vessels? **Technology:** What type of technology is used on vessels and within the container ports?	*Optional Activities* → 1) Dialogue and Discussion 2) Journal/ Diary/Log [paper or digital] 3) Create a Timeline 4) Field Trips 5) Online Collaboration [Google Drive, Facebook,	**Text Set:** primary and secondary sources of information that are credible and contextualize learning for a topic of study *Optional Sources* → Internet Newspapers Magazines/Articles Journals Books School or Public Library Videos	How might you improve and/or change a situation related to your topic of study? **Task:** 1) Make two or more recommendations related to your topic of study 2) Use evidence from the research to support your recommendations 3) Explain the benefits of your recommendations	**Persuasion:** *Ethos* (credibility) *Pathos* (emotions) *Logos* (logic) **Presentation:** *PEACES* (projection, eye contact, attire, confidence, engagement, succinctness)

(Continued)

Figure 5.21 (Continued)

			Optional Presentations →	Support your findings with evidence from your research.

Writing AS 7: Conduct short as well as more sustained research projects based on focused questions demonstrating understanding of the subject under investigation.

Speaking and Listening AS 4: Present information, findings, and supporting evidence such that listeners can follow the line of reasoning and the organization, development, and style are appropriate to task, purpose, and audience.

Language AS 1: Demonstrate command of the conventions of standard English grammar and usage when writing or speaking.

Cargo: What are specific types of cargo? What types of cargo does the United States **import and export**?

Trade: What is trade?

Elaborate Questions:

Vessels: What purpose and function do vessels serve?

Technology: How does technology impact **vessel operations**?

Cargo: Why do countries import and export goods?

Trade: How does **supply and demand** impact trade?

Sourcing Questions:
How will you access your information? What sources will you use? What makes your sources credible?
(e.g., www.aapa-ports.org and www.worldshipping.org)

E-mail, Padlet, Blogs, Twitter, TodaysMeet, & Skype]

6) Create a Blog

7) Interviews or Surveys

8) Build a Model

9) Display Board

10) Debate

11) Socratic Seminar

12) Quizzes [paper or digital]

13) Academic Games

14) Vocabulary Placemat

15) Venn Diagram

16) Collage

Television
Movies
Documentaries
Pictures
Charts and Graphs
Statistics/Data/Surveys
Personal Accounts
Interviews
Observation
Field Trip
Museums
Science Centers

Look Fours (L4s) in Research:

1) Trends Over Time

2) Multiple Perspectives

3) Technological Advances

4) Forecasting

Credibility 4 (sourcing)

*Students are encouraged to direct their recommendations to a particular audience.

Optional Presentations →

Kinesthetic:
- Music
- Play or Skit
- Experiment
- Board Game

Oral:
- Panel Discussion or Debate
- Video Recording
- PowerPoint/Prezi/Google Presentation
- Lecture

Visual:
- Website
- Poster/Illustration
- Video or Short Film
- Flow Chart or Concept Map

Written:
- Report
- Newsletter
- Brochure or Pamphlet
- Script or Short Story

Reminders:
- ☑ Essay follows the criteria in the rubric
- ☑ Essay includes a beginning, middle, and end
- ☑ Essay stays on topic
- ☑ References are included

Reflection and Commitment

1) How did this +1P experience deepen or enhance your knowledge of the topic?

2) What would you do differently next time?

3) What commitment will you make to extend this project and share it with others in your community?

Figure 5.22 +1P Sample Planning Calendar

Day 1 __/__ /20__	Day 2 __/__ /20__	Day 3 __/__ /20__	Day 4 __/__ /20__	Day 5 __/__ /20__
Plan: Project *hook* – find a creative way to draw students in through a video, picture, or guest speaker. Review 21st Century Skills, brainstorm potential topics. **Materials:** journals (digital or paper), "hook" materials, 21st CS checklist, chart paper, technology **Time Required:** 30 min. – 1 hr.	**Plan:** Review standards, project objective, and +1P planning rubric. Clarify any questions. Next, let students choose a topic of study (can be small or whole group). **Materials:** handout with standards and objective, rubric, chart paper, markers, journals, technology **Time Required:** 30 min. – 1 hr.	**Plan:** Organize student teams for topics of study. Review team roles and responsibilities and team agreement. Review and role-play the 7 Norms of Collaboration. **Materials:** handouts for 7 norms, team roles and responsibilities, and team agreement, technology **Time Required:** 30 min. – 1 hr.	**Plan:** Model big ideas, universal Concepts (UCs), and essential questions (EQs). Have student teams choose their own, or you choose if doing whole group. **Materials:** chart paper, markers, student journals, handouts with EQs and UCs, technology **Time Required:** 1 hr. (or more)	**Plan:** Have students share their big ideas, UCs, and EQs with each other to check for understanding. If whole group, have students create a tri-fold. **Materials:** students' big ideas, UCs and EQs, tri-fold handout, markers/crayons, technology **Time Required:** 30 min. – 1 hr.
Day 6 __/__ /20__	Day 7 __/__ /20__	Day 8 __/__ /20__	Day 9 __/__ /20__	Day 10 __/__ /20__
Plan: Review the presentation rubric (and presentation options), PEACES and EPL, writing assessment rubric, and reflection and commitment criteria. **Materials:** presentation rubric, writing rubric, reflection and commitment criteria, technology **Time Required:** 30 min. – 1 hr.	**Plan:** Use big ideas to generate questions using the +1P Questioning Technique and questioning storm activity. Do whole group or in student teams. **Materials:** handout for questioning technique, chart paper, markers, journals, technology **Time Required:** 1 hr.	**Plan:** Choose which questions to research. Make sure the chosen questions represent all four levels in the +1P Questioning Technique. Have teams share with each other. **Materials:** handout for questioning technique, chart paper, markers, journals, technology **Time Required:** 30 min. – 1 hr.	**Plan:** Determine learning activities (LAs) for remainder of project and encourage online collaboration. Review text sets, Look Fours (L4s), and Credibility 4 (C4). **Materials:** sample text set, handouts for L4s and C4, journals, chart paper, technology **Time Required:** 1 hr. (or more)	**Plan:** First day of research ☺. Students conduct research to find answers to their Focused Inquiry questions. Students complete a learning activity (LA) for this day. **Materials:** journals, paper or digital folder for research materials, L4s, C4, technology **Time Required:** 1 hr. (or more)

(Continued)

Figure 5.22 (Continued)

Day 11 ___/___/20___	Day 12 ___/___/20___	Day 13 ___/___/20___	Day 14 ___/___/20___	Day 15 ___/___/20___
Plan: Second day of research. Students conduct research to find answers to their Focused Inquiry questions. Students complete another LA or extend previous LA.	**Plan:** Third day of research. Students conduct research to find answers to their Focused Inquiry questions. Students complete another LA or extend previous LA.	**Plan:** Fourth day of research. Students conduct research to find answers to their Focused Inquiry questions. Students complete another LA or extend previous LA.	**Plan:** Fifth day of research – only conduct research if necessary. Complete team recommendations, determine presentation option(s), and start planning presentation.	**Plan:** Refer back to presentation rubric. Remind students to consider PEACES and EPL when planning. Continue to plan for presentation at school and home.
Materials: journals, paper or digital folder for research materials, L4s, C4, technology	**Materials:** journals, paper or digital folder for research materials, L4s, C4, technology	**Materials:** journals, paper or digital folder for research materials, L4s, C4, technology	**Materials:** journals, chart paper, paper or digital folder for research materials, L4s, C4, technology	**Materials:** journals, chart paper, paper or digital folder for research materials, L4s, C4, technology
Time Required: 1 hr. (or more)	**Time Required:** 1 hr. (or more)	**Time Required:** 1 hr. (or more)	**Time Required:** 1 hr. (or more)	**Time Required:** 1 hr. (or more)
Day 16 ___/___/20___	**Day 17 ___/___/20___**	**Day 18 ___/___/20___**	**Day 19 ___/___/20___**	**Day 20 ___/___/20___**
Plan: Continue to plan for presentation at school and home. Student teams should use the presentation rubric to practice PEACES and EPL.	**Plan:** Continue to plan for presentation at school and home. Conduct a dress rehearsal and use presentation rubric for a guide. Students choose presentation role.	**Plan:** Presentation day ☺. Student teams present to each, whole group, or present to another audience outside of the classroom. Use presentation rubric to grade.	**Plan:** Students take the writing assessment. Encourage students to use notes from journal, Boxes and Bullets, sentence frames, and evidence from their project.	**Plan:** Students write their reflection and commitment. Teacher (or students) decides how this will be demonstrated. Give a classroom celebration ☺.
Materials: journals, chart paper, paper or digital folder for research materials, L4s, C4, technology	**Materials:** presentation materials (projector, chart paper, rubrics, laptop/digital device/technology)	**Materials:** presentation materials (projector, chart paper, rubrics, laptop/digital device/technology)	**Materials:** student notes/ journals, pen/pencil, paper, technology (if typing on computer/digital device)	**Materials:** depends on the activity – chart paper, markers, pen/pencil, journals, technology
Time Required: 1 hr. (or more)	**Time Required:** 1 hr. (or more)	**Time Required:** 1 hr. (or more)	**Time Required:** 1 hr. (or more)	**Time Required:** 30 min. – 1 hr.

Note: Investigation/research can also be conducted at home.

want to keep students engaged and enthusiastic, and too many breaks may impede or slow down their progress.

Before addressing differentiation, I want to highlight interdisciplinary characteristics of the Vessel Operations unit and +1P units in general. Interdisciplinary units allow students to make connections within and across content. As a result, students learn to transfer and apply knowledge, principles, and/or values to more than one academic discipline. Interdisciplinary units also increase a student's ability to think critically and problem solve in more than one context, thus elevating student consciousness, cognitive ability, and problem-solving skills. These skills prepare students for college and career readiness and capture the essence of +1P.

Figure 5.23   Interdisciplinary Chart for Vessel Operations

Standards	Learning Activities
English Language Arts Common Core ELA/Literacy standards are already addressed in the sample unit, but more can be added.	1. Close read an article on vessel operations, annotate text, highlight transitional words, and highlight evidence of EPL. 2. Create a commercial for vessel operations using transitional words/phrases and EPL. Perform the commercial in front of the class.
Math Common Core Mathematical Practices (MPs) • MP4: Model with mathematics. • MP5: Use appropriate tools strategically. • MP6: Attend to precision.	1. Use a calculator to determine the perimeter, area, and volume of a cargo container. 2. Calculate cargo moves per minute, cargo moves per hour, or cost of cargo moves per hour. 3. Build a vessel using shapes, straws, popsicle sticks, blocks, plastic, or paper. 4. Determine the mathematical concepts and formulas used in a blueprint of a vessel. Solve for one of these formulas.
Science Next Generation Science Standards (NGSS) • Practice 2: Developing and using models • Practice 4: Analyzing and interpreting data	1. Build a ship to scale. 2. Use the scientific method to conduct an experiment on objects that float and sink in water. 3. Calculate the buoyant force on a vessel using the equation $F_b = V_s \times D \times g$ 4. Organize vessel data into charts and graphs. Interpret what the data say, what they mean, and why they matter.

(Continued)

Figure 5.23 (Continued)

Standards	Learning Activities
History/Social Studies California Department of Education (CDE) • Chronological and Spatial Thinking Construct timelines • Research, Evidence, and Point of View Access primary and secondary sources	1. Note the difference between a primary source (original photograph or painting of a vessel) and a secondary source (*Time* magazine article about vessels). 2. Critique the credibility of a source. 3. Create a timeline of vessel operations occurring over one or more centuries. An example is Columbus to the present.
Physical Education California Department of Education (CDE) • Standard 4 (K–5): Students demonstrate knowledge of physical fitness concepts, principles, and strategies to improve health performance. • Standard 2 (6–12): Students achieve a level of physical fitness for health and performance while demonstrating knowledge of fitness concepts, principles, and strategies.	1. Research how a ship crew engages in physical activity and exercise. Example questions to explore: Is there a gym on board? Are there exercise drills? How much physical activity does the ship crew endure on a daily basis? How does this relate to physical fitness concepts, principles, and strategies? 2. Create a text set (pictures, articles, videos, etc.) for a ship crew's diet and exercise.
Visual Arts California Department of Education (CDE) • Historical and Cultural Context • Aesthetic Valuing	1. Analyze past and present works of art related to ships/vessels (paintings, sketches, models, pottery, etc.). 2. Draw, paint, or create a vessel while considering elements of art, principles of design, and aesthetic qualities. Generate ideas from the above works of art.

+1P projects foster connections across the disciplines. As seen in Figure 5.23, there are numerous ways to apply interdisciplinary standards and activities, including those not stated in the chart. To achieve interdisciplinary outcomes, first plan with the content standards and then generate learning activities that align with the standards. Throughout a 20-day cycle, teachers have multiple opportunities to promote interdisciplinary learning activities. For example, if teachers decided to teach the Vessel Operations unit, they could use Figure 5.23

to assign two or more learning activities that address multiple content standards. Even as students engage in these cross-curricular learning activities, they are still participating in a cycle of inquiry and investigation around vessel operations. For optimal planning, it is recommended that teachers collaborate on the different ways to make learning activities interdisciplinary.

21ST CENTURY SKILLS

As we conclude the +1P process, it is important to revisit Wagner's (2010) 21st Century Skills. We need to ask, "How well does the framework attend to Wagner's 21st Century Skills and what is the evidence?" Fidelity to Wagner's model is indicated below:

1. **Critical Thinking and Problem Solving**—The framework promotes critical thinking through the study of real-world issues (i.e., Vessel Operations), inquiry, investigation, and reflection. Students learn to apply problem-solving skills during learning activities, research, technology (SAMR), and project recommendations.

2. **Collaboration Across Networks and Leading by Influence**—As students engage in their projects, they use technology to socially interact with peers, collaborate, and network. Students work in teams as they complete a project from beginning to end, thus building their capacity to lead by influence.

3. **Agility and Adaptability**—Students learn to adapt as they work in teams and engage in research—they are not opposed to change. Students use their agility and intellectual capacity to apply different strategies/techniques (questioning, text sets, Look Fours, Credibility 4), make recommendations, present, and reflect.

4. **Initiative and Entrepreneurialism**—Students are encouraged to be self-directed, innovative, and creative as they learn about their topic of study. Their success is dependent on their ability to take initiative, meaning they will accomplish more if they are proactive. These skills prepare students to be college and career ready.

5. **Effective Oral and Written Communication**—Effective communication is required throughout the entire +1P process.

Students are given several opportunities to practice and enhance their *oral* (dialogue and discussion with peers), *written* (journals, technology [Padlet, TodaysMeet, or Social Media], recommendations, writing assessment, reflection and commitment), and *presentation* (rhetorical devices and project presentation) skills. Students also learn to substantiate their findings/claims with evidence from their research.

6. **Accessing and Analyzing Information**—Students access information through text sets (primary and secondary sources), research, and the Internet. They learn to analyze information through strategies such as EPL (ethos, pathos, logos), VTS (visual thinking strategies), Look Fours, and Credibility 4.

7. **Curiosity and Imagination**—The curious nature of students lends itself nicely to +1P projects. Students choose a topic of study that peaks their curiosity and interest. Imaginative skills are fostered through the presentation component, where students are encouraged to be creative, original, and unique.

As demonstrated, 21st Century Skills are useful for guiding students through the +1P cycle. Teachers can introduce and explain each of seven skills before students start their project. Students need to understand the significance and relevance of the 21st Century Skills before they can apply the skills. Similarly, if students know the purpose of 21st Century Skills, they will be more inclined to use them.

DIFFERENTIATION

To close out this chapter without addressing differentiation would be unjustifiable. Due to its pervasive use in education, the term "differentiate" necessitates an operational definition. Carol A. Tomlinson, author of *The Differentiated Classroom: Responding to the Needs of All Learners*, provides a very coherent and comprehensive definition of differentiation. According to Tomlinson (1999), there are three questions to consider when differentiating curriculum and instruction. Each question includes specific strategies for achieving desired outcomes. Many of the strategies are directly aligned with the +1P process.

1. *What* is the teacher differentiating? This pertains to what the teacher is modifying in response to student needs.

a. **Content**—instructional delivery and materials needed to access information

(graphic organizers, charts, music, movement, technology, visuals,

storytelling, dialogue and discussion, humor, mnemonic devices, models, etc.)

b. **Process**—ways students understand, make meaning, and "own" knowledge

(*flexible grouping*—whole group, small group, pairs, triads, interest groups, and language ability groups; *learning activities*—experiments, games, research, journals, projects, give one-get one, field trips, homework, etc.)

c. **Product**—how students demonstrate mastery of what they know and can do as a result of learning

(*oral*—debate, lecture, presentation; *kinesthetic*—play, dance, board game; *visual*—video, collage, display board; *written*—essay, assessment, newsletter)

2. *How* is the teacher differentiating? This pertains to how the teacher differentiates in response to student readiness, interest, or learning profile.

(e.g., progress monitoring, IEPs, using data to inform instruction, acknowledging different entry points, choice activities and projects, individualized instruction/pacing plan)

3. *Why* is the teacher differentiating? This speaks to a teacher's reasons for modifying the learning experience. Key reasons include access to learning, motivation to learn, and efficiency of learning.

+1P projects differentiate **what** through *content* (because the teacher uses models, technology, scaffolds, sentence frames, L4s, C4, and rubrics), *process* (because students work in teams, they collaborate, they engage in dialogue and discussion, and participate in several learning activities), and *product* (because students make recommendations, present their projects in a variety of ways [oral, kinesthetic, visual, and written], engage in a writing assessment, reflect, and make a commitment to extend the project). The **how** is addressed through student interest, where students are given a choice of which topic to study, and the **why** is addressed through student motivation and efficiency of learning. Differentiation is not only achievable, but also critical to enhancing learning opportunities for students and heightening instructional practices of teachers. Subgroups such as gifted learners, students in special education, and English Learners benefit from these differentiation strategies. +1P enriches the learning experience for students within these subgroups because the framework can be tailored to meet their specific needs through content, process, and product.

Think about how you currently differentiate instruction for your students. Do you remember how any of your K–12 teachers differentiated instruction for you? Why does differentiation matter? How might you transfer Tomlinson's differentiation model back to your district, school, or classroom?

SUMMARY

Checkpoints 6 (recommendations and presentation) and 7 (writing assessment, reflection, and commitment) are critical components of the framework because they address accountability and ownership. All stakeholders are accountable for ensuring student success, including the students. Accountability is heightened by ownership. If we do not own what we do, say, and aspire to achieve, there is no need for a commitment on our end. Effective implementation of +1P requires collective accountability, collective ownership of accelerating achievement, and a collective commitment to prepare students to be college and career ready. To achieve these desired outcomes, instructional practices must reflect exemplary teaching and learning.

Through +1P, students acquire and apply skills in problem solving, asking and answering questions, conducting research, sourcing, critical thinking, using technology, presenting, communicating (orally, digitally, and in writing), reflecting, and making a commitment to a larger purpose—as seen in Chapters 2 through 5. Equally important is the fact that students learn the purpose of 21st Century Skills and how to apply them throughout the +1P process. When the cycle is completed, students are equipped with skills to compete locally and globally. They have also mastered skills that prepare them for college, career, and life. We accelerate achievement by investing our time, effort, and money into instructional practices that are research based, standards based, project based, inquiry based, 21st Century Skills based, interest based, motivation based, technology based and, most importantly, student centered. Together, these characteristics put the "+1" in +1 Pedagogy. The intricacies of the +1P framework, along with the high levels of cognitive demand required by students, are the type of rigor that students need to prepare for college and career readiness. The last chapter includes a conversation about mindset, exemplary teaching, and a commitment to raising the instructional bar.

 MICs

MOST IMPORTANT CONCEPTS

- Accountability
- Formative Assessment and Summative Assessment
- Common Core Assessments

  o SBAC and PARCC

- Recommendations
- Presentation

  o Persuasion (**Ethos**, **Pathos**, **Logos**—EPL)
  o Presentation (**Projection**, **Eye** Contact, **Attire**, **Confidence**, **Engagement**, **Succinctness**—PEACES)
  o Presentation Styles—Oral, Kinesthetic, Visual, and Written

- Writing Assessment

  o Rubrics and Grading
  o Student Samples

- Reflection and Commitment
- Interdisciplinary Units
- 21st Century Skills
- Differentiation

6

FINAL DESTINATION

Ready or not, change is inevitable. To keep up with our evolving world, students need to learn skills that transfer beyond the classroom. Students must learn how to collaborate, communicate, think critically, use technology, problem solve, inquire, conduct research, and think like an interdisciplinarian. +1 Pedagogy is a framework designed to apply these important skills across multiple contexts. This framework is also a conversation starter for transforming teaching and learning. As Einstein so eloquently stated, we cannot expect different results if we keep doing the same things over and over again. Adaptations to our instructional practices are necessary to keep up with our rapidly changing society and student population. What worked for students 30, 20, and even 10 years ago may need to be adapted for today's students. Notice that I said adapted and not abandoned. Certain best practices are timeless, like strategies for student engagement, enrichment, and equity. We need to embrace instructional practices that move us forward, especially those that are innovative, technology based, and interest based. The demands of the twenty-first century necessitate these instructional practices.

Educators need a collective definition of what it means to be college and career ready. Curriculum and instruction are perhaps the most influential pathways to prepare students for college, career, and life. Respectively, instructional practices that elevate consciousness, embed 21st Century Skills and technology, foster inquiry and investigation, incorporate rigor, include real-world application, and equip students to compete in a global economy are a step in the right direction. Until we believe that instruction is a catalyst for education reform, the status quo will remain the same. Teachers can leverage what, why, and how they teach to better prepare students for twenty-first-century learning. In return, students will acquire skills and knowledge that are transferrable to college and a career. Students can increase their chances of success as long as they embrace learning as an unlimited process. This last chapter emphasizes the use of self-assessment to stimulate professional growth and exemplary teaching. Final thoughts about the +1P process are also discussed.

SELF-ASSESSMENT

Assessment is not just formative and summative. It is also reflective and intrapersonal. This type of assessment is an integral part of growing up personally and professionally. To maintain a healthy balance of teaching and learning, educators should perform routine self-assessments. We can start by adopting the same metacognitive skills that we teach our students.

21ST CENTURY SKILLS CHECKLIST FOR TEACHERS AND ADMINISTRATORS

You may ask, "How do we self-assess our teaching and learning?" Rubrics, checklists, and performance metrics are basic tools we can use for self-assessment. Most schools have an evaluative tool for teaching and learning that includes quantitative measures. However, I am referring to a self-assessment that considers 21st Century Skills. These skills are just as critical for teachers as they are for students. Teachers who develop habits of mind around 21st Century Skills will be more inclined to utilize them during planning and instruction. Similarly, administrators can bolster their leadership and learning by developing habits of mind around 21st Century Skills. These skills are equally imperative to students, teachers, and administrators. For this reason, I have created a 21st Century Skills checklist for teachers and administrators. Use the checklist to inquire into your thinking and to determine next steps for your professional practice.

Figure 6.1   21st Century Skills Checklist for Teachers

Critical Thinking and Problem Solving	1. How am I thinking and teaching outside the box?
	2. How do I consider multiple perspectives?
	3. Do I ask questions that generate more questions?
	4. How do I find answers to my questions?
	5. Can I go about teaching this in a different way?
	6. What more can I say, find, or do for my students?
	7. What methods am I using to problem solve?
Collaboration Across Networks and Leading by Influence	1. How am I collaborating across networks/PLCs?
	2. How does teamwork help me collaborate?
	3. How do I use technology to interact with my peers?
	4. How do I integrate technology into my teaching?
	5. In what ways am I showing leadership?
	6. How do I lead by influence?
Agility and Adaptability	1. How do I show that I am alert and prepared?
	2. Am I being responsive and is it quick enough?
	3. How do I show that I am flexible?
	4. What does being adaptable mean to me?
	5. Why should my colleagues and I be adaptable?
Initiative and Entrepreneurialism	1. How do I show that I am self-directed?
	2. How do I show that I am taking initiative?
	3. How do I achieve success with my students?
	4. How am I enhancing my professional practice?
	5. In what ways am I being proactive and innovative?
Effective Oral and Written Communication	1. How often do I engage in collaborative dialogue?
	2. Are my conversations intellectually stimulating?
Power of Words	3. How do I present information effectively?
	4. In what ways do I express my thoughts in writing?
	5. How do I use technology to communicate?

(Continued)

Figure 6.1 (Continued)

Accessing and Analyzing Information	1. What tools and strategies am I using to access information?
	2. How does technology help me gain access?
	3. What tools and strategies am I using to analyze and interpret student data/information?
Curiosity and Imagination	1. What am I curious about and why?
	2. What am I interested in studying and why?
	3. How do I use my imagination when teaching?
	4. In what ways am I being creative in my teaching?
	5. What does it mean to be original and unique?

Figure 6.2 21st Century Skills Checklist for Administrators

Critical Thinking and Problem Solving	1. How am I thinking and leading outside the box?
	2. How do I consider multiple perspectives?
	3. Do I ask questions that generate more questions?
	4. How do I find answers to my questions?
	5. Can I go about facilitating this in a different way?
	6. What more can I say, find, or do for my staff?
	7. What methods am I using to problem solve?
Collaboration Across Networks and Leading by Influence	1. How am I building capacity to collaborate?
	2. How does teamwork help me collaborate?
	3. How do I use technology to interact with my staff?
	4. How do I facilitate the use of technology on campus?
	5. In what ways am I showing leadership?
	6. How do I lead by influence?
Agility and Adaptability	1. How do I show that I am alert and prepared?
	2. Am I being responsive and is it quick enough?
	3. How do I show that I am flexible?
	4. What does being adaptable mean to me?
	5. Why should my staff and I be adaptable?

Initiative and Entrepreneurialism	1. How do I show that I am self-directed?
	2. How do I show that I am taking initiative?
	3. How do I achieve success with my staff?
	4. How am I enhancing my professional practice?
	5. In what ways am I being proactive and innovative?
Effective Oral and Written Communication *Power of Words*	1. How often do I engage in collaborative dialogue?
	2. Are my conversations intellectually stimulating?
	3. How do I present information effectively?
	4. In what ways do I express my thoughts in writing?
	5. How do I use technology to communicate?
Accessing and Analyzing Information	1. What tools and strategies am I using to access information?
	2. How does technology help me gain access?
	3. What tools and strategies am I using to analyze and interpret student data/information?
Curiosity and Imagination	1. What am I curious about and why?
	2. What am I interested in studying and why?
	3. In what ways am I being creative in my leadership?
	4. What does it mean to be original and unique?
	5. How do I share my vision and articulate new ideas?

Think   Question   Transfer

Think about ways in which you self-assess your professional practice. Do you apply 21st Century Skills to your own professional growth? How might you transfer the 21st Century Skills checklist for teachers and administrators back to your district, school, or classroom?

MINDSET

The next self-assessment relates to mindset. Once you have taken ownership of applying 21st Century Skills to your professional practice, you need to determine how you will approach your goals. According to Dweck (2006), the right mindset motivates adults and students to reach their full potential, as well as their personal goals. Dweck's (2006) research is centered on two mindsets—*growth* and *fixed*. People with a growth mindset believe that intelligence can be developed, meaning that with effort and the right amount of training, people can substantially improve their outcomes. Those who have a growth mindset thrive when they are stretching themselves, resulting in higher levels of fulfillment and achievement. They start from where they are, confront challenges, and strive to get better over time. Alternatively, people with a fixed mindset believe that intelligence is more static. They accept their qualities "as they are," with no real desire to change or enhance these qualities. A fixed mindset is based on the belief that qualities, intelligence, and character cannot be cultivated with effort and training, making it difficult to achieve one's full potential. People with this mindset thrive when things are safely within their grasp. The minute something gets too challenging, or when they are not feeling smart or talented, they lose interest.

Dweck (2006) contends that mindsets are not everlasting; adults and children can be taught to change their mindset. What does mindset have to do with +1 Pedagogy? Everything. +1P entails a growth process around a topic of study. Teachers must value +1P as an avenue for cultivating motivation, embracing challenges, sustaining effort, learning from the successes and failures of others. Human behavior and cognition is changed as a result of teachers and students learning and growing together. This change stems from a desire to learn and improve one's circumstances. Without such a desire, it is unlikely that growth and application from learning will occur. Aside from preparing students with college- and career-ready skills, the purpose of +1P is to apply and transfer knowledge from one context to another. This transfer of knowledge increases a student's capacity to compete locally and globally because students are already accustomed to adapting, making connections, and applying concepts to real-world issues. A growth mindset is essential to sustaining these outcomes.

Think about a time when you had a fixed mindset around something. How did this mindset impact or influence your decision making? Why does mindset matter? How might you transfer Dweck's research on mindset back to your district, school, or classroom?

FINAL THOUGHTS

I am confident that the relevance of this book will extend beyond today. Why? Because +1 Pedagogy thrives on skills that are transferrable and applicable across any discipline. Students are not just engaged in the work for the sake of rigor. They learn *how* to apply knowledge in real-world contexts, utilize 21st Century Skills, conduct research, integrate technology, and reflect as true practitioners. Without a doubt, these skills elevate student consciousness and increase mastery toward college and career readiness. Educators cultivate high expectations by teaching students to go deeper for conceptual knowledge. Deeply engaging with content causes students to think critically and process through higher levels of cognitive demand. +1P deliberately raises the bar for rigor and conceptual understanding, while focusing on habits of mind that reset norms for teaching and learning.

This book is predicated on a rationale for transforming instructional practices and causing a change in human behavior. Students walk away from this process with a more in-depth understanding of their topic of study and skills that prepare them for college, career, and life. Teachers walk away with a toolkit of resources, strategies, and techniques for accelerating achievement through +1 Pedagogy. Administrators walk away with a practical guide for facilitating the implementation of +1 Pedagogy. Parents walk away with greater confidence in our school system and increased satisfaction in knowing that their student is engaged, interested, and motivated to learn. Employers walk away with a workforce that is fully equipped to apply 21st Century Skills and ready to use technology in multiple contexts. My hope is that your +1P experience inspires you to spread the good news about project-based learning across the disciplines. Learning should be fun, engaging, and cause a thirst for more knowledge. May you grow from this process, share this process with others, and practice the cycle many more times in the future. Thank you for taking this road trip to planning, managing, and assessing +1 Pedagogy. Now that you have reached the final destination, it is up to you to continue the journey.

Think about a time that you pushed the boundaries of what was possible. How did you achieve your goal? How did this +1P experience influence your instructional practices? What might be two or three takeaways from this book that you can share with your district, school, or students?

MICs

MOST IMPORTANT CONCEPTS

- Starting a Conversation
- Self-Assessment

  o 21st Century Skills Checklist for Teachers and Administrators
  o Growth Mindset vs. Fixed Mindset

- Final Thoughts

APPENDIX A

VISUAL AND PERFORMING ARTS STANDARDS

DANCE

(California Department of Education, 2015)

ARTISTIC PERCEPTION

- ✓ Processing, Analyzing, and Responding to Sensory Information Through the Language and Skills Unique to Dance
- ✓ Students perceive and respond, using the elements of dance. They demonstrate movement skills, process sensory information, and describe movement using the vocabulary of dance.

CREATIVE EXPRESSION

- ✓ Creating, Performing, and Participating in Dance
- ✓ Students apply choreographic principles, processes, and skills to create and communicate meaning through the improvisation, composition, and performance of dance.

HISTORICAL AND CULTURAL CONTEXT

- ✓ Understanding the Historical Contributions and Cultural Dimensions of Dance
- ✓ Students analyze the function and development of dance in past and present cultures throughout the world, noting human diversity as it relates to dance and dancers.

AESTHETIC VALUING

- ✓ Responding to, Analyzing, and Making Judgments About Works of Dance
- ✓ Students critically assess and derive meaning from works of dance, performance of dancers, and original works according to the elements of dance and aesthetic qualities.

CONNECTIONS, RELATIONSHIPS, APPLICATIONS

- ✓ Connecting and Applying What is Learned in Dance to Learning in Other Art Forms and Subject Areas and to Careers
- ✓ Students apply what they learn in dance to learning across subject areas. They develop competencies and creative skills in problem solving, communication, and management of time and resources that contribute to lifelong learning and career skills. They also learn about careers in and related to dance.

*These standards represent overarching themes in Visual and Performing Arts for Grades K–12. They are not grade-specific standards.

MUSIC

(California Department of Education, 2015)

ARTISTIC PERCEPTION

- ✓ Processing, Analyzing, and Responding to Sensory Information Through the Language and Skills Unique to Music Students
- ✓ Read, notate, listen to, analyze, and describe music and other aural information using the terminology of music.

CREATIVE EXPRESSION

- ✓ Creating, Performing, and Participating in Music
- ✓ Students apply vocal and instrumental musical skills in performing a varied repertoire of music. They compose and arrange music and improvise melodies, variations, and accompaniments using digital/electronic technology when appropriate.

HISTORICAL AND CULTURAL CONTEXT

- ✓ Understand the Historical Contributions and Cultural Dimensions of Music
- ✓ Students analyze the role of music in past and present cultures throughout the world, noting cultural diversity as it relates to music, musicians, and composers.

AESTHETIC VALUING

- ✓ Responding to, Analyzing, and Making Judgments About Works of Music
- ✓ Students critically assess and derive meaning from works of music and the performance of musicians according to the elements of music, aesthetic qualities, and human responses.

CONNECTIONS, RELATIONSHIPS, APPLICATION

- ✓ Connecting and Applying What is Learned in Music to Learning in Other Art Forms and Subject Areas and to Careers
- ✓ Students apply what they learn in music across subject areas. They develop competencies and creative skills in problem solving, communication, and management of time and resources that contribute to lifelong learning and career skills. They also learn about careers in and related to music.

*These standards represent overarching themes in Visual and Performing Arts for Grades K–12. They are not grade-specific standards.

THEATRE

(California Department of Education, 2015)

ARTISTIC PERCEPTION

- ✓ Processing, Analyzing, and Responding to Sensory Information Through the Language and Skills Unique to Theatre
- ✓ Students observe their environment and respond using the elements of theatre. They also observe formal and informal works of theatre, film/video, and electronic media and respond using the vocabulary of theatre.

CREATIVE EXPRESSION

- ✓ Creating, Performing, and Participating in Theatre
- ✓ Students apply processes and skills in acting, directing, designing, and script writing to create formal and informal theatre, films/videos, and electronic media productions and to perform in them.

HISTORICAL AND CULTURAL CONTEXT

- ✓ Understand the Historical Contributions and Cultural Dimensions of Theatre
- ✓ Students analyze the role of theatre, film/video, and electronic media in past and present cultures throughout the world, noting cultural diversity as it relates to theatre.

AESTHETIC VALUING

- ✓ Responding to, Analyzing, and Critiquing Theatrical Experiences
- ✓ Students critique and derive meaning from works of theatre, film/video, electronic media, and theatrical artists on the basis of aesthetic qualities.

CONNECTIONS, RELATIONSHIPS, APPLICATIONS

- ✓ Connecting and Applying What is Learned in Theatre, Film/Video, and Electronic Media to Other Art Forms and Subject Areas and to Careers
- ✓ Students apply what they learn in theatre, film/video, and electronic media across subject areas. They develop competencies and creative skills in problem solving, communication, and management of time and resources that contribute to lifelong learning and career skills. They also learn about careers in and related to theatre.

*These standards represent overarching themes in Visual and Performing Arts for Grades K–12. They are not grade-specific standards.

APPENDIX B

Big Ideas	Universal Concepts	Essential Questions	Writing Assessment
economics, politics, supply and demand, **invest**, interest rates, inflation, SEC, **competition**, Federal Reserve, **bull/bear market**, NASDAQ, S&P, DOW, options, futures, charts, systems, **laws**, **technology**, **capitalism**, **trading**, currency, and commodities	**Competition** advances an **economy**. **Technology** influences how people act and interact.	Is **capitalism** good for an **economy**? How do **laws** impact **trade**?	

Project Objective

Standards

Students will **analyze** the **purpose and function** of the stock market. They will gather information from the **Internet, media, videos, charts,** and **articles**. Students will present their findings to their classmates (or other audience) in a presentation, write a **short essay** about their findings and topic of study, and reflect on the process.

Standards	Focused Inquiry	Learning Activities	Investigation (Research)	Recommendations	Presentation	Writing Assessment
CCR Anchor Standards: **Reading AS 7** Integrate and evaluate content presented in diverse media and formats . . . **Writing AS 6** Use technology, including the Internet, to produce and publish writing and to interact and collaborate with others.	**General Questions** What is the stock **market**? What is **competition**? What does it mean to **invest**? What is **capitalism**? **Specific Questions** *Bull/Bear Market:* What is the difference between a bull market and a bear market? How many bear market cycles	*Optional Activities* ➜ 1) Dialogue and Discussion 2) Journal/Diary/Log [paper or digital] 3) Timeline 4) Analysis of Laws 5) Online Collaboration	**Text Set:** primary and secondary sources of information that are credible and contextualize learning for a topic of study	How might you improve and/or change a situation related to your topic of study? **Task:** 1) Make two or more recommendations related to your topic of study 2) Use evidence from the research to support your recommendations	**Persuasion:** *Ethos* (credibility) *Pathos* (emotions) *Logos* (logic) **Presentation:** *PEACES* (projection, eye contact, attire, confidence, engagement, succinctness)	Students will write a short essay about their topic of study. They will respond to the following questions: 1) Why is this topic important to study (refer to the Universal Concepts and Essential Questions)?

	Elaborate Questions	*Optional Sources* →		*Optional Presentations* →	
Writing AS 7 Conduct short as well as more sustained research projects based on focused questions demonstrating understanding of the subject under investigation. **Speaking and Listening AS 4** Present information, findings, and supporting evidence such that listeners can follow the line of reasoning . . . **History/Social Studies** *Chronological and Spatial Thinking* (explain how major events are related . . . in time; construct timelines)	does it take to enter a recession? *Competition:* What types of competition exist in a stock market? *Laws:* What laws pertain to the stock market? *Investing:* What different types of investments can be made in the stock market? **Elaborate Questions** *Bull/Bear Market:* What impact do bull/bear markets have on the economy? *Competition:* How does competition bring the best products to the market?	[Google Drive, E-mail, Facebook, Padlet, Blogs, Twitter, Skype, or TodaysMeet] 6) Create a Blog 7) Interviews or Surveys 8) Analyze Data and Financial Statements 9) Display Board 10) Quizzes [paper or digital] 11) Academic Games 12) Vocabulary Practice 13) Debate 14) Solve for P/E Ratios, Book Value, Intrinsic Value, etc. 15) Dummy Accounts	Internet Newspapers Magazines/Articles Economic Journals Books School or Public Library Videos Television Movies Documentaries Pictures Charts and Graphs Statistics/Data/Surveys Personal Accounts Interviews Observations	3) Explain the benefits of your recommendations *Students are encouraged to direct their recommendations to a particular audience.	**Kinesthetic:** • Music or Song • Play or Skit • Demonstrate a Trade • Board Game **Oral:** • Panel Discussion or Debate • Video Recording • PowerPoint/Prezi/Google Presentation • Lecture **Visual:** • Website • Poster/Illustration • Video or Short Film • Advertise a Stock **Written:** • Report • Newsletter • Brochure or Pamphlet • Script or Short Story	2) What are three or more major findings from your research? 3) What is the significance of each finding? Support your findings with evidence from your research. **Reminders:** ☑ Essay follows the criteria in the rubric ☑ Essay includes a beginning, middle, and end ☑ Essay stays on topic ☑ References are included

(Continued)

Mathematical Practices		Look Fours (L4s)		Reflection and Commitment
MP4: Model with mathematics. **MP5:** Use appropriate tools strategically. **MP7:** Look for and make use of structures **MP8:** Look for and express regularity in repeated reasoning. **NGSS Sci. & Engr. Practices** **Practice 4:** Analyzing and interpreting data	**Laws:** What happens when you break laws in the stock market? **Investing:** Why should people invest in the stock market? How do businesses invest differently from individuals? **Sourcing Questions** How will you access your information? What sources will you use? What makes your sources credible?	**in Research:** 1) Trends Over Time 2) Multiple Perspectives 3) Technological Advances 4) Forecasting **Credibility 4** (sourcing)		1) How did this +1P experience deepen or enhance your knowledge of the topic? 2) What would you do differently next time? 3) What commitment will you make to extend this project and share it with others in your community?

Teacher's Name: Date:

+1P Unit Plan—Roller Coasters

Big Ideas	Universal Concepts	Essential Questions
theme parks, roller coasters, speed (acceleration & velocity), height, area, force, design, volume, weight/mass, distance, **patterns, technology, engineering,** innovation, and systems	**Patterns** have repetitive structures. **Technology** requires innovation.	What does it take to become an expert in **engineering?** How does **technology** influence safety?

Standards	Project Objective	Writing Assessment
	Students will **compare** and **contrast** the **trends over time** for roller coasters. They will gather information from the **Internet, observations (field trip to a theme park), videos,** and **articles.** Students will present their findings to their classmates (or other audience) in a presentation, write a **short essay** about their topic of study, and reflect on the process.	Students will write a short essay about their topic of study. They will respond to the following questions: 1) Why is this topic important to study (refer to the Universal Concepts

CCR Anchor Standards:	Focused Inquiry	Learning Activities	Investigation (Research)	Recommendations	Presentation
Reading AS 7 Integrate and evaluate content presented in diverse media and formats, including visually and quantitatively, as well as in words. **Writing AS 6** Use technology, including the Internet,	**General Questions:** What is a **roller coaster?** What is a **theme park?** What is a **pattern?** What is an **engineer?** **Specific Questions:** *Roller Coasters:* What are some specific types of roller coasters? Which theme parks	*Optional Activities* → 1) Dialogue and Discussion 2) Journal/Diary/Log [paper or digital] 3) Create a Timeline 4) Field Trips	**Text Set:** primary and secondary sources of information that are credible and contextualize learning for a topic of study	How might you improve and/or change a situation related to your topic of study? **Task:** 1) Make two or more recommendations related to your topic of study	**Persuasion:** *Ethos* (credibility) *Pathos* (emotions) *Logos* (logic) **Presentation:** PEACES (projection, eye contact, attire, confidence, engagement, succinctness)

(Continued)

		Optional Sources →		2) Use evidence from the research to support your recommendations 3) Explain the benefits of your recommendations *Students are encouraged to direct their recommendations to a particular audience.	Optional Presentations →	and Essential Questions)? 2) What are three or more major findings from your research? 3) What is the significance of each finding? Support your findings with evidence from your research.
to produce and publish writing and to interact and collaborate with others. **Writing AS 7** Conduct short as well as more sustained research projects based on focused questions demonstrating understanding of the subject under investigation. **Speaking and Listening AS 4** Present information, findings, and supporting evidence such that listeners can follow the line of reasoning . . . **Mathematical Practices** **MP4:** Model with mathematics	have the biggest roller coasters? *Technology:* What type of technology is used on roller coasters? *Patterns:* What specific patterns do you see in roller coasters? *Engineering:* What type of engineer designs and builds roller coasters? **Elaborate Questions:** *Roller Coasters:* Why are roller coasters attractive? *Technology:* How does technology influence the design of a roller coaster? *Patterns:* Why do roller coasters have patterns?	5) Online Collaboration [Google Drive, Facebook, E-mail, Padlet, Blogs, Twitter, TodaysMeet, or Skype] 6) Create a Blog 7) Interviews or Surveys 8) Build a Model 9) Display Board 10) Experiment 11) Quizzes [paper or digital] 12) Academic Games 13) Vocabulary Placemat 14) Solving for Speed, Force, and/or Area 15) Collage of Roller Coasters Over Time	Internet Newspapers Magazines/Articles Sci. and Engr. Journals Books School or Public Library Videos Television Movies Documentaries Pictures Charts and Graphs Statistics/Data/Surveys Personal Accounts Interviews		**Kinesthetic:** • Music • Play or Skit • Experiment • Board Game **Oral:** • Panel Discussion or Debate • Video Recording • PowerPoint/Prezi/Google Presentation • Lecture **Visual:** • Website • Poster/Illustration • Video or Short Film • Flow Chart or Concept Map **Written:** • Report • Newsletter • Brochure or Pamphlet • Script or Short Story	**Reminders:** ☑ Essay follows the criteria in the rubric ☑ Essay includes a beginning, middle, and end ☑ Essay stays on topic ☑ References are included

					Reflection and Commitment
MP5: Use appropriate tools strategically	Engineering: How are engineers contracted to work on roller coasters?		Observation		1) How did this +1P experience deepen or enhance your knowledge of the topic?
MP7: Look for and make use of structures			Field Trip		
	Sourcing Questions:		Museums		
NGSS Sci. & Engr. Practices	How will you access your information? What sources will you use? What makes your sources credible?		Science Centers		2) What would you do differently next time?
Practice 2: Developing and using models			Look Fours (L4s) in Research:		
			1) Trends Over Time		
Practice 4: Analyzing and interpreting data			2) Multiple Perspectives		3) What commitment will you make to extend this project and share it with others in your community?
Practice 5: Using mathematics and computational thinking			3) Technological Advances		
			4) Forecasting		
			Credibility 4 (sourcing)		

209

Teacher's Name: +1P Unit Plan—Paintings by Famous Painters Date:

Big Ideas	Universal Concepts	Essential Questions
art, artist, artistic design, paintbrush, color wheel, elements of art, auctions, art museums, collections, fame, value (price), creativity, patterns, culture, society, beauty, and painter	A painting's artistic beauty is defined by culture and society. Art is timeless.	Why is some art (paintings) worth more than others? How does art appeal to emotions?

Standards	Project Objective				Writing Assessment
	Students will analyze the purpose and function of elements of art in paintings by famous painters (Picasso's Starry Night, Leonardo de Vinci's Mona Lisa, Norman Rockwell's Ruby Bridges, Jean-Michel Basquiat's The Rugged Male, etc.). They will gather information from the Internet, field trips to museums, videos, pictures, and articles. Students will present their findings to their classmates (or other audience) in a presentation, write a short essay about their findings and topic of study, and reflect on the process.				Students will write a short essay about their topic of study. They will respond to the following questions: 1) Why is this topic important to study (refer to the Universal Concepts and Essential Questions)?

CCR Anchor Standards:	Focused Inquiry	Learning Activities	Investigation (Research)	Recommendations	Presentation
Reading AS 7 Integrate and evaluate content presented in diverse media and formats, including visually and quantitatively, as well as in words. **Writing AS 6** Use technology, including the Internet, to produce and publish writing and to interact and collaborate with others.	**General Questions:** What is **art**? What is **fame**? What is a **color wheel**? What are the **elements of art**? **Specific Questions** *Art:* What are some specific types of art? *Elements of Art:* What are examples of each element of art?	*Optional Activities* → 1) Dialogue and Discussion 2) Journal/Diary/Log [paper or digital] 3) Document Analysis 4) Field Trips 5) Online Collaboration	**Text Set:** primary and secondary sources of information that are credible and contextualize learning for a topic of study *Optional Sources* → Internet Newspapers Magazines/Articles	How might you improve and/or change a situation related to your topic of study? **Task:** 1) Make two or more recommendations related to your topic of study 2) Use evidence from the research to support your recommendations	**Persuasion:** *Ethos* (credibility) *Pathos* (emotions) *Logos* (logic) **Presentation:** *PEACES* (projection, eye contact, attire, confidence, engagement, succinctness)

Writing AS 7				Optional Presentations →	2) What are three or more major findings from your research?

Writing AS 7

Conduct short as well as more sustained research projects based on focused questions demonstrating understanding of the subject under investigation.

Speaking and Listening AS 4

Present information, findings, and supporting evidence such that listeners can follow the line of reasoning . . .

History/Social Studies

Chronological and Spatial Thinking (construct timelines)

Research, Evidence, Point of View (assess primary and secondary sources)

Value (price): Who prices paintings? What are the five highest sold paintings?

Fame: Who are 10 famous painters?

Elaborate Questions

Art: How do painters generate ideas for their art? What motivates a painter?

Elements of Art: How are elements of art manifested in famous paintings? How do the elements of art help one evaluate a painting?

Value (price): What determines the value of a painting?

[Google Drive, Facebook, E-mail, Padlet, Blogs, Twitter, TodaysMeet, or Skype]

6) Create a Blog
7) Interviews or Surveys
8) Create a Painting
9) Display Board
10) Quizzes [paper or digital]
11) Academic Games
12) Vocabulary Practice
13) Debate
14) Collage [Famous painters and paintings]
15) Create a Timeline

Arts Journals

Books

School or Public Library

Videos

Television

Movies

Documentaries

Pictures

Charts and Graphs

Statistics/Data/Surveys

Personal Accounts

Interviews

Observation

Field Trip

Museums

Art Exhibits

Look Fours (L4s) in Research:

1) Trends Over Time
2) Multiple Perspectives

---

3) Explain the benefits of your recommendations

*Students are encouraged to direct their recommendations to a particular audience.

Optional Presentations →

Kinesthetic:
- Music or Song
- Play or Skit
- Demonstrate a Painting
- Board Game

Oral:
- Panel Discussion or Debate
- Video Recording
- PowerPoint/Prezi/Google Presentation
- Lecture

Visual:
- Website
- Poster/Illustration
- Video or Short Film
- Advertisement

Written:
- Report
- Newsletter
- Brochure or Pamphlet
- Script or Short Story

---

2) What are three or more major findings from your research?

3) What is the significance of each finding? Support your findings with evidence from your research.

Reminders:

☑ Essay follows the criteria in the rubric

☑ Essay includes a beginning, middle, and end

☑ Essay stays on topic

☑ References are included

(Continued)

(Continued)

VAPA—Visual Arts			Reflection and Commitment
Historical and Cultural Context (analyze role . . . of visual arts in past and present cultures . . .) *Aesthetic Valuing* (analyze . . . meaning from works of art . . . according to elements of art, principles of design . . .)	*Fame:* How does fame influence our perception of a painting? **Sourcing Questions** How will you access your information? What sources will you use? What makes your sources credible?	3) Technological Advances 4) Forecasting **Credibility 4** (sourcing)	**Reflection and Commitment** 1) How did this +1P experience deepen or enhance your knowledge of the topic? 2) What would you do differently next time? 3) What commitment will you make to extend this project and share it with others in your community?

Teacher's Name: +1P Unit Plan—Formal and Informal Communication   Date:

Big Ideas	Universal Concepts	Essential Questions	Writing Assessment
formal, informal, communication, memo, e-mail, flyers and brochures, **reading,** writing, speaking and listening, **media, social media, relationships,** websites, policies, bulletins, newsletters, employee handbook, and phone calls	**Media** and **social media** provide a means of communication. **Relationships** take on different forms.	How do **relationships** influence **communication?** How does **reading** connect us to the world?	Students will write a short essay about their topic of study. They will respond to the following questions: 1) Why is this topic important to study

Standards	Project Objective		
	Students will **analyze** the **purpose and function** of formal and information communication in a business setting. They will gather information from the **Internet, business documents, field trip, interviews,** and **articles.** Students will present their findings to their classmates (or other audience) in a presentation, write a short essay about their findings and topic of study, and reflect on the process.		

CCR Anchor Standards:	Learning Activities	Investigation (Research)	Recommendations	Presentation
Reading AS 7 Integrate and evaluate content presented in diverse media and formats . . . **Writing AS 6** Use technology, including the Internet, to produce and publish writing and to interact	**Focused Inquiry** **General Questions** How do you define **formal** and **informal?** What is **communication?** What is the difference between **media** and **social media?** *Optional Activities* → 1) Dialogue and Discussion 2) Journal/Diary/Log [paper or digital] 3) Document Analysis 4) Field Trips	**Text Set:** primary and secondary sources of information that are credible and contextualize learning for a topic of study	How might you improve and/or change a situation related to your topic of study? **Task:** 1) Make two or more recommendations related to your topic of study	**Persuasion:** *Ethos* (credibility) *Pathos* (emotions) *Logos* (logic) **Presentation:** *PEACES* (projection, eye contact, attire, confidence, engagement, succinctness)

(Continued)

(Continued)

Standards	Specific / Elaborate Questions	Optional Sources →	(sources, continued)	Recommendations	Optional Presentations →	(Questions, continued)
and collaborate with others. **Writing AS 7** Conduct short as well as more sustained research projects based on focused questions . . . **Speaking and Listening AS 1** Prepare for and participate effectively in a range of conversations and collaborations with diverse partners . . . **Speaking and Listening AS 4** Present information, findings, and supporting evidence such that listeners can follow the line of reasoning and the organization, development, and style are appropriate	**Specific Questions** *Formal and Informal:* What are some specific types of formal and informal documents? *Communication:* What are different types of communication? *Media/Social Media:* What are different forms of media and social media? *Relationships:* What are different types of business relationships? **Elaborate Questions** *Formal and Informal:* Why do businesses use both formal and informal communication? *Communication:* How do people	5) Online Collaboration [Google Drive, E-mail, Facebook, Padlet, Blogs, Twitter, Skype, or TodaysMeet] 6) Create a Blog 7) Interviews or Surveys 8) Create a Formal and Informal Business Document 9) Display Board 10) Quizzes [paper or digital] 11) Academic Games 12) Vocabulary Practice 13) Grammar and Syntax Practice 14) Collage of Formal and Informal Communications	Internet Newspapers Magazines/Articles Communication Journals Books School or Public Library Videos Television Movies Documentaries Pictures Charts and Graphs Statistics/Data/Surveys Personal Accounts Interviews Observations	2) Use evidence from the research to support your recommendations 3) Explain the benefits of your recommendations *Students are encouraged to direct their recommendations to a particular audience.	**Kinesthetic:** • Music or Song • Play or Skit • Puppet Show • Board Game **Oral:** • Panel Discussion or Debate • Video Recording • PowerPoint/Prezi/Google Presentation • Lecture **Visual:** • Website • Poster/Illustration • Video or Short Film • Diagram **Written:** • Report • Newsletter • Brochure or Pamphlet • Script or Short Story	(refer to the Universal Concepts and Essential Questions)? 2) What are three or more major findings from your research? 3) What is the significance of each finding? Support your findings with evidence from your research. **Reminders:** ☑ Essay follows the criteria in the rubric

to task, purpose, and audience. **Language AS 1** Demonstrate command of the conventions of standard English grammar and usage when writing or speaking. **History/Social Studies** *Chronological and Spatial Thinking* (construct timelines for formal and informal communication over time)	respond to different types of communication? *Media/Social Media:* What biases exist in media and social media? *Relationships:* Why is it important to establish relationships? **Sourcing Questions** How will you access your information? What sources will you use? What makes your sources credible?	Field Trip Museums **Look Fours (L4s) in Research:** 1) Trends Over Time 2) Multiple Perspectives 3) Technological Advances 4) Forecasting **Credibility 4** (sourcing)		☑ Essay includes a beginning, middle, and end ☑ Essay stays on topic ☑ References are included **Reflection and Commitment** 1) How did this +1P experience deepen or enhance your knowledge of the topic? 2) What would you do differently next time? 3) What commitment will you make to extend this project and share it with others in your community?

Big Ideas	Universal Concepts	Essential Questions	Writing Assessment
physical fitness, agents, **competition**, trainers, attire, sleep, contracts, diet, injuries, college, sponsors and brands, media, **nutrition**, sportsmanship, discipline, **public relations/media**, travel, insurance, **exercise**, leadership, reputation, and **statistics**	**Nutrition** and **exercise** are interdependent. **Competition** takes on different forms.	Can **physical fitness** change our lives? What does it take to become a professional athlete?	Students will write a short essay about their topic of study. They will respond to the following questions: 1) Why is this topic important to study (refer to the Universal Concepts and Essential Questions)?

Standards		Project Objective	
	Students will **analyze** the basics of physical fitness and study the **trends over time** of professional sports. They will gather information and data from the **Internet**, a task-oriented **field trip, articles,** and **videos.** Students will present their findings to their classmates (or other audience) in a **digital presentation,** write a **short essay** about their findings and topic of study, and reflect on the process.		

CCR Anchor Standards:	Focused Inquiry	Learning Activities	Investigation (Research)	Recommendations	Presentation
Reading AS 7 Integrate and evaluate content presented in diverse media and formats, including visually and quantitatively, as well as in words. **Writing AS 6** Use technology, including the Internet, to produce and publish writing and to interact and	**General Questions** What is an athlete? What is **competition**? Who are some professional athletes? **Specific Questions** *Statistics:* What are different types of athletic statistics and how are they recorded? *Competition:* What are different levels of competition?	*Optional Activities* → 1) Dialogue and Discussion 2) Journal/ Diary/Log [paper or digital] 3) Statistical Analysis 4) Field Trips 5) Online Collaboration	**Text Set:** primary and secondary sources of information that are credible and contextualize learning for a topic of study	How might you improve and/or change a situation related to your topic of study? **Task:** 1) Make two or more recommendations related to your topic of study 2) Use evidence from the research to support your recommendations	**Persuasion:** *Ethos* (credibility) *Pathos* (emotions) *Logos* (logic) **Presentation:** *PEACES* (projection, eye contact, attire, confidence, engagement, succinctness)

			Optional Sources →		Optional Presentations →
collaborate with others. **Writing AS 7** Conduct short as well as more sustained research projects based on focused questions demonstrating understanding of the subject under investigation. **Speaking and Listening AS 4** Present information, findings, and supporting evidence such that listeners can follow the line of reasoning . . . **Physical Education Standard 4:** Students demonstrate knowledge of physical fitness	**Physical Fitness:** What are the basic components of physical fitness? **Public Relations/Media:** What are different media outlets for professional sports? **Elaborate Questions** **Statistics:** How do statistics impact the career of a professional athlete? **Competition:** What role does sportsmanship play in competition? What happens when professional athletes are not challenged? **Physical Fitness:** How do professional athletes maintain and monitor physical fitness?	[Google Drive, Facebook, E-mail, Padlet, Blogs, Twitter, TodaysMeet, or Skype] 6) Create a Blog 7) Interviews or Surveys 8) Portrait of an Athlete [drawn or painted] 9) Display Board 10) Quizzes [paper or digital] 11) Academic Games 12) Vocabulary Practice 13) Collage 14) Poetry 15) Sports Articles 16) Timeline	Internet Newspapers Magazines/Articles Sports Journals Books School or Public Library Videos Television Movies Documentaries Pictures Charts and Graphs Statistics/Data/Surveys Personal Accounts Interviews Observations Field Trip	3) Explain the benefits of your recommendations *Students are encouraged to direct their recommendations to a particular audience.	**Kinesthetic:** • Music or Song • Play or Skit • Mock Game • Board Game **Oral:** • Panel Discussion or Debate • Video Recording • PowerPoint/Prezi/Google Presentation • Mock Interview or Press Conference **Visual:** • Website • Poster/Illustration • Video or Short Film • Statistical Charts **Written:** • Report • Newsletter • Brochure or Pamphlet • Script or Short Story

2) What are three or more major findings from your research?

3) What is the significance of each finding? Support your findings with evidence from your research.

Reminders:

☑ Essay follows the criteria in the rubric

☑ Essay includes a beginning, middle, and end

☑ Essay stays on topic

☑ References are included

(Continued)

(Continued)

			Reflection and Commitment
concepts, principles, and strategies to improve health performance. **History/Social Studies** Students construct various time lines of key events, people, and periods of the historical era they are studying. **NGSS Sci. & Engr. Practices** Practice 4: Analyzing and interpreting data	*Public Relations/ Media:* What is the relationship between media and professional athletes? How does the media influence a professional athlete's reputation? **Sourcing Questions** How will you access your information? What sources will you use? What makes your sources credible?	Hall of Fame Museum **Look Fours (L4s) in Research:** 1) Trends Over Time 2) Multiple Perspectives 3) Technological Advances 4) Forecasting **Credibility 4** (sourcing)	1) How did this +1P experience deepen or enhance your knowledge of the topic? 2) What would you do differently next time? 3) What commitment will you make to extend this project and share it with others in your community?

Teacher's Name: +1P Unit Plan—Nephrology   Date:

Big Ideas	Universal Concepts	Essential Questions
kidneys, medications, potassium/sodium/creatinine, dialysis, lab work, diseases (End Stage Renal Disease), **transplants**, **career**, **nephrologist**, interventional nephrologist, HIPAA, **nutrition/diet**, medical school/boards, fellowship, residency, and **technology**	**Nutrition** and **diet** have costs and benefits. **Technology** increasingly meets human health needs.	What makes a healthy **kidney**? What is the future of **kidney transplants**? How does a person prepare for a **career** in nephrology?

Project Objective

Students will **analyze** the **trends over time** for a career in nephrology. They will also **identify and describe** the **purpose and function** of kidneys. They will gather information and data from the **Internet**, a **field trip** to a nephrology practice, **articles**, and **videos**. Students will present their findings in a **digital presentation**, write a **short essay** about their findings and topic of study, and reflect on the process.

Standards	Focused Inquiry	Learning Activities	Investigation (Research)	Recommendations	Presentation	Writing Assessment
CCR Anchor Standards: **Reading AS 7** Integrate and evaluate content presented in diverse media and formats, including visually and quantitatively . . . **Writing AS 6** Use technology, including the Internet, to produce	**General Questions** What is a **nephrologist**? What is **dialysis**? What is a **career**? Who are famous **nephrologists**? **Specific Questions** *Medical School:* How much education/training does a nephrologist need?	*Optional Activities* ➜ 1) Dialogue and Discussion 2) Journal/Diary/Log [paper or digital] 3) Statistical Analysis of an Anonymous	**Text Set:** primary and secondary sources of information that are credible and contextualize learning for a topic of study	How might you improve and/or change a situation related to your topic of study? **Task:** 1) Make two or more recommendations related to your topic of study	**Persuasion:** *Ethos* (credibility) *Pathos* (emotions) *Logos* (logic) **Presentation:** *PEACES* (projection, eye contact, attire, confidence, engagement, succinctness)	Students will write a short essay about their topic of study. They will respond to the following questions: 1) Why is this topic important to study (refer to the Universal Concepts and Essential Questions)?

(Continued)

(Continued)

Standards	Guiding Questions	Optional Sources →	Recommendations	Optional Presentations →
and publish writing and to interact and collaborate with others. **Writing AS 7** Conduct short as well as more sustained research projects based on focused questions . . . **Speaking and Listening AS 4** Present information, findings, and supporting evidence such that listeners can follow the line of reasoning . . . **Physical Education Standard 4:** Students demonstrate knowledge of physical fitness concepts, principles, and strategies to improve health performance.	*Diseases:* What are different types of kidney diseases? *Technology:* What specific technology is used for a dialysis machine? *Nutrition/Diet:* What foods, drinks, and recreational drugs negatively impact kidney function? What foods and drinks positively impact kidney function? **Elaborate Questions** *Medical School:* Why are nephrologists required to continue their education? *Diseases:* Why are lab results important for monitoring kidney disease? Which diseases can result in kidney failure?	Patient's Medical Record 4) Field Trip 5) Online Collaboration [Google Drive, E-mail, Facebook, Padlet, Blogs, Twitter, Skype, or TodaysMeet] 6) Create a Medical Blog for Nephrology 7) Interview with Nephrologist and/or Interventional Nephrologist 8) Display Board of Kidney functions and/or diseases 9) Experiment Internet Newspapers Magazines/Articles Medical Journals Books School/Public Library Videos Television Movies Documentaries Pictures Charts and Graphs Statistics/Data/Survey Personal Accounts Interviews Field Trip Dialysis Clinic	2) Use evidence from the research to support your recommendations 3) Explain the benefits of your recommendations *Students are encouraged to direct their recommendations to a particular audience.	2) What are three or more major findings from your research? 3) What is the significance of each finding? **Kinesthetic:** • Music or Song • Play or Skit • Mock Game • Board Game **Oral:** • Panel Discussion or Debate • Video Recording • PowerPoint/Prezi/Google Presentation • Mock Interview or Press Conference **Visual:** • Website • Poster/Illustration • Video or Short Film • Statistical Charts **Written:** • Report • Newsletter • Brochure or Pamphlet • Script or Short Story

Mathematical Practices	Technology / Sourcing Questions	Vocabulary & Activities	Look Fours (L4s) in Research	Reminders & Reflection
Mathematical Practices **MP4:** Model with mathematics. **MP6:** Attend to precision. **MP7:** Look for and make use of structure. **NGSS Sci. & Engr. Practices** **Practice 1:** Asking questions (for science) and defining problems (for engineering) **Practice 4:** Analyzing and interpreting data	*Technology:* What would happen if there were a power outage during dialysis treatment? *Nutrition/Diet:* Why does nutrition/diet matter to kidney health? **Sourcing Questions** How will you access your information? What sources will you use? What makes your sources credible?	10) Vocabulary Practice 11) Timeline 12) Diet/Menu for a Strong Kidney	**Look Fours (L4s) in Research:** 1) Trends Over Time 2) Multiple Perspectives 3) Technological Advances 4) Forecasting **Credibility 4** (sourcing)	Support your findings with evidence from your research. **Reminders:** ☑ Essay follows the criteria in the rubric ☑ Essay includes a beginning, middle, and end ☑ Essay stays on topic ☑ References are included **Reflection and Commitment** 1) How did this +1P experience deepen or enhance your knowledge of the topic? 2) What would you do differently next time? 3) What commitment will you make to extend this project and share it with others in your community?

(Continued)

Teacher's Name: **1P Unit Plan—Teaching**   Date:

Big Ideas	Universal Concepts	Essential Questions
research, **systems**, stakeholders (**teachers**, students, parents, administrators), **policies/laws, learning**, instruction, **technology**, environment, curriculum, culture, diversity, unions, salary, grades, report cards, assessments, gen. ed., spec. ed., GATE, standards, planning, management, **career, credential, school,** accountability	**Teaching** is essential to **learning.** **Systems** can be disturbed. **Technology** has costs and benefits.	What is the true purpose of a **teacher?** How does a person prepare for a **career** in teaching? How can **technology** be used to inspire **learning?** **Writing Assessment**

Project Objective

Students will **analyze** the **trends over time** for a career in teaching, **analyze policies/laws** that have changed the landscape of education, and **compare and contrast technological advances** in education. They will gather information from the **Internet,** their school, **articles,** and **videos.** Students will present their findings in a **digital presentation,** write a **short essay** about their findings, and reflect on the process.

Standards	Focused Inquiry	Learning Activities	Investigation (Research)	Recommendations	Presentation	Writing Assessment
CCR Anchor Standards: **Reading AS 7** Integrate and evaluate content presented in diverse media and formats, including visually and quantitatively… **Writing AS 6** Use technology, including the Internet, to produce and	**General Questions** What is a **teacher?** Who are some famous **teachers?** What is a **system?** What is a **career?** **Specific Questions** *Credentialing/Teaching:* How much education/training does a teacher need to be credentialed?	*Optional Activities* → 1) Dialogue and Discussion 2) Journal/Diary/Log [paper or digital] 3) Analyze Data from a Report Card or Cum.	**Text Set:** primary and secondary sources of information that are credible and contextualize learning for a topic of study	How might you improve and/or change a situation related to your topic of study? **Task:** 1) Make two or more recommendations related to your topic of study	**Persuasion:** *Ethos* (credibility) *Pathos* (emotions) *Logos* (logic) **Presentation:** *PEACES* (projection, eye contact, attire, confidence, engagement, succinctness)	Students will write a short essay about their topic of study. They will respond to the following questions: 1) Why is this topic important to study (refer to the Universal Concepts

		Optional Sources →		Optional Presentations →	and Essential Questions)?
publish writing and to interact and collaborate with others. **Writing AS 7** Conduct short as well as more sustained research projects based on focused questions . . . **Speaking & Listening AS 4** Present information, findings, and supporting evidence such that listeners can follow the line of reasoning . . . **History/Social Studies** Students construct various time lines of key events, people, and periods of the historical era they are studying. **Mathematical Practices**	What assessments are required? What are different teaching specialties? *Technology:* What types of technologies are used in a school? How about a classroom? *Systems:* What general systems are in place at schools? *Policies/Laws:* What are three to four policies/laws that have directly impacted K–12 education? **Elaborate Questions** *Credentialing/Teaching:* Why are teachers required to have a teaching credential? *Technology:* Why are more schools and	4) Field Trip to Another School 5) Online Collaboration [Google Drive, E-mail, Facebook, Padlet, Blogs, Twitter, Skype, TodaysMeet] 6) Create an Education Blog 7) Interview Teachers and Students 8) Display Board of School Systems 9) Create/Build a Model of a School 10) Vocabulary Practice 11) Timeline	Internet Newspapers Magazines/Articles Education Journals Books School/Public Library Videos Television Movies Documentaries Pictures Charts and Graphs Statistics/Data/Survey Personal Accounts Interviews Field Trip	2) Use evidence from the research to support your recommendations 3) Explain the benefits of your recommendations *Students are encouraged to direct their recommendations to a particular audience.	**Kinesthetic:** • Music or Song • Play or Skit • Mock Game • Board Game **Oral:** • Panel Discussion or Debate • Video Recording • PowerPoint/Prezi/Google Presentation • Mock Interview or Press Conference **Visual:** • Website • Poster/Illustration • Video or Short Film • Statistical Charts **Written:** • Report • Newsletter • Brochure or Pamphlet • Script or Short Story	2) What are three or more major findings from your research? 3) What is the significance of each finding? Support your findings with evidence from your research. **Reminders:** ☑ Essay follows the criteria in the rubric ☑ Essay includes a beginning, middle, and end ☑ Essay stays on topic ☑ References are included

(Continued)

(Continued)

				Reflection and Commitment
MP4: Model with mathematics. MP5: Use appropriate tools strategically. MP6: Attend to precision. **NGSS Sci. & Engr. Practices** **Practice 2:** Developing and Using Models **Practice 4:** Analyzing and Interpreting Data	districts investing in technology? *Systems:* What would happen if schools did not have systems in place? *Policies/Laws:* What purpose do policies/laws serve in our schools? **Sourcing Questions** How will you access your information? What sources will you use? What makes your sources credible?	12) Collage of Technology Over Ttime 13) Create a Rubric	**Look Fours (L4s) in Research:** 1) Trends Over Time 2) Multiple Perspectives 3) Technological Advances 4) Forecasting **Credibility 4** (sourcing)	1) How did this +1P experience deepen or enhance your knowledge of the topic? 2) What would you do differently next time? 3) What commitment will you make to extend this project and share it with others in your community?

Big Ideas	Universal Concepts	Essential Questions
practice, instrument(s), **patterns**, perseverance, talent, harmony, performance, scales, notes, lyrics/rhythm/beats, **culture**, critics, concert, recording, contracts, **technology**, experience, **creativity**, coaching, expenses, **career**, artistry, competition, and **innovation**	**Patterns** follow a structure. **Technology** influences **music**. **Innovation** requires **creativity**.	Why is **music** considered a universal language? How does **music** influence human behavior? How does a person prepare for a **career** in music?

Standards		Writing Assessment
		Students will write a short essay about their topic of study. They will respond to the following questions: 1) Why is this topic important to study

Project Objective

Students will **identify** and **describe trends over time** in music, **analyze the cause and effect** of music on human behavior, and **compare and contrast** different careers in music. They will gather information from the Internet, **articles/magazines, songs**, and **videos**. Students will present their findings in a **digital presentation**, write a **short essay** about their findings, and reflect on the process.

CCR Anchor Standards:	Focused Inquiry	Learning Activities	Investigation (Research)	Recommendations	Presentation
Reading AS 7 Integrate and evaluate content presented in diverse media and formats . . . **Writing AS 6** Use technology, including the Internet, to produce and publish writing	**General Questions** What is a **musician**? Who are some famous **musicians**? What is a **pattern**? What is a **career**? **Specific Questions** *Practice and Careers:* How much time does a professional	*Optional Activities* → 1) Dialogue and Discussion 2) Journal/Diary/Log [paper or digital] 3) Write a Song/Verse	**Text Set:** primary and secondary sources of information that are credible and contextualize learning for a topic of study	How might you improve and/or change a situation related to your topic of study? **Task:** 1) Make two or more recommendations related to your topic of study	**Persuasion:** *Ethos* (credibility) *Pathos* (emotions) *Logos* (logic) **Presentation:** *PEACES* (projection, eye contact, attire, confidence, engagement, succinctness)

(Continued)

(Continued)

Standards / Questions	Optional Sources		Optional Presentations
and to interact and collaborate with others. **Writing AS 7** Conduct short as well as more sustained research projects based on focused questions . . . **Speaking & Listening AS 4** Present information, findings, and supporting evidence . . . **History/Social Studies** Students construct various timelines . . . **Mathematical Practices** **MP6:** Attend to precision. **MP7:** Look for and make use of structure. musician practice in a week? What are different careers in music? *Technology:* What types of technologies do musicians use? *Patterns:* What are different patterns in music? *Culture:* How is music expressed in different cultures? **Elaborate Questions** *Practice and Careers:* Why do musicians practice their craft? What makes a music career last over time? *Technology:* How has technology enhanced music? What impact does technology have on musicians?	4) Field Trip to Concert or Music Museum 5) Online Collaboration [Google Drive, E-mail, Facebook, Padlet, Blogs, Twitter, Skype, TodaysMeet] 6) Create a Music Blog 7) Interview a Musician 8) Display Board of Music Over Time 9) Create/Build an Instrument 10) Vocabulary Practice 11) Analyze Lyrics to a Song	*Optional Sources* → Internet Newspapers Magazines/Articles Music Journals Books School/Public Library Videos Television Movies Documentaries Pictures Charts and Graphs Statistics/Data/Survey Personal Accounts Interviews Field Trip Museum	*Optional Presentations* → **Kinesthetic:** • Dance/Choreography • Play or Skit • Music Video • Concert **Oral:** • Panel Discussion or Debate • Recite Lyrics • PowerPoint/Prezi/Google Presentation • Mock Interview or Press Conference **Visual:** • Website • Poster/Illustration • Video or Short Film • Create a Costume **Written:** • Report • Newsletter/Blog • Brochure or Pamphlet • Write a Song

2) Use evidence from the research to support your recommendations

3) Explain the benefits of your recommendations

*Students are encouraged to direct their recommendations to a particular audience.

(refer to the Universal Concepts and Essential Questions)?

2) What are three or more major findings from your research?

3) What is the significance of each finding? Support your findings with evidence from your research.

Reminders:
☑ Essay follows the criteria in the rubric

NGSS Sci. & Engr. Practices	Patterns / Culture / Sourcing Questions	Products	Look Fours (L4s) in Research	Reflection and Commitment
Practice 2: Developing and Using Models **Practice 4:** Analyzing and Interpreting Data **VAPA—Music** *Connections, Relationships, Applications* (Students apply what they learn in music across disciplines . . . They also learn about careers in and related to music.)	*Patterns:* How have musical patterns changed over time? *Culture:* Why are some cultures more influential than others when it comes to music? **Sourcing Questions** How will you access your information? What sources will you use? What makes your sources credible?	12) Collage of the Music Industry 13) Make a Music Video 14) Statistics in Music [Sales & Popularity]	**Look Fours (L4s) in Research:** 1) Trends Over Time 2) Multiple Perspectives 3) Technological Advances 4) Forecasting **Credibility 4** (sourcing)	☑ Essay includes a beginning, middle, and end ☑ Essay stays on topic ☑ References are included **Reflection and Commitment** 1) How did this +1P experience deepen or enhance your knowledge of the topic? 2) What would you do differently next time? 3) What commitment will you make to extend this project and share it with others in your community?

Teacher's Name: Date:

+1P Unit Plan

Standards	Big Ideas	Universal Concepts		Essential Questions	
		Project Objective			
	Focused Inquiry	Learning Activities	Investigation (Research)	Recommendations	Presentation	Writing Assessment
						Reflection and Commitment

Big Ideas	Universal Concepts			Essential Questions	
Standards		Project Objective			**Writing Assessment**
	Focused Inquiry	**Investigation (Research)**	**Recommendations**	**Presentation**	Students will write a short essay about their topic of study. They will respond to the following questions:
	Learning Activities	**Text Set:** primary and secondary sources of information that are credible and contextualize learning for a topic of study	How might you improve and/or change a situation related to your topic of study?	**Persuasion:** *Ethos* (credibility) *Pathos* (emotions) *Logos* (logic)	1) Why is this topic important to study (refer to the Universal Concepts and Essential Questions)?
	Optional Activities →	*Optional Sources* →	**Task:**	**Presentation:**	
	General Questions:	Internet	1) Make two or more recommendations related to your topic of study	*PEACES* (projection, eye contact, attire, confidence, engagement, succinctness)	2) What are three or more major findings from your research?
	1)	Newspapers	2) Use evidence from the research to support your recommendations	*Optional Presentations* →	3) What is the significance of each finding? Support your findings with evidence from your research.
	2)	Magazines / Articles	3) Explain the benefits of your recommendations	**Kinesthetic:**	
	Specific Questions: 3)	Journals	*Students are encouraged to direct their	• Music	
	4)	Books		• Play or Skit	
	Elaborate Questions: 5)	School or Public Library		• Experiment	
	6)	Videos		• Board Game	
	Sourcing Questions: 7)	Television		**Oral:**	
	How will you access your information? 8)			• Panel Discussion or Debate	
	What sources will you use? 9)			• Video Recording	
	What makes your sources credible? 10)				

(Continued)

(Continued)

recommendations to a particular audience.	• PowerPoint/Prezi/Google Presentation • Interactive Lecture **Visual:** • Website • Poster/Illustration • Video or Short Film • Flow Chart or Concept Map **Written:** • Report • Newsletter • Brochure or Pamphlet • Script or Short Story **Reflection and Commitment** 1) How did this +1P experience deepen or enhance your knowledge of the topic? 2) What would you do differently next time? 3) What commitment will you make to extend this project and share it with others in the community?	**Reminders:** ☑ Essay follows the criteria in the rubric ☑ Essay includes a beginning, middle, and end ☑ Essay stays on topic ☑ References are included
Movies Documentaries Pictures Charts and Graphs Statistics/Data/Surveys Personal Accounts Interviews Observations Field Trips Museums Science Centers **Look Fours (L4s) in Research:** 1) Trends Over Time 2) Multiple Perspectives 3) Technological Advances 4) Forecasting **Credibility 4** (sourcing)		

230

Day 1 ___/___/20___	Day 2 ___/___/20___	Day 3 ___/___/20___	Day 4 ___/___/20___	Day 5 ___/___/20___
Plan: Project *hook*—find a creative way to draw students in through a video, picture, or guest speaker. Review 21st Century Skills, brainstorm potential topics. **Materials:** journals (digital or paper), "hook" materials, 21st CS checklist, chart paper, technology **Time Required:** 30 min. – 1 hr.	**Plan:** Review standards, project objective, and +1P planning rubric. Clarify any questions. Next, let students choose a topic of study (can be small or whole group). **Materials:** handout with standards and objective, rubric, chart paper, markers, journals, technology **Time Required:** 30 min. – 1 hr.	**Plan:** Organize student teams for topics of study. Review team roles and responsibilities and team agreement. Review and role-play the 7 Norms of Collaboration. **Materials:** handouts for 7 norms, team roles and responsibilities, and team agreement, technology **Time Required:** 30 min. – 1 hr.	**Plan:** Model big ideas, universal Concepts (UCs), and essential questions (EQs). Have student teams choose their own, or you choose if doing whole group. **Materials:** chart paper, markers, student journals, handouts with EQs and UCs, technology **Time Required:** 1 hr. (or more)	**Plan:** Have students share their big ideas, UCs, and EQs with each other to check for understanding. If whole group, have students create a tri-fold. **Materials:** students' big ideas, UCs and EQs, tri-fold handout, markers/crayons, technology **Time Required:** 30 min. – 1 hr.

Day 6 ___/___/20___	Day 7 ___/___/20___	Day 8 ___/___/20___	Day 9 ___/___/20___	Day 10 ___/___/20___
Plan: Review the presentation rubric (and presentation options), PEACES and EPL, writing assessment rubric, and reflection and commitment criteria. **Materials:** presentation rubric, writing rubric, reflection and commitment criteria, technology **Time Required:** 30 min. – 1 hr.	**Plan:** Use big ideas to generate questions using the +1P Questioning Technique and questioning storm activity. Do whole group or in student teams. **Materials:** handout for questioning technique, chart paper, markers, journals, technology **Time Required:** 30 min. – 1 hr.	**Plan:** Choose which questions to research. Make sure the chosen questions represent all four levels in the +1P Questioning Technique. Have teams share with each other. **Materials:** handout for questioning technique, chart paper, markers, journals, technology **Time Required:** 30 min. – 1 hr.	**Plan:** Determine learning activities (LAs) for remainder of project and encourage online collaboration. Review text sets, Look Fours (L4s), and Credibility 4 (C4). **Materials:** sample text set, handouts for L4s and C4, journals, chart paper, technology **Time Required:** 1 hr. (or more)	**Plan:** First day of research ☺. Students conduct research to find answers to their Focused Inquiry questions. Students complete a learning activity (LA) for this day. **Materials:** journals, paper or digital folder for research materials, L4s, C4, technology **Time Required:** 1 hr. (or more)

(Continued)

(Continued)

Day 11 ___/___/20___	Day 12 ___/___/20___	Day 13 ___/___/20___	Day 14 ___/___/20___	Day 15 ___/___/20___
Plan: Second day of research. Students conduct research to find answers to their Focused Inquiry questions. Students complete another LA or extend previous LA. **Materials:** journals, paper or digital folder for research materials, L4s, C4, technology **Time Required:** 1 hr. (or more)	**Plan:** Third day of research. Students conduct research to find answers to their Focused Inquiry questions. Students complete another LA or extend previous LA. **Materials:** journals, paper or digital folder for research materials, L4s, C4, technology **Time Required:** 1 hr. (or more)	**Plan:** Fourth day of research. Students conduct research to find answers to their Focused Inquiry questions. Students complete another LA or extend previous LA. **Materials:** journals, paper or digital folder for research materials, L4s, C4, technology **Time Required:** 1 hr. (or more)	**Plan:** Fifth day of research—only conduct research if necessary. Complete team recommendations, determine presentation option(s), and start planning presentation. **Materials:** journals, chart paper, paper or digital folder for research materials, L4s, C4, technology **Time Required:** 1 hr. (or more)	**Plan:** Refer back to presentation rubric. Remind students to consider PEACES and EPL when planning. Continue to plan for presentation at school and home. **Materials:** journals, chart paper, paper or digital folder for research materials, L4s, C4, technology **Time Required:** 1 hr. (or more)
Day 16 ___/___/20___	**Day 17 ___/___/20___**	**Day 18 ___/___/20___**	**Day 19 ___/___/20___**	**Day 20 ___/___/20___**
Plan: Continue to plan for presentation at school and home. Student teams should use the presentation rubric to practice PEACES and EPL. **Materials:** journals, chart paper, paper or digital folder for research materials, L4s, C4, technology **Time Required:** 1 hr. (or more)	**Plan:** Continue to plan for presentation at school and home. Conduct a dress rehearsal and use presentation rubric for a guide. Students choose presentation role. **Materials:** presentation materials (projector, chart paper, rubrics, laptop/digital device/technology) **Time Required:** 1 hr. (or more)	**Plan:** Presentation day ☺. Student teams present to each other, whole group, or present to another audience outside of the classroom. Use presentation rubric to grade. **Materials:** presentation materials (projector, chart paper, rubrics, laptop/digital device/technology) **Time Required:** 1 hr. (or more)	**Plan:** Students take the writing assessment. Encourage students to use notes from journal, Boxes and Bullets, sentence frames, and evidence from their project. **Materials:** student notes/journals, pen/pencil, paper, technology (if typing on computer/digital device) **Time Required:** 1 hr. (or more)	**Plan:** Students write their reflection and commitment. Teacher (or students) decides how this will be demonstrated. Give a classroom celebration ☺. **Materials:** depends on the activity—chart paper, markers, pen/pencil, journals, technology **Time Required:** 30 min. – 1 hr.

Note: Investigation/research can also be conducted at home.

+1P Planning Calendar

Day 1 __/__/20__	Day 2 __/__/20__	Day 3 __/__/20__	Day 4 __/__/20__	Day 5 __/__/20__
Plan: Materials: Time Required:	Plan: Materials: Time Required:	Plan: Materials: Time Required:	Plan: Materials: Time Required:	Plan: Materials: Time Required:
Day 6 __/__/20__	Day 7 __/__/20__	Day 8 __/__/20__	Day 9 __/__/20__	Day 10 __/__/20__
Plan: Materials: Time Required:	Plan: Materials: Time Required:	Plan: Materials: Time Required:	Plan: Materials: Time Required:	Plan: Materials: Time Required:
Day 11 __/__/20__	Day 12 __/__/20__	Day 13 __/__/20__	Day 14 __/__/20__	Day 15 __/__/20__
Plan: Materials: Time Required:	Plan: Materials: Time Required:	Plan: Materials: Time Required:	Plan: Materials: Time Required:	Plan: Materials: Time Required:
Day 16 __/__/20__	Day 17 __/__/20__	Day 18 __/__/20__	Day 19 __/__/20__	Day 20 __/__/20__
Plan: Materials: Time Required:	Plan: Materials: Time Required:	Plan: Materials: Time Required:	Plan: Materials: Time Required:	Plan: Materials: Time Required:

Note: Investigation/research can also be conducted at home.

233

REFERENCES

Ambrose, S. A., Bridges, M. W., DiPietro, M., Lovett, M. C., & Norman, M. K. (2010). *How learning works: Seven research-based principles for smart teaching.* San Francisco, CA: Jossey-Bass.

Anderson, L. W., & Krathwohl , D. R., et al (Eds.). (2001). *A Taxonomy for learning, teaching, and assessing: A revision of Bloom's taxonomy of educational objectives.* New York, NY: Longman.

Atkins-Sayre, W. (2014). *Teaching with PechaKucha presentations.* The University of Southern Mississippi Speaking Center. Retrieved March 8, 2014, from http://www.usm.edu/speaking-center/creating-your-presentation

Barak, M., & Dori, Y. J. (2005). Enhancing undergraduate students' chemistry understanding through project-based learning in an IT environment. *Science Education, 89*(1), 117–139.

Bell, S. (2010). Project-based learning for the 21st century: Skills for the future. *The Clearing House, 83,* 39–43.

Bloom, B. S. (1984). *Taxonomy of educational objectives.* Boston, MA: Allyn & Bacon.

Boaler, J. (1997). *Experiencing school mathematics: Teaching styles, sex, and settings.* Buckingham, UK: Open University Press.

Bonwell, C. C., & Eison, J. A. (1991). *Active learning: Creating excitement in the classroom. AEHE-ERIC Higher Education Report No. 1.* Washington, DC: Jossey-Bass.

Boss, S. (2012). How project-based learning builds 21st century skills. *Edutopia.* Retrieved January 22, 2015, from http://www.edutopia.org/blog/21st-century-skills-pbl-suzie-boss

Burke, J. C. (2004). Achieving accountability in higher education: Balancing public, academic, and market demands. In J. C. Burke (Ed.), *The many faces of accountability* (pp. 1–24). San Francisco, CA: Jossey-Bass.

Bushweller, K. (2002). Report says e-learning redefining K-12 education. *Education Week, 21*(36), 10.

California Department of Education. (2015). *History/social studies standards.* Retrieved from http://www.cde.ca.gov/be/st/ss/documents/histsocscistnd.pdf#search=standards%20+%20history&view=FitH&pagemode=none

California Department of Education. (2015). *Physical education standards.* Retrieved from http://www.cde.ca.gov/be/st/ss/documents/pestandards.pdf#search=standards%20+%20pe&view=FitH&pagemode=none

California Department of Education. (2015). *Visual and performing arts standards*. Retrieved from http://www.cde.ca.gov/be/st/ss/documents/ vpastandards.pdf#search=standards%20+%20arts&view=FitH& pagemode=none

Calkins, L., Hohne, K. B., & Gillette, C. (2013). *Boxes and bullets: Personal and reflective essays*. Portsmouth, NH: Firsthand-Heinemann.

Cappiello, M. A., & Dawes, E. T. (2012). *Teaching with text sets*. Huntington Beach, CA: Shell Education.

ChanLin, L. (2008). Technology integration applied to project-based learning in science. *Innovations in Education and Teaching International, 45*(1), 55–65.

Coley, R. (1997, September). Technology's impact. *Online Electronic School*. Retrieved January 6, 2015, from http://www.electronic-school.com/ 0997f3.html

Common Core State Standards Initiative. (2015). Retrieved January 4, 2015, from http://www.corestandards.org/

Covey, S. R. (1989). *The 7 habits of highly effective people*. New York, NY: FranklinCovey.

Danielson, C. (2007). *Enhancing professional practice: A framework for teaching* (2nd ed.). Alexandria, VA: ASCD.

Dembo, M. H., & Eaton, M. J. (2000). Self-regulation of academic learning in middle-level schools. *The Elementary School Journal, 100*, 473–490.

Dobler, E. (2012). Flattening classroom walls: Edmodo takes teaching and learning across the globe. *Reading Today*. Retrieved January 6, 2015, from http://www.dentonisd.org/cms/lib/TX21000245/Centricity/Domain/ 3150/Flattening%20Classroom%20Walls.pdf

Dweck, C. S. (2006). *Mindset: The new psychology of success*. New York, NY: Ballantine Books.

Eccles, J. S., & Wigfield, A. (2002). Motivational beliefs, values, and goals. *Annual Review of Psychology, 53*, 109–132.

Educational Technology and Mobile Learning. (2014). *A comprehensive guide to the use of Edmodo with students*. Retrieved December 29, 2014, from http:// www.educatorstechnology.com/2014/03/a-comprehensive-guide -to-use-of-edmodo.html

Everette, M. (2013). A guide to the eight mathematical practice standards. Retrieved December 29, 2014, from http://www.scholastic.com/teachers/ top-teaching/2013/03/guide-8-mathematical-practice-standards

Fernandez, C., & Chokshi, S. (2002). A practical guide to translating lesson study for a U.S. setting. *Phi Delta Kappan, 84*(2), 128–34.

Fletcher, G. H. (2010). Race to the top: No district left behind. *T.H.E. Journal 37*(10), 17–18.

Garmston, R. J., & Wellman, B. M. (2009). *The adaptive school: A sourcebook for developing collaborative groups* (2nd ed.). Norwood, MA: Christopher-Gordon Publishers.

Garrison, C., & Ehringhaus, M. (2007). Formative and summative assessments in the classroom. Retrieved December 29, 2015, from http://ccti .colfinder.org/sites/default/files/formative_and_summative_assess ment_in_the_classroom.pdf

Guskey, T. R. (2000). *Evaluating professional development*. Thousand Oaks, CA: Corwin.

Harris, J., Cohen, P., & Flaherty, T. (2008, July). *Eight elements of high school improvement: A mapping framework.* Retrieved February 7, 2015, from http://www.betterhighschools.org/docs/NHSCEightElements7-25-08.pdf

Hentschke, G. C., & Wohlstetter, P. (2004). Cracking the code of accountability. *University of Southern California Urban,* Spring/Summer, 17–19.

Houghton Mifflin Harcourt. (2015). *Assessment 101: PARCC & SBAC.* Retrieved March 21, 2015, from http://www.hmhco.com/classroom/professional-and-school-resources/common-core/common-core-state-standards/assessment-101-parcc-and-sbac

Jimenez-Eliaeson, T. (2010). Knowledge transposed: Learning globally, applying locally. *Educational Facility Planner, 45*(1), 5–9.

Keany, M. (2013). Comparing the PARCC and Smarter Balanced Assessments. *School Leadership 2.0.* Retrieved February 15, 2015, from http://www.schoolleadership20.com/forum/topics/comparing-the-parcc-and-smarter-balanced-assessments

Kilpatrick, W. H. (1918). The project method. *Teachers College Record, 19*(4), 319–335.

Lamb, A., Johnson, L., & Smith, N. (1997). Wondering, wiggling, and weaving: A new model for project and community based learning on the web. *Learning and Leading With Technology, 24*(7), 6–13.

Larmer, J., & Mergendoller, J. R. (2010). *The main course, not dessert: How are students reaching 21st century goals with 21st century project based learning?* Retrieved December 29, 2014, from http://groups.ascd.org/resource/documents/122463CCSS_PBL_Handout_1_Main_Course.pdf

Laur, D. (2011). *Project based learning with Edmodo.* Retrieved February 7, 2015, from http://blog.edmodo.com/2011/12/29/project-based-learning-with-edmodo/

Lesson Study Research Group. (2015). Retrieved February 20, 2015, from http://www.tc.columbia.edu/lessonstudy/whatislessonstudy.html

Martyn, M. (2003). The hybrid online model: Good practice. *Educause Quarterly, 1,* 18–23.

Marzano, R. J. (2011). The art and science of teaching: Making the most of instructional rounds. *Educational leadership, 68*(5), 80–81.

Marzano, R. J., & Simms, J. A. (2014). *Questioning sequences in the classroom.* Bloomington, IN: Marzano Research Laboratory.

Mayer, R. E. (2011). *Applying the science of learning.* Boston, MA: Pearson Education.

McTighe, J., Seif, E., & Wiggins, G. (2010). You can teach for meaning. In F.W. Parkay, G. Hass, & E. J. Anctil (Eds.), *Curriculum leadership: Readings for developing quality educational programs* (9th ed., pp. 372–377). Upper Saddle River, NJ: Pearson Education, Inc.

McTighe, J., & Wiggins, G. (2013). *Essential questions: Opening doors to student understanding.* Alexandria, VA: ASCD.

Means, B., Toyama, Y., Murphy, R., Bakia, M., & Jones, K. (2010). *Evaluation of evidence-based practices in online learning: A meta-analysis and review of online learning studies.* Report prepared for the U.S. Department of Education, Office of Planning, Evaluation, and Policy Development. Washington, DC.

Moodle. (2013). [Main page of Moodle Docs]. Retrieved December 29, 2014, from http://docs.moodle.org/24/en/Main_Page

National Research Council. (2012). *A framework for K-12 science education: Practices, cross cutting concepts, and core ideas.* Washington, DC: The National Academies Press.

Newell, R. (2003). *Passion for learning: How project-based learning meets the needs of 21st-century students.* Lanham, MD: Scarecrow.

Pearlman, B. (2002). Designing, and making, the new American high school. *Technos, 11*(1), 12–19.

Pintrich, P. R. (2003). A motivational science perspective on the role of student motivation in learning and teaching contexts. *Journal of Educational Psychology, 95*(4), 667–686.

Puentedura, R. R. (2006). *Transformation, Technology, and Education.* Retrieved February 7, 2015, from http://hippasus.com/resources/tte/

Ravitz, J., & Blazevski, J. (2010, October 28). *Assessing the impact of online technologies on PBL use in US high schools.* Paper presented at the Annual Meetings of the Association for Educational Communications and Technology, Anaheim, CA.

Reynolds, G. (2008). *Presentation Zen: Simple ideas on presentation design and delivery.* Berkeley, CA: New Riders.

Rheingold, H. (2007). *Using participatory media and public voice to encourage civic engagement.* The John D. and Catherine T. MacArthur Foundation Series on Digital Media and Learning: 97–118.

Ribble, M. (2015). Nine themes of digital citizenship. Retrieved November 16, 2015, from http://www.digitalcitizenship.net/Nine_Elements.html

Roebuck, K. (2011). *Web content management systems (WCMS): High-impact strategies – what you need to know: Definitions, adoptions, impact, benefits, maturity, vendors.* Brisbane, Australia: Emereo Pty Limited.

Santrock, J. W. (2001). *A topical approach to lifespan development.* New York, NY: McGraw-Hill.

Schon, D. A. (1987). *Educating the reflective practitioner: Toward a new design for teaching and learning in the professions.* San Francisco, CA: Jossey-Bass.

Schrum, L. (2005). E-learning and K-12. *Encyclopedia of Distance Learning, 2,* 737–742.

Schubert, W. H. (2010). Perspectives on four curriculum traditions. In F. W. Parkay, G. Hass, and E. J. Anctil (Eds.), *Curriculum leadership: Readings for developing quality educational programs* (9th ed., pp. 20–24). Boston, MA: Pearson, Allyn and Bacon.

Slavin, R. E. (2006). *Educational Psychology: Theory and Practice* (8th ed.). Boston, MA: Allyn & Bacon.

Sousa, D. A. (2006). *How the brain learns* (3rd ed.). Thousand Oaks, CA: Sage.

Spector, J. M. (2008). Theoretical foundations. In J. M. Spector, M. D. Merrill, J. van Merrienboer, & M. P. Driscoll (Eds.), *Handbook of research on educational communication and technology* (3rd ed., pp. 21–28). New York, NY: Lawrence Erlbaum.

Stiggins, R. J., & Chappuis, J. (2005). Using student-involved classroom assessment to close achievement gaps. *Theory Into Practice, 44*(1), 11–18.

Stommel, J. (2013, March). *Decoding digital pedagogy, pt. 2: (Un)Mapping the terrain.* Retrieved December 29, 2014, from http://www.hybridpedagogy.com/Journal/files/Unmapping_the_Terrain_of_Digital_Pedagogy.html

Szabo, M., & Flesher, K. (2002). *CMI theory and practice: Historical roots of learning management systems.* Presented at the E-Learn 2002 World Conference on E-Learning in Corporate, Government, Healthcare, and Higher Education. Norfolk, VA: Association for the Advancement of Computing in Education (AACE).

Teemant, A., Smith, M. E., Pinnegar, S., & Egan, M. W. (2005). Modeling sociocultural pedagogy in distance education. *Teachers College Record, 107*(8), 1675–1698.

Thomas, J. W. (2000). *A review of research on project-based learning.* Retrieved February 7, 2015, from http://www.bie.org/index.php/site/RE/pbl_research/29

Tobin, K., Tippins, D. J., & Gallard, A. J. (1994). Research on instructional strategies for teaching science. In D. L. Gabel (Ed.), *Handbook of research on science teaching and learning,* New York, NY: Macmillan.

Tomlinson, C. A. (1999). *The differentiated classroom: Responding to the needs of all learners.* Alexandria, VA: ASCD.

Tomlinson, C. A., Kaplan, S. N., Purcell, J. H., Leppien, J. H., Burns, D. E., & Strickland, C. A. (2005). *The parallel curriculum in the classroom, book 2: Units for application across the content areas, K-12.* New York, NY: Corwin.

Trilling, B., & Fadel, C. (2009). *21st century skills: Learning for life in our times.* San Francisco, CA: Jossey-Bass.

Tyler, R. W. (1949). *Basic principles of curriculum and instruction.* Chicago, IL: University of Chicago Press.

Ullman, E. (2013). *What does project-based learning really look like?* Retrieved April 5, 2015, from http://www.k12blueprint.com/content/what-does-project-based-learning-really-look-like

USC Hybrid High School. (2013). Retrieved December 30, 2014, from http://uschybridhigh.org/the-program/technology/

U.S. Department of Education, National Center for Education Statistics. (2010). *Teachers' Use of Educational Technology in U.S. Public Schools: 2009.* Retrieved April 11, 2015, from http://nces.ed.gov

Wagner, T. (2010). *The global achievement gap: Why even our best schools don't teach the new survival skills our children need and what we can do about it.* New York, NY: Basic Books.

Walker, A., & Leary, H. (2009). A problem based learning meta analysis: Differences across problem types, implementation types, disciplines, and assessment levels. *Interdisciplinary Journal of Problem-based Learning, 3*(1), 12–43. Retrieved April 11, 2015, from http://docs.lib.purdue.edu/ijpbl/vol3/iss1/3

White, M. (2005). *The content management handbook.* London, England: Facet Publishing.

Wikipedia. (n.d.a.). *Mobile App.* Retrieved January 3, 2015, from https://en.wikipedia.org/wiki/Mobile_app

Wikipedia. (n.d.a.). *Blackboard Inc.* Retrieved January 3, 2015, from https://en.wikipedia.org/wiki/Blackboard_Inc.

Wikipedia. (n.d.a.). *Edmodo*. Retrieved March 1, 2015, from https://en.wiki pedia.org/wiki/Edmodo

Wikipedia. (n.d.a.). *Google Drive*. Retrieved December 30, 2015, from https://en.wikipedia.org/wiki/Google_Drive

Wolk, S. (1994). Project-based learning: Pursuits with a purpose. *Educational Leadership, 52*(3), 42–45.

Yetkiner, Z. E., Anderoglu, H., & Capraro, R. M. (2008). *Research summary: Project-based learning in middle grade mathematics*. Retrieved June 7, 2015, from http://www.nmsa.org/Research/ResearchSummaries/Project BasedLearninginMath/tabid/1570/Def.ault.aspx

Yost, D. S., Sentner, S. M., & Forlenza-Bailey, A. (2000). An examination of the construct of critical reflection: Implications for teacher education programming in the 21st century. *Journal of Teacher Education, 51*(1), 39–49.

Zimmerman, B. J. (1989). A social-cognitive view of self-regulated academic learning. *Journal of Educational Psychology, 81*(3), 329–339.

INDEX

Accountability, 136–140, 152, 165
Adaptability, 10, 11 (figure), 185,
      193–195 (figure)
Adapted Taxonomy, 86 (figure), 86–87
Administrator skills checklist,
      194–195 (figure)
Aesthetic valuing
   see Visual and performing arts
      standards
Agility, 10, 11 (figure), 185,
      193–195 (figure)
Ambrose, S. A., 97
Anchor standards
   see College and Career Ready (CCR)
      Anchor Standards
Anderoglu, H., 14
Anderson, L. W., 86–87
Apps (applications), 130, 130 (figure)
Art, 210–212 (figure)
Artistic expression
   see Visual and performing arts
      standards
Assessment practices
   accountability, 136–140
   Common Core assessments, 142–144
   formative and summative
      assessments, 140–142
   +1 Pedagogy™ (+1P) checkpoints,
      34 (figure)
   purpose, 135–136
   self-assessments, 192, 193–195
      (figure), 196
   see also Writing assessment
      component
Athletics unit plan, 216–218 (figure)
Atkins-Sayre, W., 152
Attire, 26, 37 (figure), 150 (figure),
      153 (figure), 155, 172–173 (figure),
      175 (figure)
   see also Unit plan rubrics

Attributions, 59
Authentic learning, 13, 15–16, 18, 21–22
Autonomy, 15

Bakia, M., 111
Barak, M., 13
Beauty, 64 (figure), 210–212 (figure)
Beginning competency, 35, 36–37 (figure)
Beliefs, 59
Bell, S., 112
Big Ideas
   characteristics, 25
   completed sample unit, 179 (figure)
   planning strategies, 34 (figure),
      36 (figure), 60–61, 61 (figure),
      63–64 (figure), 65, 65 (figure)
   +1 Pedagogy™ (+1P) framework,
      25 (figure)
   Questioning Technique, 80–82,
      81 (figure), 82 (figure), 237 (figure)
   Team Agreement, 92 (figure),
      238 (figure)
   unit plan rubrics, 204–230 (figure)
   visual reminder, 103–104 (figure)
Bitly, 117–118, 118 (figure)
Blackboard Learn, 124–125, 130,
      130 (figure)
Blazevski, J., 14, 15
Blended learning systems, 110–111
Blogs, 127
Bloom, B. S., 85
Bloom's Taxonomy, 85–86, 86 (figure)
Boaler, J., 15
Bonwell, C. C., 13
Boss, S., 130
Boxes and Bullets Strategy,
      170, 170 (figure)
Bridges, M. W.
   see Ambrose, S. A.

Burke, J. C., 136
Burns, D. E., 62
Bushweller, K., 110, 111

California Department of Education,
     48, 49, 51, 184 (figure), 199,
     200, 201
Calkins, L., 170
Cappiello, M. A., 94, 95
Capraro, R. M., 14
Cell phones, 126–127, 130
Centrality, 15
Change, 63 (figure)
ChanLin, L., 14, 112
Chappuis, J., 140
Chat rooms, 127, 128 (figure), 129 (figure)
Checkpoints
     assessment strategies, 34 (figure),
          37 (figure)
     Big Ideas, 34 (figure), 36 (figure),
          60–61, 63–64 (figure),
          65, 65 (figure)
     essential questions, 34 (figure),
          36 (figure), 66–67, 68–69 (figure),
          70 (figure), 70–71
     focused inquiry, 34 (figure),
          36 (figure), 80–84, 81 (figure),
          82 (figure), 85 (figure)
     investigation and research,
          34 (figure), 37 (figure), 94–100,
          101 (figure), 102
     learning activities, 34 (figure),
          36 (figure), 85–89, 89 (figure),
          93, 94 (figure)
     management strategies, 34 (figure)
     planning strategies, 34 (figure),
          35, 36–37 (figure), 38
     presentation component, 34 (figure),
          37 (figure), 148–149, 150 (figure),
          151 (figure), 152 (figure), 152–154,
          153 (figure)
     project management, 90–91,
          91–93 (figure), 93
     project objectives, 34 (figure),
          36 (figure), 76–79, 77 (figure),
          78 (figure)
     recommendations component,
          34 (figure), 37 (figure), 144–145,
          146 (figure), 147 (figure), 147–148
     reflection and commitment
          component, 37 (figure),
          171, 176 (figure), 176–177
     standards, 34 (figure), 35, 38–39,
          40–41 (figure), 42–55, 54 (figure)

topic selection, 34 (figure), 56–58,
     57 (figure)
universal concepts, 34 (figure),
     36 (figure), 62, 63–64 (figure),
     65 (figure), 65–66
writing assessment, 156–158,
     158 (figure), 159 (figure), 160, 160
     (figure), 161 (figure), 162–163
Chokshi, S., 138
Chronological thinking
     see History/social studies standards
Citing sources, 100, 101 (figure),
     104 (figure), 180 (figure)
Cloud management systems (CMS),
     112–123
Cloze essay, 158, 160, 160 (figure)
Cognitive Process Dimension, The, 86
Cognitive processes, 85–89
Cohen, P., 14
Coley, R., 107
Collaboration
     benefits, 137
     blended learning programs, 111
     College and Career Ready (CCR)
          Anchor Standards, 40–41 (figure),
          42, 54, 54 (figure), 103–104 (figure)
     computer-mediated technology,
          125–127, 129, 130–131
     digital pedagogy, 111–112
     instructional rounds, 139
     lesson logs, 164 (figure)
     lesson study, 138
     online options, 89 (figure),
          164 (figure)
     planning strategies, 181 (figure), 185
     +1 Pedagogy™ (+1P) process, 20, 179
          (figure), 187, 191
     professional development, 27–28
     project-based learning, 13–15,
          17 (figure)
     project management, 90–91,
          91–93 (figure), 93
     social networks, 9, 11 (figure), 125–127,
          129, 185, 193–195 (figure)
     student motivation, 59
     Team Agreement, 238 (figure)
     unit plan rubrics, 204–230 (figure)
     see also Cloud management systems
          (CMS)
College and career readiness, 191–192
College and Career Ready (CCR) Anchor
     Standards, 38, 39, 40–41 (figure),
     42–44, 54 (figure), 103–104 (figure),
     179–180 (figure), 204–230 (figure)

Commitment component
see Reflection and commitment component
Common Core assessments, 142–144
Common Core State Standards (CCSS), 38–39, 40–41 (figure), 44, 54 (figure), 103–104 (figure), 157, 179–180 (figure)
Common Core State Standards Initiative, 43, 44
Communication platforms, 127–128, 128 (figure), 129 (figure)
Communication skills, 10, 11 (figure), 185–186, 193–195 (figure), 213–215 (figure)
Community, 64 (figure)
Competency measures, 35, 36–37 (figure)
Competition, 63 (figure), 204–206 (figure), 216–218 (figure)
Computer-mediated technology
apps (applications), 130, 130 (figure)
assessment practices, 142–144
benefits, 63 (figure), 130–132
cloud management systems (CMS), 112–123, 115 (figure)
digital pedagogy, 110–112
instructional practices, 107–108
learning management systems, 122, 123–125
parental involvement, 122, 126
SAMR model, 108 (figure), 108–109
social media, 125–129, 128 (figure), 129 (figure)
Conceptual understanding, 86
Confidence, 26, 37 (figure), 150 (figure), 153 (figure), 155, 172–173 (figure), 175 (figure)
see also Unit plan rubrics
Conflict, 63 (figure)
Consistency, 22
Constructive investigation, 15
Constructivist learning, 13, 15–16
Contextual learning, 17–18
CourseSites, 124
Covey, S. R., 22
Creative expression
see Visual and performing arts standards
Creativity, 10, 12 (figure), 186, 225–227 (figure)
Credibility 4 (C4) strategy, 99–100, 101 (figure), 104 (figure), 150 (figure), 180 (figure)

Critical thinking skills, 9, 11 (figure), 185, 193–195 (figure)
Cultural contributions
see Visual and performing arts standards
Culture, 210–212 (figure)
Curiosity, 10, 12 (figure), 186, 193–195 (figure)
Cyberschools, 110

Dance standards, 199–200
Danielson, C., 137
Data collection management, 95–96
Dawes, E. T., 94, 95
Decision rights, 137
Dembo, M. H., 97
Department of Motor Vehicles (DMV), 135
Diet, 219–221 (figure)
Differentiation strategies, 186–188
Digital Citizenship (DC), 126
Digital devices, 19
Digital pedagogy, 110–112
DiPietro, M.
see Ambrose, S. A.
Distance learning, 110
Dobler, E., 114
Doctorow, Edgar Lawrence (E.L.), 156
Dori, Y. J., 13
Dweck, C. S., 196
Dynamic Learning Maps (DLM), 142

Eaton, M. J., 97
Eccles, J. S., 59
Edmodo, 114–116, 115 (figure), 122, 123, 130, 130 (figure)
Education, 64 (figure)
Educational Technology and Mobile Learning, 114
Egan, M. W., 17
Ehringhaus, M., 140
Eison, J. A., 13
Elaborate questions, 80–84, 81 (figure), 82 (figure), 85 (figure), 104 (figure), 180 (figure), 237 (figure)
see also Unit plan rubrics
eLearning, 110
Emerging competency, 35, 36–37 (figure)
Engagement, 26, 37 (figure), 150 (figure), 153 (figure), 155, 172–173 (figure)
see also Unit plan rubrics
English Language Arts (ELA) standards, 183 (figure), 235 (figure)

Entrepreneurialism, 10, 11 (figure), 185, 193–195 (figure)
Essential questions
  authentic learning, 15
  characteristics, 26
  completed sample unit, 179 (figure)
  investigation and research, 98
  planning strategies, 34 (figure), 36 (figure), 66–67, 68–69 (figure), 70 (figure), 70–71
  +1 Pedagogy™ (+1P) framework, 25 (figure)
  Team Agreement, 92 (figure), 238 (figure)
  unit plan rubrics, 204–230 (figure)
Ethos, pathos, and logos (EPL), 26, 37 (figure), 149, 150 (figure), 153 (figure), 153–156, 172 (figure), 174 (figure)
  see also Unit plan rubrics
Everette, M., 43
Exercise, 216–218 (figure)
Eye contact, 26, 37 (figure), 150 (figure), 153 (figure), 155, 172–173 (figure), 175 (figure)
  see also Unit plan rubrics

Facebook, 125, 126
Fadel, C., 39
Family, 64 (figure)
Famous painters unit plan, 210–212 (figure)
Fernandez, C., 138
Fixed mindset, 196
Flaherty, T., 14
Flesher, K., 123
Fletcher, G. H., 39
Flexibility, 10, 11 (figure), 185, 187, 193–195 (figure)
Florida Virtual School (FVS), 110
Focused inquiry
  benefits, 105
  characteristics, 26, 80
  completed sample unit, 179–180 (figure)
  planning strategies, 34 (figure), 36 (figure)
  +1 Pedagogy™ (+1P) framework, 25 (figure)
  Questioning Technique, 80–84, 81 (figure), 82 (figure), 85 (figure), 97, 98, 179–180 (figure), 204–230 (figure)
  unit plan rubrics, 204–230 (figure)
  visual reminder, 103–104 (figure)

Forlenza-Bailey, A., 171
Formative assessments, 140–142
Friendship, 64 (figure)

Gallard, A. J., 16
Garmston, R. J., 92 (figure), 93, 238 (figure)
Garrison, C., 140
General questions, 80–84, 81 (figure), 82 (figure), 85 (figure), 103 (figure), 179 (figure), 237 (figure)
  see also Unit plan rubrics
Gillette, C., 170
Gmail accounts, 121
Goals, 59
GoDaddy, 123
Gonzalez, V., 40–41 (figure)
Google +, 127
Google Apps, 121
Google Classroom, 122
Google Docs, 119 (figure), 119–121, 120 (figure)
Google Drive, 116, 118–123, 119 (figure), 121 (figure), 122 (figure), 130, 130 (figure)
Google Sites, 123
Grading systems, 163–165, 164 (figure), 165 (figure), 170–171
Graphic organizers, 170
Growth mindset, 196
Guskey, T. R., 27, 28, 29, 30

Haiku, 123
Hands-on learning, 16
Harris, J., 14
Hentschke, G. C., 137
Historical contributions
  see History/social studies standards; Visual and performing arts standards
History/social studies standards, 47–51, 184 (figure), 205 (figure), 236 (figure)
Hohne, K. B., 170
Houghton Mifflin Harcourt, 142, 143
Hybrid learning, 110

iChat, 127
Imagination, 10, 12 (figure), 186, 193–195 (figure)
Information, 137
Information access and analysis, 10, 12 (figure), 186, 193–195 (figure)

Initiative-taking behavior,
10, 11 (figure), 185, 193–195 (figure)
Innovation, 63 (figure),
225–227 (figure)
Inquiry-based learning, 16–17,
17 (figure), 79–84, 85 (figure),
179–180 (figure)
Instagram, 125
Instructional rounds, 139
Intentional professional development,
28 (figure)
Interdisciplinary units, 183,
183–184 (figure), 184–185,
235–236 (figure)
Interest, 59
Investigation/research component
authentic learning, 15
characteristics, 26
completed sample unit,
179–180 (figure)
credibility, 99–100, 101 (figure),
104 (figure), 150 (figure)
Look Fours (L4s), 26, 98–99,
99 (figure), 101 (figure),
104 (figure), 180 (figure)
metacognitive skills, 97–98
planning strategies, 34 (figure),
37 (figure)
+1 Pedagogy™ (+1P) framework,
25 (figure)
practice activity, 102
purpose, 94
text sets, 94–97, 96 (figure),
101 (figure), 103–104 (figure),
179–180 (figure), 204–230 (figure)
unit plan rubrics, 204–230 (figure)
visual reminder, 103–104 (figure)
see also History/social studies
standards; Recommendations
component

Jimenez-Eliaeson, T., 13, 130
Johnson, L., 16
Jones, K., 111
Journals, 98
Justice, 64 (figure)

Kaplan, S. N., 62, 64 (figure)
Keany, M., 143
Kilpatrick, W. H., 13
Kinesthetic presentation style,
152 (figure), 153 (figure), 155,
180 (figure), 187
see also Unit plan rubrics
Krathwohl , D. R., 86–87

Lakein, A., 7
Lamb, A., 16
Language anchor standards,
40–41 (figure), 42, 54, 54 (figure),
104 (figure), 180 (figure)
see also Unit plan rubrics
Larmer, J., 15
Laur, D., 116
Leading by influence, 9, 11 (figure), 185
Learning activities
benefits, 105
characteristics, 26
completed sample unit,
179–180 (figure)
differentiation strategies, 187
grading systems, 164 (figure),
165 (figure)
interdisciplinary units, 183–184
(figure), 235–236 (figure)
learning logs, 163, 164 (figure),
242 (figure)
meaningful learning, 85–89
planning strategies, 34 (figure),
36 (figure)
+1 Pedagogy™ (+1P) framework,
25 (figure)
sample activities, 89 (figure)
team roles and responsibilities, 93
templates, 94 (figure)
unit plan rubrics, 204–230 (figure)
visual reminder, 103–104 (figure)
Learning logs, 163, 164 (figure),
242 (figure)
Learning management systems,
122, 123–125
Leary, H., 14
Leppien, J. H., 62
Lesson study, 138–139
Lesson Study Research Group, 138
Listening anchor standards,
40–41 (figure), 42, 54, 54 (figure),
104 (figure), 180 (figure)
see also Unit plan rubrics
Literacy standards
see Standards
Look Fours (L4s), 26, 98–99,
99 (figure), 101 (figure),
104 (figure), 180 (figure)
Lovett, M. C.
see Ambrose, S. A.
Loyalty, 64 (figure)

Martyn, M., 110
Marzano, R. J., 80, 139

Mastery level assessment, 20
Mathematical practices (MPs),
    43–44, 183 (figure), 206 (figure),
    208–209 (figure), 221 (figure),
    224 (figure), 226 (figure),
    235 (figure)
  see also Next Generation Science
    Standards (NGSS)
Mayer, R. E., 59
McTighe, J., 18
Meaningful learning, 13, 15–16, 18,
    21–22, 87–88
Means, B., 111
Media, 64 (figure), 213–218 (figure)
Mergendoller, J. R., 15
Metacognitive skills, 97–98
Mindsets, 196
Minds-on learning, 16
Mixed-mode instruction, 110
Mobile devices, 126–127, 130
Mobile learning, 110–111
Moodle, 130, 130 (figure)
Moodle (Modular Object Oriented
    Developmental Learning
    Environment), 123–124
Motivation, 59–60
Multiple outcomes, 22
Murphy, R., 111
Museum of Contemporary Art
    (MOCA), 96
Musician unit plan, 225–227 (figure)
Music standards, 200–201

National Academy of Sciences, 44
National Center and State
    Collaborative Partnership
    (NCSC), 142
National Center for Education Statistics
    (NCES), 107
National High School Center, 14
National Middle School
    Association, 14
National Research Council, 44, 44–47
National University, 110
Nephrology unit plan,
    219–221 (figure)
Newell, R., 14
Next Generation Science Standards
    (NGSS), 44–47, 183 (figure),
    206 (figure), 236 (figure)
Norman, M. K.
  see Ambrose, S. A.
Norms, 92 (figure), 93, 238 (figure)
Nutrition, 64 (figure), 216–221 (figure)

Objectives Organizer, 77 (figure), 77–78
Ongoing professional development,
    28 (figure)
Online learning, 110–111
Oral communication skills, 10, 11
    (figure), 148–149, 155, 185–186,
    193–195 (figure)
  see also Presentation component
Oral presentation style, 152 (figure),
    153 (figure), 155, 180 (figure), 187
  see also Unit plan rubrics
Order, 63 (figure)
Ott, Maria G., x
Outstanding competency,
    35, 36–37 (figure)

Padlet, 127, 128–129, 129 (figure)
Paintings unit plan,
    210–212 (figure)
PARCC (Partnership for Assessment of
    Readiness for College and
    Careers), 142–144
Parental involvement, 122, 126
Participatory instructional methods,
    110–112
Partnerships, 59
Patterns, 63 (figure), 207–209 (figure),
    225–227 (figure)
PEACES (projection, eye contact, attire,
    confidence, engagement, and
    succinctness), 26, 37 (figure),
    150 (figure), 153 (figure), 153–156,
    172–173 (figure), 175 (figure)
  see also Unit plan rubrics
Pearlman, B., 14
PechaKucha, 149, 151 (figure), 152,
    154, 156
Performance expectations,
    35, 36–37 (figure)
Persuasive skills, 148–149, 150 (figure),
    153 (figure), 153–156
  see also Unit plan rubrics
Philosophical rationale, 24
Physical education standards, 51–52,
    184 (figure), 216–218 (figure),
    236 (figure)
Physical fitness, 216–218 (figure)
Pinnegar, S., 17
Pinterest, 125
Pintrich, P. R., 59
Planning strategies
  checkpoints, 33, 34 (figure)
  history and social studies, 47–51,
    205 (figure)

language arts, 38–39, 40–41 (figure), 42, 54, 54 (figure)
literacy standards, 38, 53–54, 54 (figure)
mathematics, 43–44, 206 (figure)
physical education, 51–52
practice activity, 54–55
recommendations and guidelines, 21–23
rubrics, 36–37 (figure)
sample planning calendar, 231–233 (figure)
science and engineering, 44–47, 206 (figure)
templates, 33, 34 (figure), 35, 243–244 (figure)
unit plan rubrics, 204–230 (figure)
visual and performing arts, 52–53, 199–202
see also Standards
+1 Pedagogy™ (+1P)
apps (applications), 130, 130 (figure)
assessment practices, 135–144
background, 1–2
benefits, 12–13, 188–189, 191–192, 197–198
cloud management systems (CMS), 112–123, 115 (figure)
completed sample unit, 179–180 (figure)
contextual learning, 17–18
differentiation strategies, 186–188
digital pedagogy, 111–112
essential components, 3 (figure), 24–27, 25 (figure)
framework, 3 (figure), 24–25, 25 (figure)
historical context, 13–14
implementation guidelines, 4–5, 19–21
interdisciplinary units, 183, 183–184 (figure), 184–185, 235–236 (figure)
learning management systems, 123–125
motivation, 59–60
philosophical and psychological rationale, 24
professional development, 27–29, 28 (figure)
project characteristics, 16–17, 17 (figure)
purpose, 2–4, 17–18
road map, 8, 74, 134

SAMR model, 108 (figure), 108–109
social media, 125–129, 128 (figure), 129 (figure)
topic selection, 34 (figure), 56–58, 57 (figure)
20-day cycle planning calendar, 178, 181–182 (figure), 183, 231–233 (figure)
unit plan rubrics, 204–230 (figure)
visual reminder, 103–104 (figure)
see also Checkpoints; Computer-mediated technology; Planning strategies; Project management; Questioning Technique; specific components
POEM (planning, organizing, executing, and monitoring) strategy, 75–76, 76 (figure), 93, 97, 98
Power, 63 (figure)
Practice activity
Big Ideas, 61
essential questions, 70–71
focused inquiry, 83–84, 85 (figure)
investigation and research, 102
learning activities, 88–89
presentation component, 154–156
project objectives, 78–79
recommendations component, 145
reflection and commitment component, 177
standards, 54–55
topic selection, 58
universal concepts, 65–66
writing assessment, 162–163
Presentation component
characteristics, 26, 148–149, 152 (figure), 152–154
completed sample unit, 179–180 (figure)
criteria chart, 150 (figure), 153 (figure)
differentiation strategies, 187
planning strategies, 34 (figure), 37 (figure)
+1 Pedagogy™ (+1P) framework, 25 (figure)
rubrics, 170–171, 172–175 (figure)
sample activities, 153 (figure)
templates, 151 (figure)
unit plan rubrics, 204–230 (figure)
visual reminder, 103–104 (figure)
Problem-solving skills, 9, 11 (figure), 185, 193–195 (figure)

Professional athletes unit plan,
216–218 (figure)
Professional development, 27–29, 28
(figure), 138–139
Project-based learning, 13–16
Projection, 26, 37 (figure), 150 (figure),
153 (figure), 155, 172–173 (figure),
175 (figure)
see also Unit plan rubrics
Project management
investigation and research, 34
(figure), 37 (figure), 94–100, 101
(figure), 102, 103–104 (figure)
POEM (planning, organizing,
executing, and monitoring)
strategy, 75–76, 76 (figure),
93, 97, 98
Team Agreement, 91, 92–93 (figure),
238 (figure)
team roles and responsibilities,
90–91, 91 (figure), 92–93 (figure),
93, 239 (figure)
teamwork, 90–91, 93
Project objectives
benefits, 105
characteristics, 26, 76–79
completed sample unit,
179–180 (figure)
Objectives Organizer, 77 (figure),
77–78
planning strategies, 34 (figure),
36 (figure)
+1 Pedagogy™ (+1P) framework,
25 (figure)
sample objectives, 78 (figure)
Team Agreement, 92 (figure), 238
(figure)
unit plan rubrics, 204–230 (figure)
visual reminder, 103–104 (figure)
Projects, general, 16–17, 17 (figure)
Psychological rationale, 24
Public relations, 216–218 (figure)
Puentedura, R. R., 108–109
Purcell, J. H., 62

QR (Quick Response) Codes, 116–117,
117 (figure), 118
Questioning Technique
characteristics, 80–83, 81 (figure)
completed sample unit,
179–180 (figure)
investigation and research, 98
sample activities, 82 (figure),
83–84

template, 85 (figure), 237 (figure)
unit plan rubrics, 204–230 (figure)
visual reminder, 103–104 (figure)
Visual Thinking Strategy (VTS), 97

Ravitz, J., 14, 15
Reading anchor standards,
40–41 (figure), 42, 54, 54 (figure),
103 (figure), 179 (figure)
see also Unit plan rubrics
Real-world learning, 15, 21–22
Recommendations component
characteristics, 26, 144–145, 147–148
completed sample unit,
179–180 (figure)
planning strategies, 34 (figure),
37 (figure)
+1 Pedagogy™ (+1P) framework,
25 (figure)
sample activities, 147 (figure)
template, 146 (figure),
240–241 (figure)
unit plan rubrics, 204–230 (figure)
visual reminder, 103–104 (figure)
Reflection and commitment component
characteristics and functional role,
27, 171, 176–177
completed sample unit, 180 (figure)
planning strategies, 34 (figure),
37 (figure)
+1 Pedagogy™ (+1P) framework,
25 (figure)
sample activities, 176 (figure)
unit plan rubrics, 204–230 (figure)
visual reminder, 103–104 (figure)
Relationships, 63 (figure),
213–215 (figure)
Retention of knowledge, 21–22
Reynolds, G., 149
Rheingold, H., 111
Rhetoric, 149
Ribble, M., 126
Roebuck, K., 113
Roller coaster unit plan, 207–209 (figure)
Rubrics
grading systems, 163–165,
164 (figure), 165 (figure)
language arts standards,
40–41 (figure)
Objectives Organizer, 77 (figure)
planning strategies, 35,
36–37 (figure), 54–55
presentation component, 170–171,
172–175 (figure)

Questioning Technique, 81 (figure),
    83–84, 85 (figure), 237 (figure)
sample planning calendar,
    231–233 (figure)
unit plans, 204–230 (figure)
writing assessment, 163–165,
    164 (figure), 165 (figure),
    166–169 (figure), 170–171

Sample planning calendar, 231–233
    (figure)
SAMR model, 108 (figure), 108–109
Santrock, J. W., 79
SBAC (Smarter Balanced Assessment
    Consortium), 142, 143–144
Scaffolding strategies, 160, 162,
    170 (figure), 170–171, 171 (figure)
Schon, D. A., 171
Schrum, L., 110
Schubert, W. H., 18
Science and engineering standards
    see Next Generation Science
        Standards (NGSS)
SCORM (Sharable Content Object
    Reference Model), 124
Seif, E., 18
Self-assessments, 192,
    193–195 (figure), 196
Self-directed learning, 97, 98
Sentence starters, 170, 171 (figure)
Sentner, S. M., 171
Service, 64 (figure)
Seven habits of success, 22–23
Seven Norms of Collaboration,
    92 (figure), 93, 238 (figure)
Shared accountability, 137
Shortened URLs, 116–118, 117 (figure),
    118 (figure)
Simms, J. A., 80
Skills checklist, 192, 193–195 (figure)
Skype, 127
Slavin, R. E., 79
Smartphones, 126–127, 130
Smith, M. E., 17
Smith, N., 16
Snapchat, 125
Social justice, 63 (figure)
Social media, 111–112, 125–129,
    128 (figure), 129 (figure),
    213–215 (figure)
Social networks, 9, 11 (figure), 185,
    193–195 (figure)
Social studies standards
    see History/social studies standards

Society, 210–212 (figure)
Source citations, 100, 101 (figure),
    104 (figure), 180 (figure)
Sourcing questions, 80–84, 81 (figure),
    82 (figure), 85 (figure), 104 (figure),
    180 (figure), 237 (figure)
    see also Unit plan rubrics
Sousa, D. A., 88
Spatial thinking
    see History/social studies
        standards
Speaking anchor standards,
    40–41 (figure), 42, 54, 54 (figure),
    104 (figure), 180 (figure)
    see also Unit plan rubrics
Specific questions, 80–84, 81 (figure),
    82 (figure), 85 (figure),
    103–104 (figure), 179–180 (figure),
    237 (figure)
    see also Unit plan rubrics
Spector, J. M., 24
Stakeholders, 136–137
Stake, R., 133
Standards
    accountability, 136–140
    characteristics, 25
    College and Career Ready (CCR)
        Anchor Standards, 38–39,
        40–41 (figure), 42–44, 54 (figure),
        204–230 (figure)
    completed sample unit,
        179–180 (figure)
    history and social studies,
        47–51, 205 (figure)
    interdisciplinary units, 183–184
        (figure), 235–236 (figure)
    language arts, 40–41 (figure), 42, 44,
        53–54, 54 (figure)
    mathematics, 43–44, 206 (figure)
    physical education, 51–52
    planning strategies, 34 (figure),
        35, 36 (figure), 38
    +1 Pedagogy™ (+1P) framework,
        25 (figure)
    science and engineering, 44–47,
        206 (figure)
    unit plan rubrics, 204–230 (figure)
    visual and performing arts, 52–53,
        199–202
    visual reminder, 103–104 (figure)
Stiggins, R. J., 140
Stock market unit plan,
    204–206 (figure)
Stommel, J., 14, 111

Strickland, C. A., 62
Structures, 63 (figure)
Struggling learners, 20
Student learning experience, 55–56
  see also Motivation
Student mastery, 20
Student teams, 90–91, 91–93 (figure), 93
Study lessons, 138–139
Succinctness, 26, 37 (figure),
     150 (figure), 153 (figure), 155,
     172–173 (figure), 175 (figure)
  see also Unit plan rubrics
Summative assessments, 140–142
Survival, 64 (figure)
Systematic professional development,
     28 (figure)
Systems, 63 (figure), 222–224 (figure)
Szabo, M., 123

Teacher skills checklist, 193–194 (figure)
Teaching unit plan, 222–224 (figure)
Teamwork, 90–91, 91–93 (figure),
     93, 238–239 (figure)
Technology
  apps (applications), 130, 130 (figure)
  assessment practices, 142–144
  benefits, 63 (figure), 130–132
  cloud management systems (CMS),
     112–123, 115 (figure)
  computer usage, 107–108
  digital pedagogy, 110–112
  learning management systems, 122,
     123–125
  parental involvement, 122, 126
  SAMR model, 108 (figure), 108–109
  social media, 125–129, 128 (figure),
     129 (figure)
  unit plan rubrics, 204–209 (figure),
     219–227 (figure)
Teemant, A., 17
Templates
  Big Ideas, 63–64 (figure)
  learning activities, 89, 94 (figure)
  planning strategies, 33, 34 (figure),
     35, 243–244 (figure)
  presentation component, 151 (figure)
  Questioning Technique, 85 (figure),
     237 (figure)
  recommendations component,
     146 (figure), 240–241 (figure)
  universal concepts, 63–64 (figure)
Text sets, 94–97, 96 (figure),
     101 (figure), 103–104 (figure),
     179–180 (figure), 204–230 (figure)

Theatre standards, 201–202
Theme park unit plan,
     207–209 (figure)
Thinking skills, 85–89
Thomas, J. W., 15, 16
Time concerns, 22
Tippins, D. J., 16
Tobin, K., 16
TodaysMeet, 127, 128 (figure)
Tomlinson, C. A., 62, 186
Topic selection, 34 (figure), 56–58,
     57 (figure), 92 (figure)
Toyama, Y., 111
Trilling, B., 39
Truth, 64 (figure)
20-day cycle planning calendar,
     178, 181–182 (figure), 183,
     231–233 (figure)
21st century skills
  background, 1–2
  college and career readiness,
     191–192
  computer-mediated technology,
     63 (figure), 107–132
  essential skills, 9–10, 11–12 (figure),
     12, 185–186, 193–195 (figure)
  skills checklist, 192,
     193–195 (figure)
  20-day cycle planning calendar,
     178, 181–182 (figure), 183,
     231–233 (figure)
  see also +1 Pedagogy™ (+1P); Unit
     plan rubrics
Twitter, 125, 126
Tyler, R. W., 21–22, 24, 31, 56, 62

Ullman, E., 113
Unit plan rubrics, 204–230 (figure)
Universal concepts
  characteristics, 26
  completed sample unit,
     179 (figure)
  planning strategies, 34 (figure),
     36 (figure), 62, 63–64 (figure),
     65 (figure), 65–66
  +1 Pedagogy™ (+1P) framework,
     25 (figure)
  Team Agreement, 92 (figure),
     238 (figure)
  unit plan rubrics, 204–230 (figure)
  visual reminder, 103–104 (figure)
University of Phoenix, 110
University of Southern
     California, 111

URL (Uniform Resource Locator),
116–118, 117 (figure), 118 (figure)
USC Hybrid High School, 111
U.S. Department of Education, 111
Values, 137

Virtual learning, 110
see also Computer-mediated
technology
Visual and performing arts standards,
52–53, 184 (figure), 199–202,
210–212 (figure), 236 (figure)
Visual presentation style,
152 (figure), 153 (figure), 155,
180 (figure), 187
see also Unit plan rubrics
Visual text sets, 96 (figure), 96–97
Visual Thinking Strategy (VTS),
96 (figure), 96–97

Wagner, T., 9, 12, 185
Walker, A., 14
Web-enhanced instruction, 110, 123
see also Computer-mediated
technology
Weebly, 123
Wellman, B. M., 92 (figure),
93, 238 (figure)
White, M., 113
Wigfield, A., 59
Wiggins, G., 18
Wikipedia, 114, 116, 124, 130
Wikis, 127
Wohlstetter, P., 137
Wolk, S., 13, 14
WordPress, 123

Writing anchor standards,
40–41 (figure), 42, 54, 54 (figure),
103–104 (figure), 179–180 (figure)
see also Unit plan rubrics
Writing assessment component
characteristics and importance,
26–27, 156–158, 160,
162–163
completed sample unit,
179–180 (figure)
criteria checklists, 165,
166–169 (figure)
grading systems, 163–165, 164
(figure), 165 (figure), 170–171
planning strategies, 34 (figure),
37 (figure)
+1 Pedagogy™ (+1P) framework,
25 (figure)
rubrics, 163–165, 164 (figure), 165
(figure), 166–169 (figure), 170–171
sample activities, 158 (figure), 159
(figure), 160 (figure), 161 (figure)
scaffolding strategies, 170 (figure),
170–171, 171 (figure)
unit plan rubrics, 204–230 (figure)
visual reminder, 103–104 (figure)
Written communication skills, 10, 11
(figure), 185–186, 193–195 (figure)
Written presentation style, 152 (figure),
153 (figure), 155, 180 (figure), 187
see also Unit plan rubrics

Yetkiner, Z. E., 14
Yost, D. S., 171

Zimmerman, B. J., 55

CORWIN

A SAGE Publishing Company

Helping educators make the greatest impact

CORWIN HAS ONE MISSION: to enhance education through intentional professional learning.

We build long-term relationships with our authors, educators, clients, and associations who partner with us to develop and continuously improve the best evidence-based practices that establish and support lifelong learning.

Solutions you want. Experts you trust. Results you need.